IMAGES
of America

POLK COUNTY
GEORGIA

IMAGES
of America

POLK COUNTY
GEORGIA

Gordon D. Sargent

ARCADIA
PUBLISHING

ISBN 978-0-7385-6865-2

Published by Arcadia Publishing
Charleston, South Carolina

Printed in the United States of America

Library of Congress Catalog Card Number: 98-85880

For all general information contact Arcadia Publishing at:
Telephone 843-853-2070
Fax 843-853-0044
E-Mail sales@arcadiapublishing.com
For customer service and orders:
Toll-Free 1-888-313-2665

Visit us on the Internet at www.arcadiapublishing.com

Contents

INTRODUCTION

Before the arrival of white settlers in the Cherokee Nation, 9,000 Native Americans lived in villages along the creeks of the northwest corner of Georgia. In the 1830s, they were probably the most civilized—according to white men's standards—of any Indian tribe, with an organized government, an alphabet for their Cherokee tongue, and even a newspaper, the bilingual *Cherokee Phoenix*, published at New Echota, Georgia.

The first recorded white visitor to the area was Col. Benjamin Hawkins, the superintendent of Indian affairs, who traveled through the frontier territory from South Carolina to Alabama in the winter of 1796. Entering the northeast corner of what is now Polk County, he journeyed with two interpreters south along Euharlee Creek through an area which was then called "Clean Town" (later Aragon, Rock Mart, and Van Wert). When Paulding County (a portion of which later became Polk County) was formed in 1832, it included three principal Native American towns: Clean Town, Cedar Town, and Char'le Town. Hawkins's party continued across Dugdown Mountain to the Tallapoosa River through what is today Haralson County.

White trappers, gold prospectors, and a handful of settlers were making forays into Native American territory, all the time urging the government to acquire more land. About 1826, two scouts visited the Cedar Town area: Linton Walthall and Hampton Whatley. Six years later, according to traditional history, both men established trading posts—Walthall on a rise above the Big Spring and Whatley in the southern end of town, near Tanyard Branch.

As the state of Georgia opened the ten counties formed from the Cherokee Nation by means of land grants and lotteries, settlers from eastern Georgia, the Carolinas, and Virginia pointed their wagons west toward the new lands. Many pioneers were attracted by rich farmlands and abundant water supplies, especially in Paulding County, which was created on December 3, 1832. The county offered fertile land in the beautiful Cedar Valley and the valley of Euharlee Creek. Ironically, these hardy frontiersmen often found the Cherokee Indians ready to help their new neighbors in clearing lands and building cabins.

More of a threat to life and property than Cherokee Indians was the company of thieves located in Clean Town and known as the Pony Club. Their horse-stealing raids were often accompanied by burning and murder. Some farmers grew discouraged and simply pulled up stakes to move again to safer areas. Others banded together as the Slick Club, and after a few years were successful in ridding the county of the Pony Club.

When the time came for the Cherokees to leave the territory, as required by treaty, many refused. Consequently, in 1838 Federal troops under Gen. Winfield Scott were ordered into the territory to forcibly remove the unfortunate Native Americans.

After being rounded up, they were imprisoned in concentration camps. Paulding County had one of the 14 stockades in northwest Georgia built to imprison the Cherokees. The location of Fort Cedar Town, as it was called, has been lost in the mists of time, but some speculate that it might be the 150 log huts of Char'le Town, which, according to legend, were located on Cedar Creek south of Cedar Town.

After a few months in 1838, the Cherokees were forcibly removed west to the Oklahoma Territory on the infamous Trail of Tears. Law and order gradually came to Paulding County, and two decades of prosperity followed. The growing numbers of farmers labored long and hard to clear the land, build homes, and put in crops. Some of the newcomers set out to build extensive plantations with dozens of slaves to labor in the fields; others came to get rich by speculating in land.

In the area of Clean Town along Euharlee Creek, the town of Van Wert, named for Isaac Van Wert, a hero of the American Revolution, was established in 1832 and incorporated as the county seat on December 27, 1838. Van Wert was the center of population in Paulding County, and it soon had 100 people, a courthouse, one church, two hotels, two or three stores, a blacksmith shop, and an academy.

The early settlers wasted little time in establishing churches and schools. Wilson Whatley built the first fine home in Cedar Town below Tanyard Branch, and it was here that his wife started teaching a few children.

Mrs. Sarah Heard Whatley worked for the establishment of a full-time school, the Cedar Town Academy. By 1837, this first school in Cedar Valley was opened in a residence on what is now Brooks Street, with the Rev. John Wood as instructor. The same year, the Cedar Town Academy building was constructed and about 50 pupils were given elementary instruction. In the Euharlee Valley, Van Wert established their school, Williams Academy, in 1838.

Another early school, the Mosely Academy, was established on Cave Spring Road by Col. Benjamin T. Mosely, with the aid of George West and William Peek. The school opened in 1845 and became a noted school for boys, which drew students from around the state.

The citizens of the western, more prosperous portion of Paulding County presumably had grown tired of paying taxes to support their poorer eastern cousins, and in response, the Georgia General Assembly created Polk County on December 20, 1851. The new county was carved from the counties of Paulding, Floyd, and Bartow.

For a few years Van Wert remained the seat of county government but now was located on the extreme eastern boundary of Polk County. Consequently, Cedar Town was chosen as the county seat and incorporated by an act of the General Assembly on February 8, 1854. The corporate limits extended three-fourths of a mile in every direction from the courthouse on the public square. City limits were farther expanded to one mile in 1873.

The "peculiar institution" of slavery in Polk County history is recorded in the 1860 slave census. Although some extremely large slave holdings are claimed today for some prosperous Polk County plantations, the largest slaveholders, the Prior family, had only 117 slaves with 31 slave cabins. In 1860 the population of whites in Polk County was 6,295; the census of slaves lists 1,171 individuals, although not by name.

The Civil War would bring great privations to the people of Polk County. In 1861, the General Assembly met in Milledgeville to consider if Georgia should leave the Union. On January 19, representatives from every county voted 208 to 89 to pass the Ordinance of Secession. Polk County sent two representatives, W.E. West and T.W. Dupree, who voted against secession. However, they joined with other Georgians to sign the ordinance.

The people of Polk County lost so much during the war that when peace finally came, recovery was slow and difficult. The small farmers were able to return to their earlier way of life, but the large plantation owners, who had depended on their slaves for labor, lost their aristocratic way of life.

The African Americans, too, had little besides their new freedom and now faced starvation. They had no choice but to return to their former masters for help, not to labor as slaves, but to rent land for a share of their cotton and corn crops. Out of this situation, tenant farming for both blacks and whites came into being. From their hundreds of idle acres, the landowners parceled out as much land as the tenant could reasonably farm.

By the early 1870s, Northern profit-minded businessmen, having seen the abundant resources of the South during the war, began developments to exploit these resources. In Polk County, they opened mines for iron ore and slate and built iron furnaces to produce pig iron. This stimulated land speculation and the building of railroads.

Chartered in 1866, Polk County's first railroad, the Selma, Rome & Dalton, built their road from Cave Spring southwest to Alabama, crossing the extreme northwestern corner of the county. By 1871 a furnace at Etna situated on the new railroad was producing pig iron from the rich brown iron deposits in the area.

However, the railroad across the eastern portion of the county did not progress so quickly. The Cartersville and Van Wert Railroad was also incorporated in 1866 but by 1871 had laid only 18 miles of track from Cartersville to Taylorsville. The proposed route through Polk County was to pass northwest of Van Wert across land owned by Seaborn Jones, a director of the railroad company. Jones had the land along the right-of-way surveyed and a new town laid out: Rock Mart, named for the expected market in locally mined slate. By some accounts, Van Wert refused to grant a right-of-way to the railroad, and Seaborn Jones provided the land as well as money for a depot in Rock Mart.

By the turn of the century, textile mills were up and running. In 1896 Charles Adamson organized the Cedartown Cotton Manufacturing Company to make high-grade hosiery yarn. Two years later a number of New York businessmen established the Aragon Mills about 4 miles north of Rockmart. The county was moving away from agriculture into industrial employment, and into prosperity.

From the early settlers in 1832, 100 years of blood, sweat, and tears changed a frontier wilderness into comfortable, prosperous communities. This evolution is recorded by the photographs in this history book. We are indebted to the individuals who have shared their family materials and made this pictorial history possible. The Polk County Historical Society gratefully receives materials for its archival collections and gladly makes them available for study. (Polk County Historical Society, 205 North College Street, Cedartown, GA 30125.)

One

The Early Years

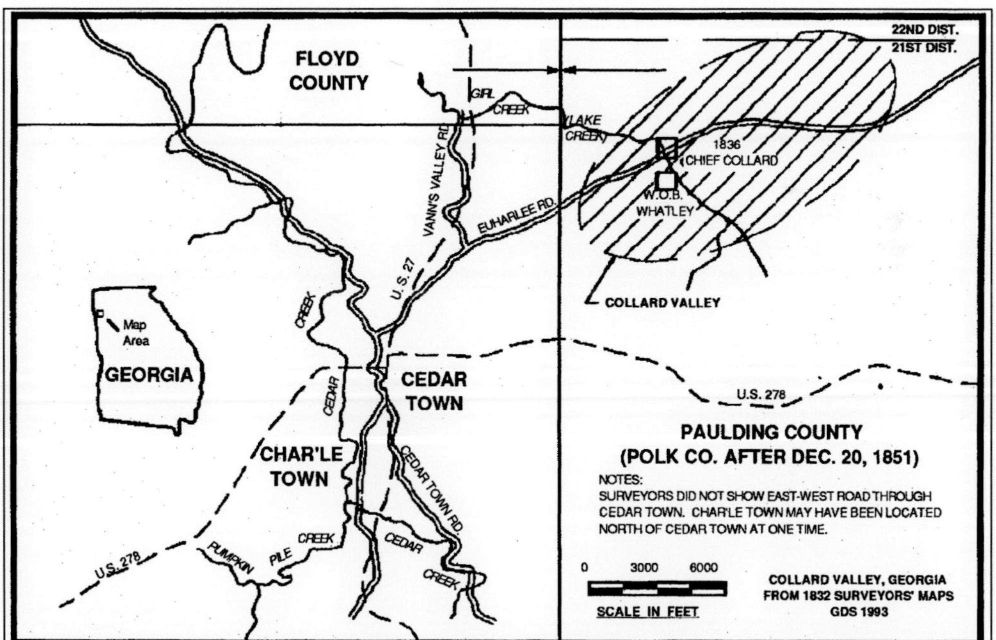

This 1832 map locates the W.O.B. Whatley home and his next-door neighbor, Chief Collard, the Cherokee Indian namesake of the lovely fertile valley. The site of the early Whatley home is well known; however, Chief Collard can be located only from Whatley family legends, as recalled by Whatley's great-great-grandson, Wayne Gammon. Collard's cabin was located a few hundred yards up the road, where the road crosses the creek. One Whatley/Gammon family legend recounts how Collard and his sons frightened the new mother, wife of W.O.B. Whatley, when they paid a neighborly visit to see her first-born.

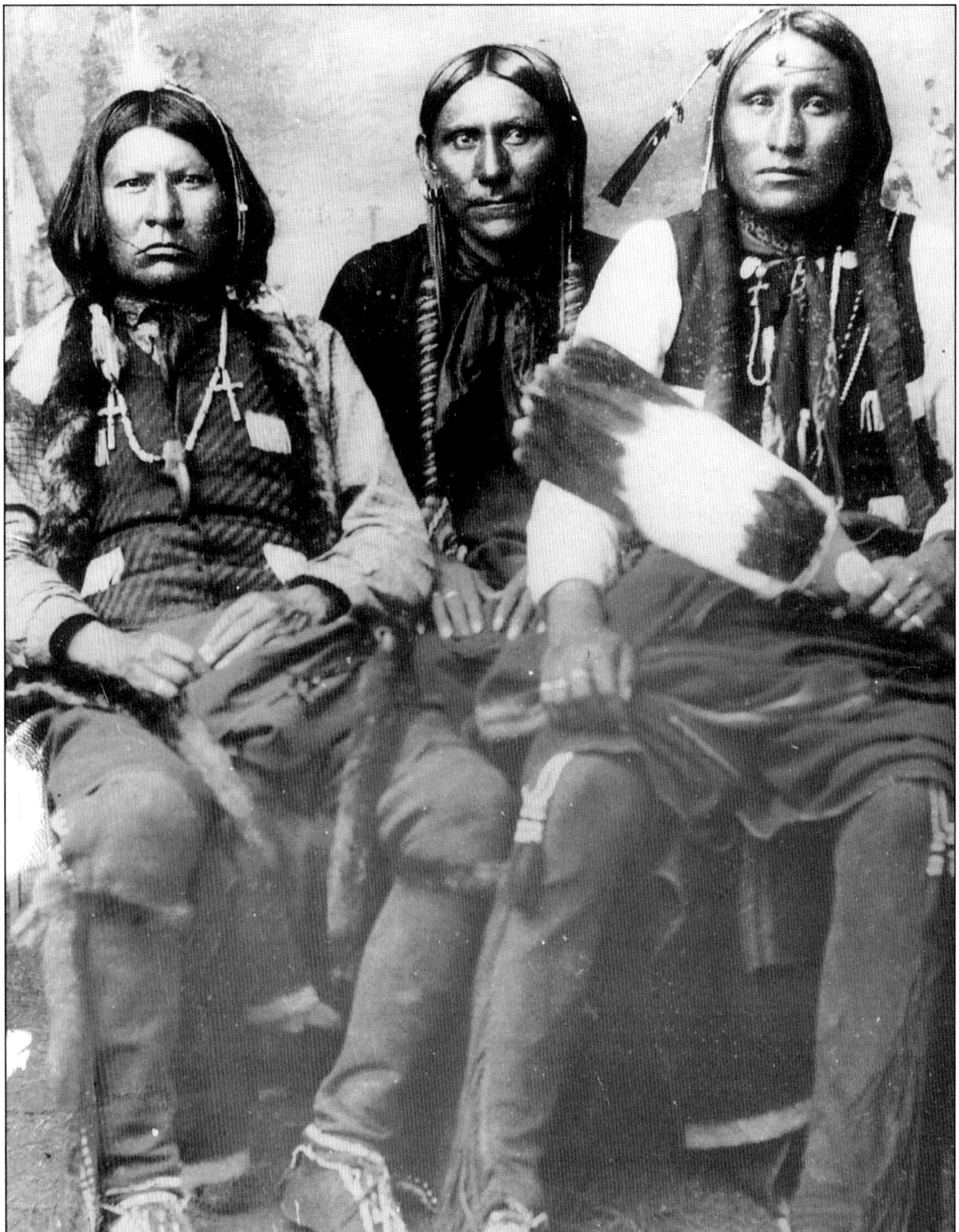

Chief Collard lived peacefully in Cedar Town among white settlers until the Cherokee Indians were rounded up and driven from northwest Georgia in 1838. Later, Collard and his sons apparently posed for a photographer in their new Oklahoma home. He and one son wear Christian crosses on their necklaces, possibly indicating a conversion by missionaries who had been working the territory since 1801. After the Civil War, the sons visited Whatley's daughter, Martha Cordelia Whatley Whitehead, and presented her with their photograph. This rare image of three Cherokees from Cedar Valley was handed down in the family to Miss Annie Jane Zuker of Rockmart, W.O.B. Whatley's great-granddaughter.

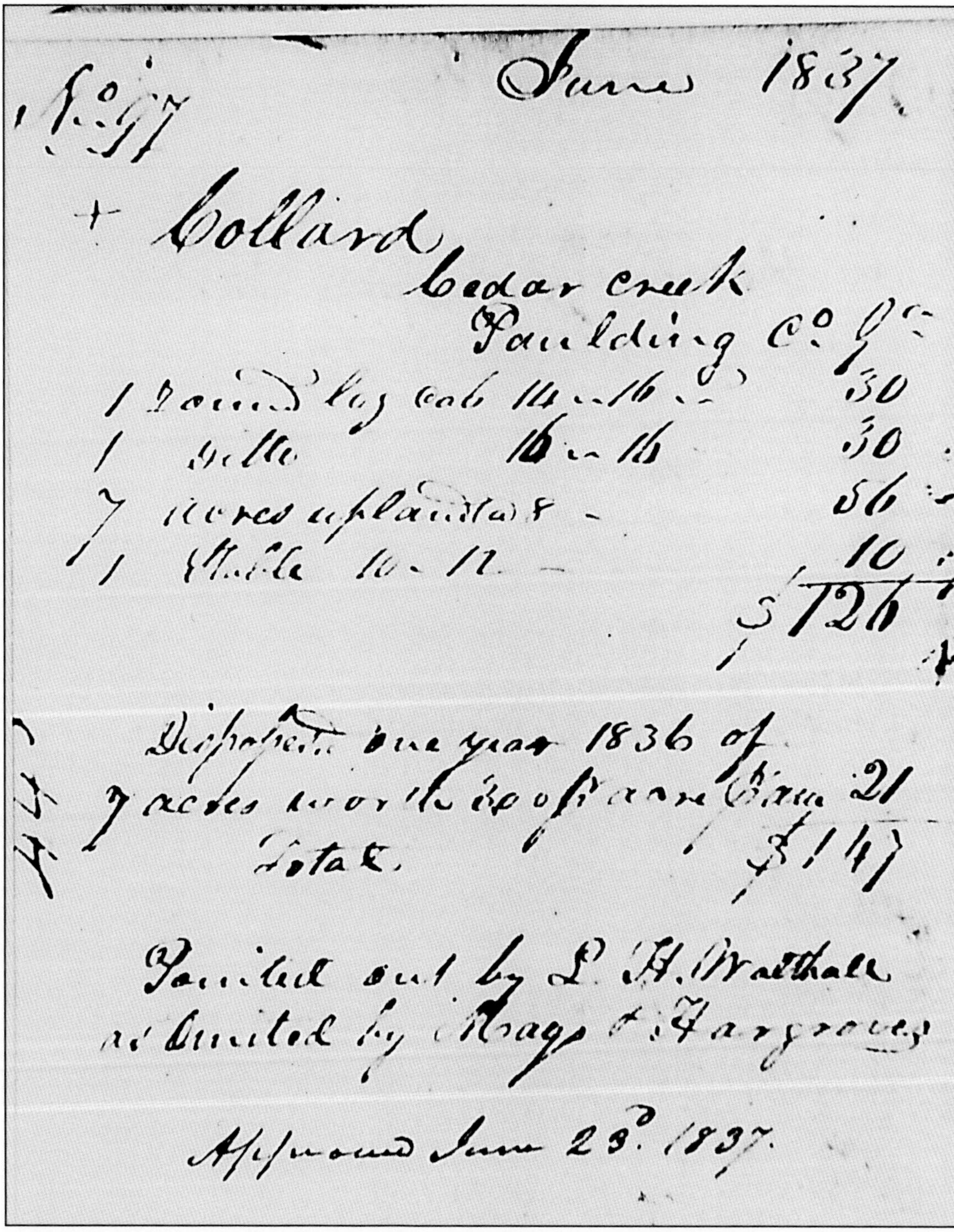
No. 97 June 1837

+ Collard

Cedar creek

Paulding Co. Ga

1	Round log cab 14 x 16	30
1	ditto 16 x 16	30
7	acres upland at 8	56
1	Stable 10 x 12	10
		$126

Dispossessed one year 1836 of 7 acres worth 3.00 per acre Rent 21

Total $147

Pointed out by L. H. Walthall as omitted by Mays & Hargroves

Approved June 23d 1837.

Valuations were made of Native American improvements to compensate them when they were force-marched west on the Trail of Tears. This 1837 document for Collard (with his signature marked with an "X") shows that he had been dispossessed of 7 acres the previous year, probably his farm next to the Whatleys in Collard Valley. After that loss, he relocated to Cedar Creek and cleared another farm described here, only to be driven off again by Federal troops. The agents, Shaw and McMillin, noted that their visit to Collard had been "pointed out by L.H. Walthall as omitted by Mays and Hargrove." Walthall guided the agents to Native Americans whose improvements had been omitted the previous year.

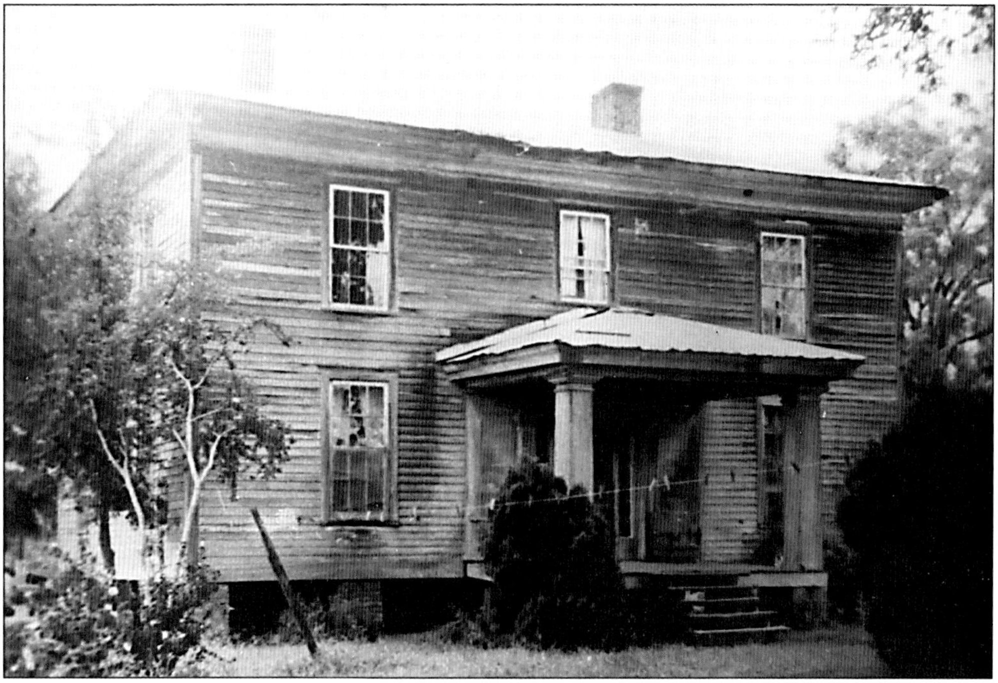

The Whatley house, scene of Chief Collard's visit, survived Cherokee Indian times, the Civil War, and the ravages of the elements until one night in 1978, when the venerable home burned to the ground. This once elegant 1830s home, pictured here in 1970, was built by Wilson Ornan Burwell Whatley in Collard Valley. Whatley's wife was the daughter of Governor Lumpkin, who may have given the couple their first home as a wedding present.

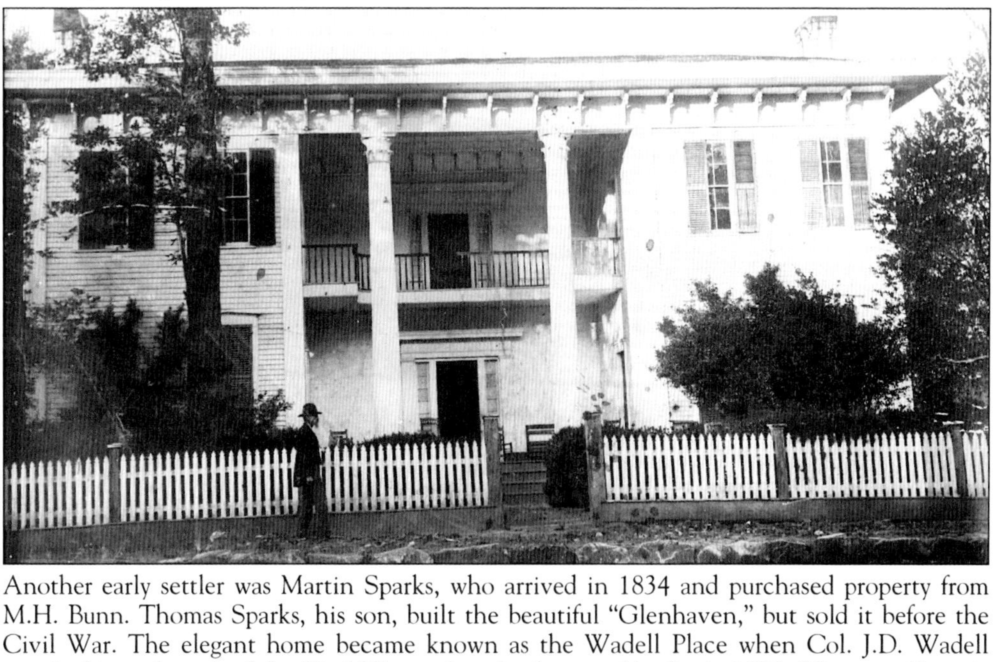

Another early settler was Martin Sparks, who arrived in 1834 and purchased property from M.H. Bunn. Thomas Sparks, his son, built the beautiful "Glenhaven," but sold it before the Civil War. The elegant home became known as the Wadell Place when Col. J.D. Wadell acquired it, and survived the Civil War, only to be destroyed by fire in 1925. (Courtesy Georgia Department of Archives and History.)

L.H. Walthall, who had guided Federal agents to Collard's farm, was an early settler living south of Cedar Town at Lime Branch, where he donated one acre in 1857 for a church. He became a lawyer and noted citizen of Cedar Town. (The daguerreotype original was copied by Watson Dyer, and his print was restored by the Leslie-Barrett Studio in Knoxville to remove rust spots and other flaws.)

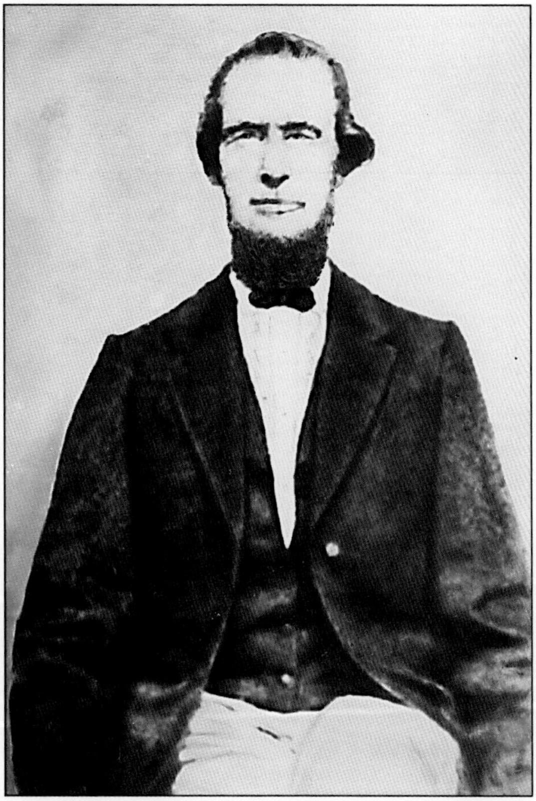

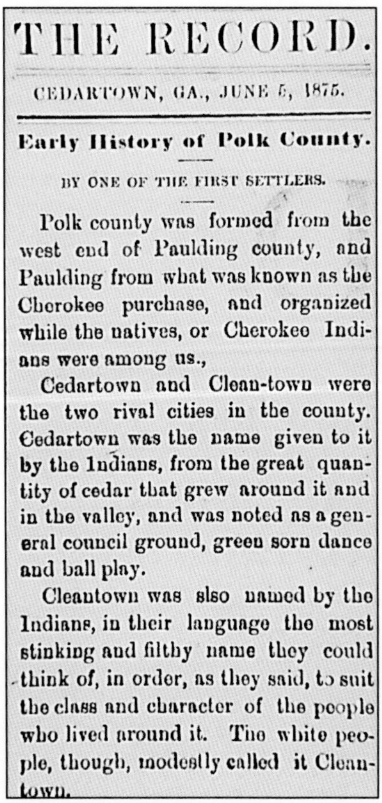

THE RECORD.

CEDARTOWN, GA., JUNE 5, 1875.

Early History of Polk County.

BY ONE OF THE FIRST SETTLERS.

Polk county was formed from the west end of Paulding county, and Paulding from what was known as the Cherokee purchase, and organized while the natives, or Cherokee Indians were among us.,

Cedartown and Clean-town were the two rival cities in the county. Cedartown was the name given to it by the Indians, from the great quantity of cedar that grew around it and in the valley, and was noted as a general council ground, green sorn dance and ball play.

Cleantown was also named by the Indians, in their language the most stinking and filthy name they could think of, in order, as they said, to suit the class and character of the people who lived around it. The white people, though, modestly called it Cleantown.

The byline for this early history was anonymous. Who wrote this nine-chapter history which appeared in sequential issues of the 1875 *Record*? Several contemporary sources, some even with quotes from the anonymous Polk County history, claim that Lemuel Hampton Walthall was the author. And yet, the author of this history refers to Walthall several times in the third person. After more than a hundred years, the identity of this mysterious author is unlikely to be revealed.

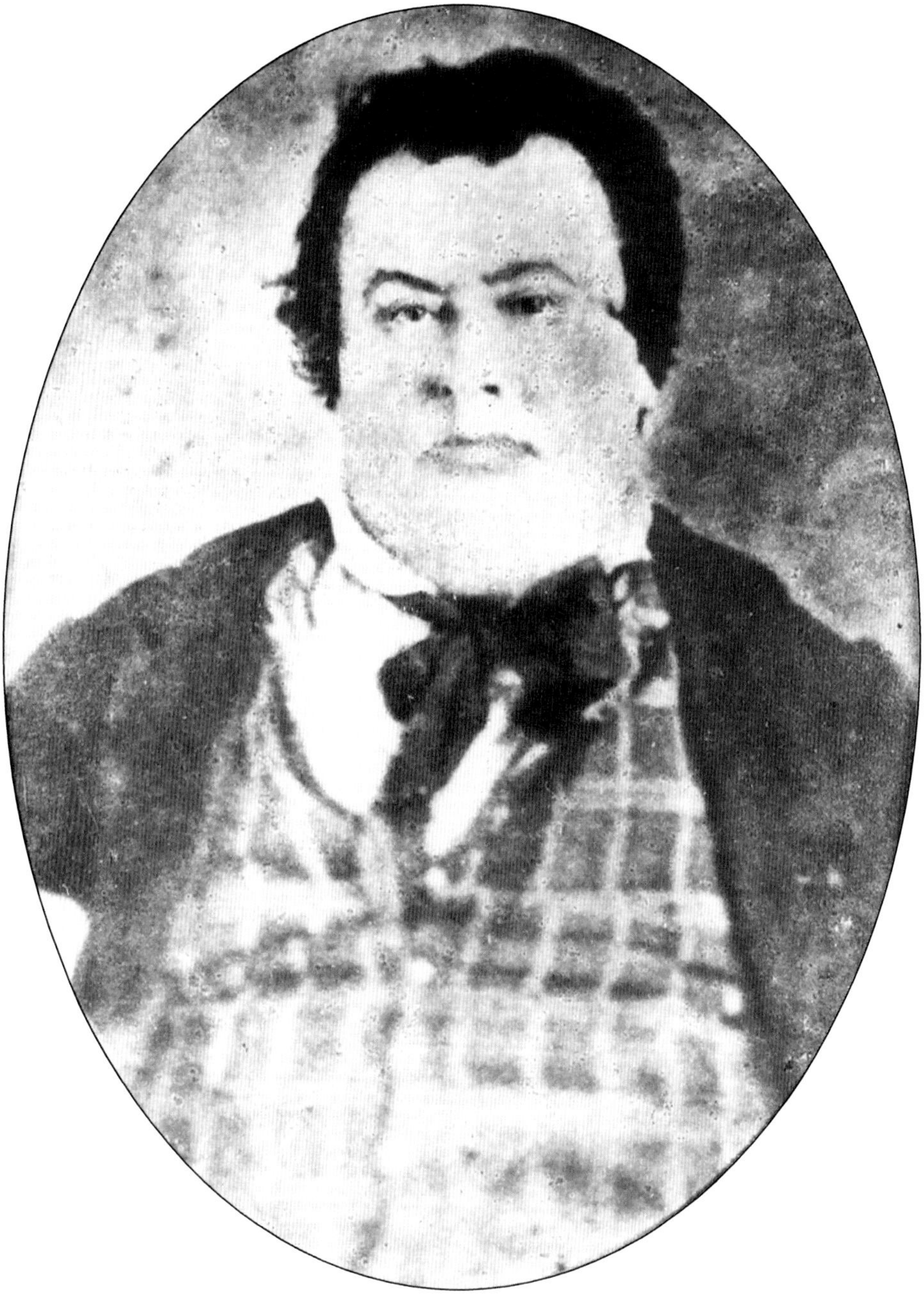

Augustin Young purchased a tract of land about 5 miles southeast of Cedar Town, and, helped by his slaves and nearby friendly Cherokee Indians, he cleared the land in 1833, planted a few crops, and built a two-story frame house along with slave quarters. The next year he moved his wife with six children and household goods from Stone Mountain, Georgia, to Paulding County. Young became a successful farmer, and in this image, he looks quite prosperous. He was a large, fleshy man standing 6 feet tall and weighing 225 pounds.

By a strange coincidence, when Catherine Pounds Young and her husband reached the end of their days, the couple died on the same day. On February 2, 1868, at 7:00 a.m., Mrs. Young passed away. Augustin, with his friend and lawyer, Lem Walthall, sitting at his bedside and his wife's remains lying upstairs, died just 14 hours later. Augustin and Catherine were buried together in the Young family cemetery—in the same grave.

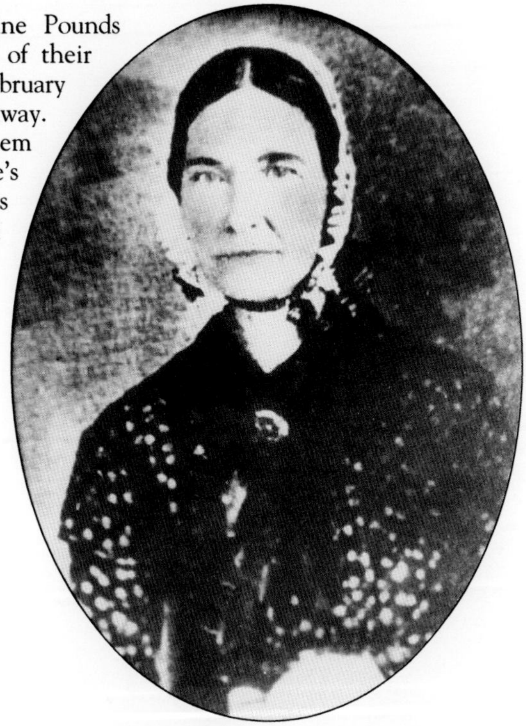

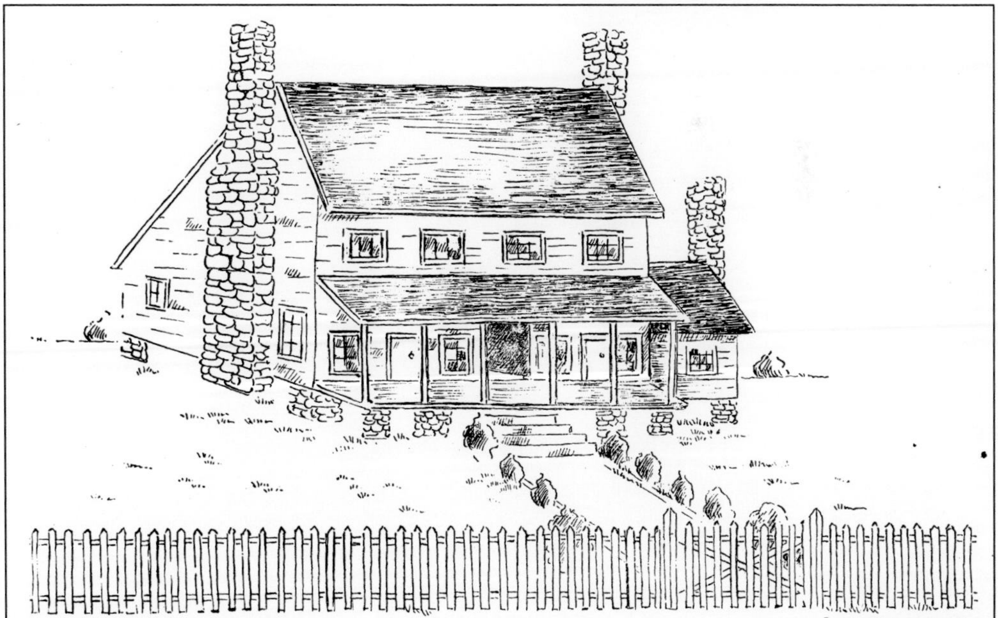

The Young homestead, shown in this primitive sketch, was built several years after Augustin built his first home. With the passing years, he continued to buy more land and slaves until he became one of the county's most prosperous planters. The large plantation near Antioch, reportedly lying on the stagecoach route, probably provided accommodations to travelers, and consequently became known as Young's Station.

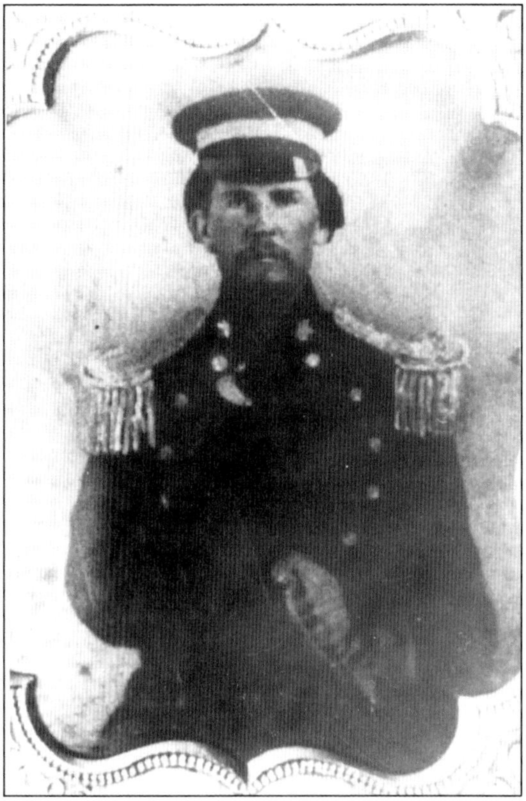

Capt. Milton H. Hanie built a mill for Asa Prior in 1849. He was also known to have completed at least one other gristmill in his home town of Cave Spring. When the Civil War began, he raised a company in Floyd County—Company C, 1st Georgia Volunteer Cavalry—and led his men through several campaigns until the final surrender.

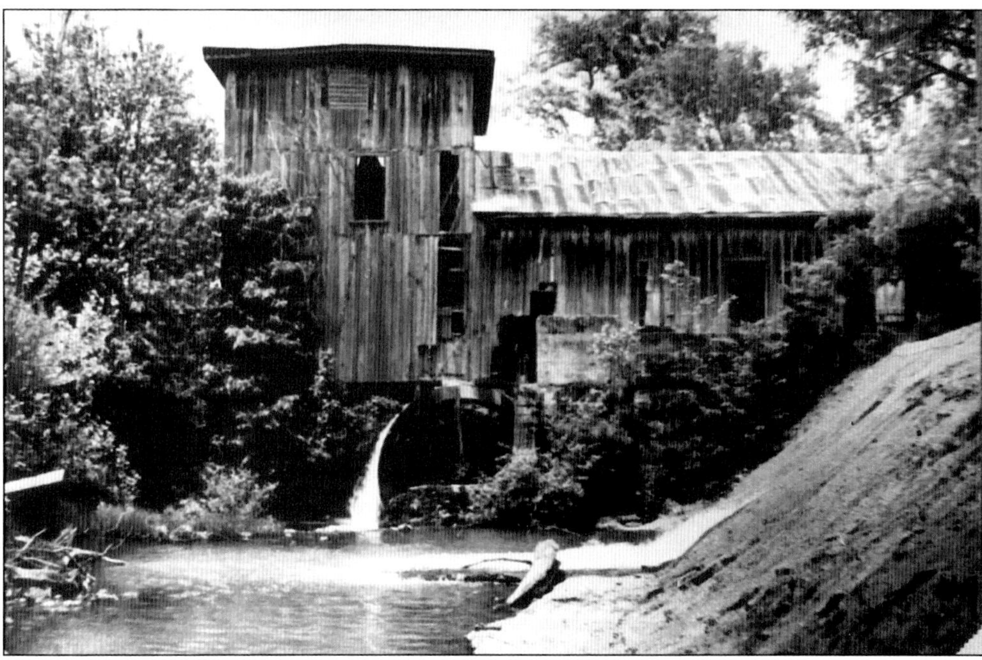

The old mill built by Hanie on Cedar Creek, shown here *c.* 1960, ground corn for Cedartown residents for almost 100 years. Known as the Benedict Mill, it is one of the county's few surviving gristmills and one of Polk County's most treasured landmarks.

Seaborn Jones might be called the "Father of Rockmart." The owner of several hundred acres of land, he was instrumental in the founding of Rock Mart. He provided land for the first railroad, five churches, a public square, a city park, and Rose Hill Cemetery, in which he reserved one site for himself. His gravestone is the tallest monument in the cemetery and stands on the highest site.

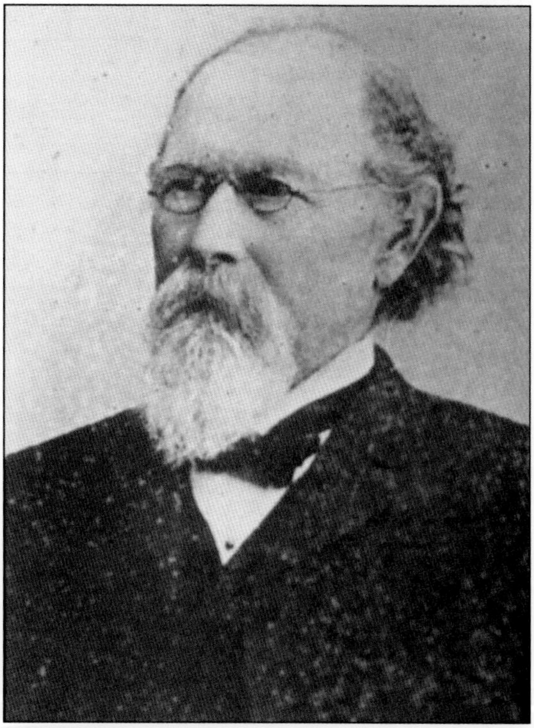

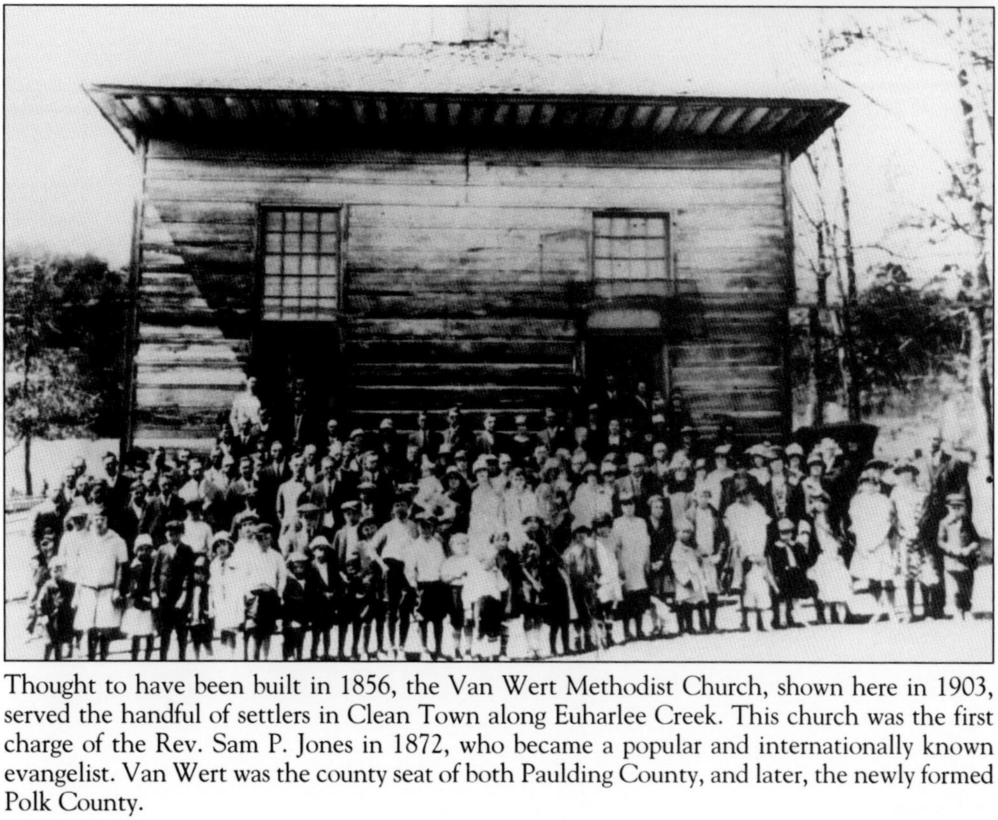

Thought to have been built in 1856, the Van Wert Methodist Church, shown here in 1903, served the handful of settlers in Clean Town along Euharlee Creek. This church was the first charge of the Rev. Sam P. Jones in 1872, who became a popular and internationally known evangelist. Van Wert was the county seat of both Paulding County, and later, the newly formed Polk County.

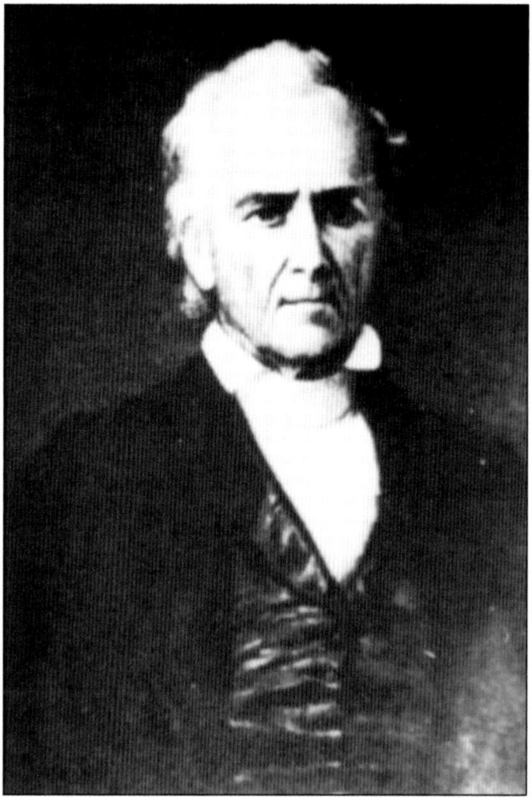

The Reverend Humphrey Posey served as a missionary to the Cherokee Indians for several years and often greeted arriving settlers. He held combined services for settlers and Cherokees, and according to church records, he organized the first two Baptist churches: Cedar Town in 1835 and Van Wert in 1840. The first Christian service held in Cedar Valley was conducted by Posey in the home of Wilson Whatley.

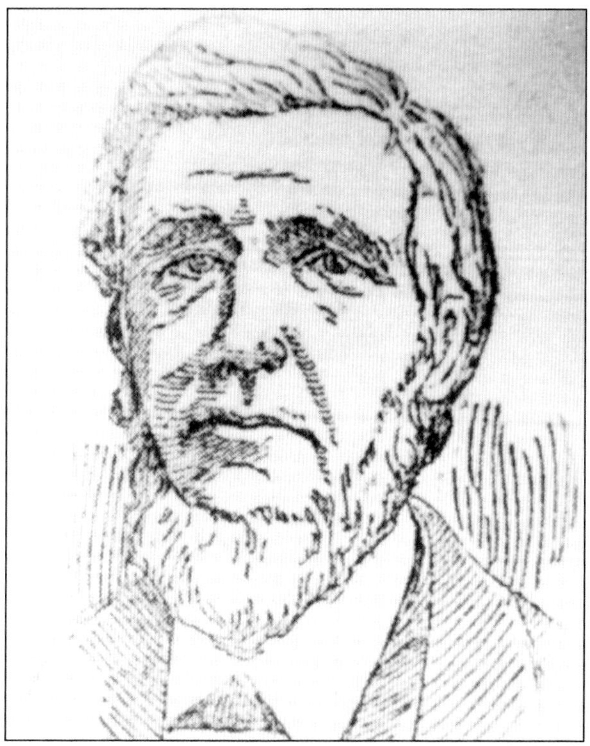

In 1840, the Baptist church had been floundering for several years when the Rev. Jesse Wood arrived in Cedar Town to breathe new life into the congregation. The Baptists were inspired to build their church that same year. Under Wood's leadership, during a period of 12 years, the church became one of the largest and most influential in Georgia.

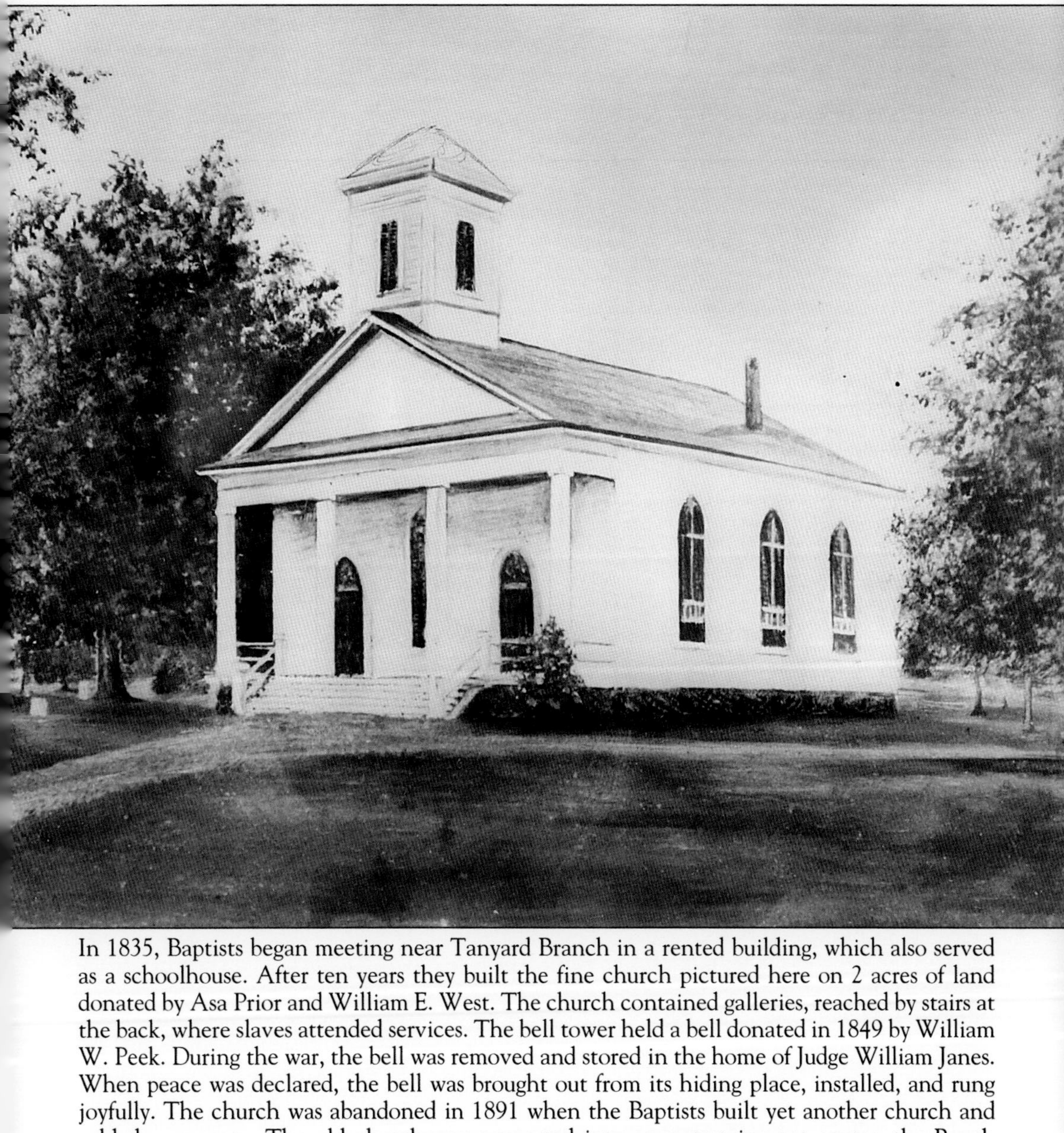

In 1835, Baptists began meeting near Tanyard Branch in a rented building, which also served as a schoolhouse. After ten years they built the fine church pictured here on 2 acres of land donated by Asa Prior and William E. West. The church contained galleries, reached by stairs at the back, where slaves attended services. The bell tower held a bell donated in 1849 by William W. Peek. During the war, the bell was removed and stored in the home of Judge William Janes. When peace was declared, the bell was brought out from its hiding place, installed, and rung joyfully. The church was abandoned in 1891 when the Baptists built yet another church and sold the property. The old church was converted into an entertainment center, the Baugh Opera House, where a variety of meetings and shows were held, although it is doubtful if any operas were ever staged. The 1845 church was demolished in 1901, after a new city hall was built with an auditorium, called the Lyceum.

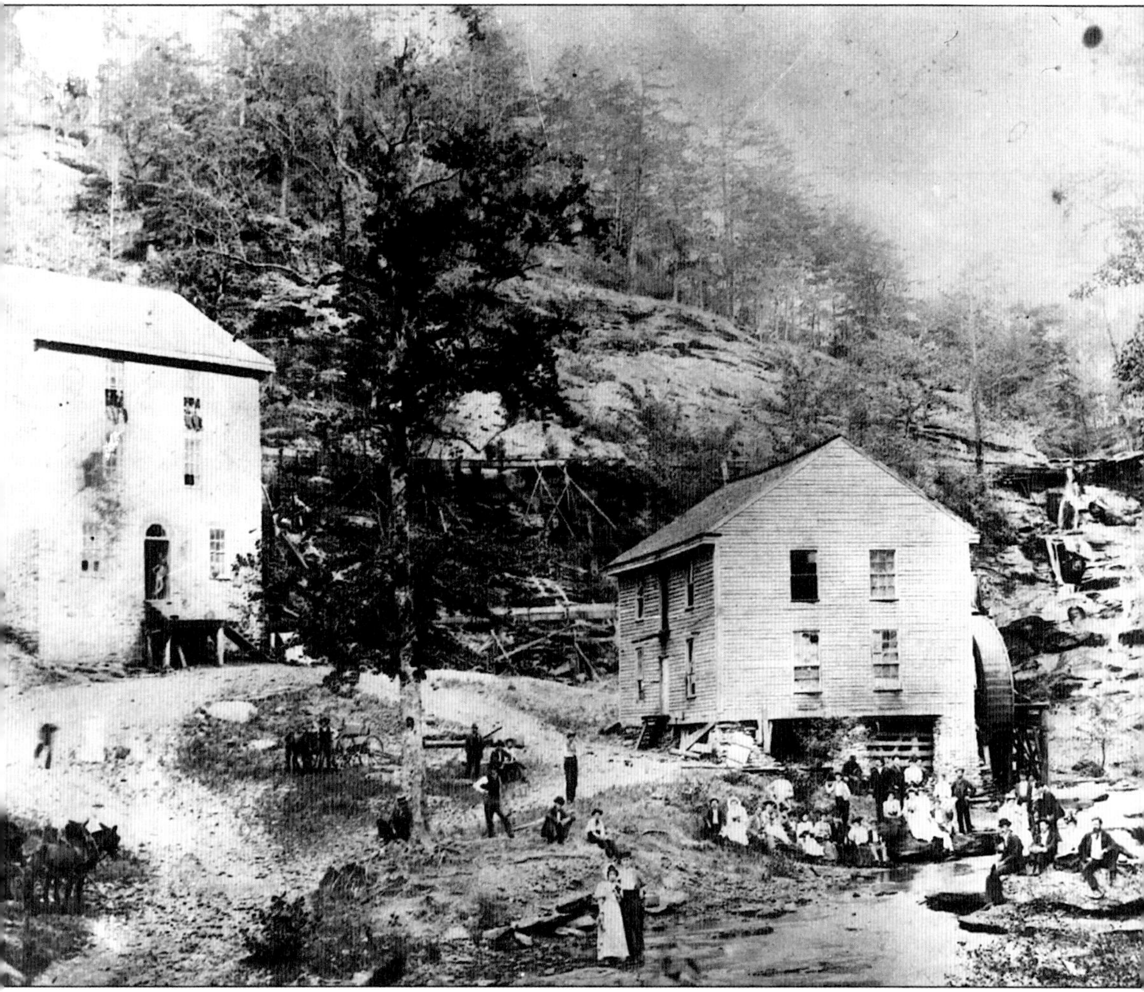

Generations of picnickers and campers have enjoyed this beautiful site of the old mill, now in ruins, and the cascading Hightower Falls, which becomes Euharlee Creek. John Wilson erected a wooden gristmill on this site in 1832 with the help of his Cherokee friends. Hightower purchased the mill, and following a visit to a relative in South Carolina where he saw similar plants in operation, he erected the stone structure shown in this 1905 view. A grain mill was installed on the first floor, a carding plant on the second, and a storage room on the third floor. Because the original dam did not provide enough power for carding and milling, Hightower raised the dam several feet, reportedly using the first cement in the county, and installed a larger wooden water race and wheel. He later built a separate cotton "engine," or gin, located in the wooden building on the right.

Elias Dorsey Hightower arrived from Greene County in 1846 and settled near Hightower Falls. Besides the mill and a successful farm, Hightower also operated a tanyard, kept bees, and raised sheep on the mountain above the falls, for which he brought experienced shepherds from Wales to tend the flock.

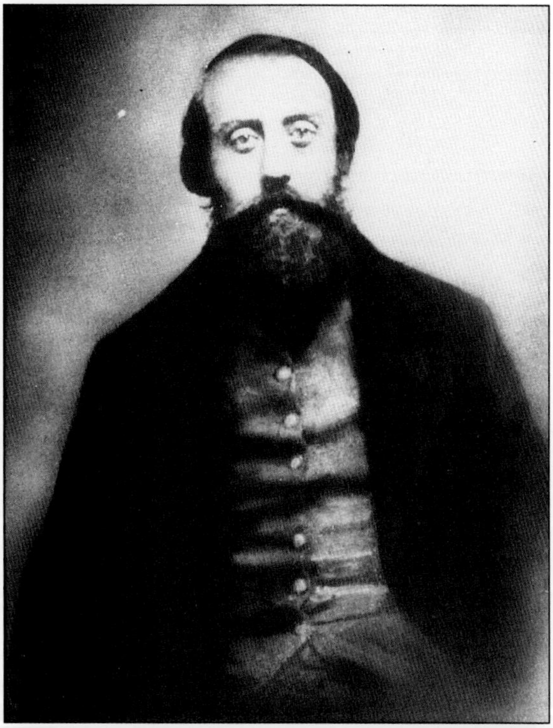

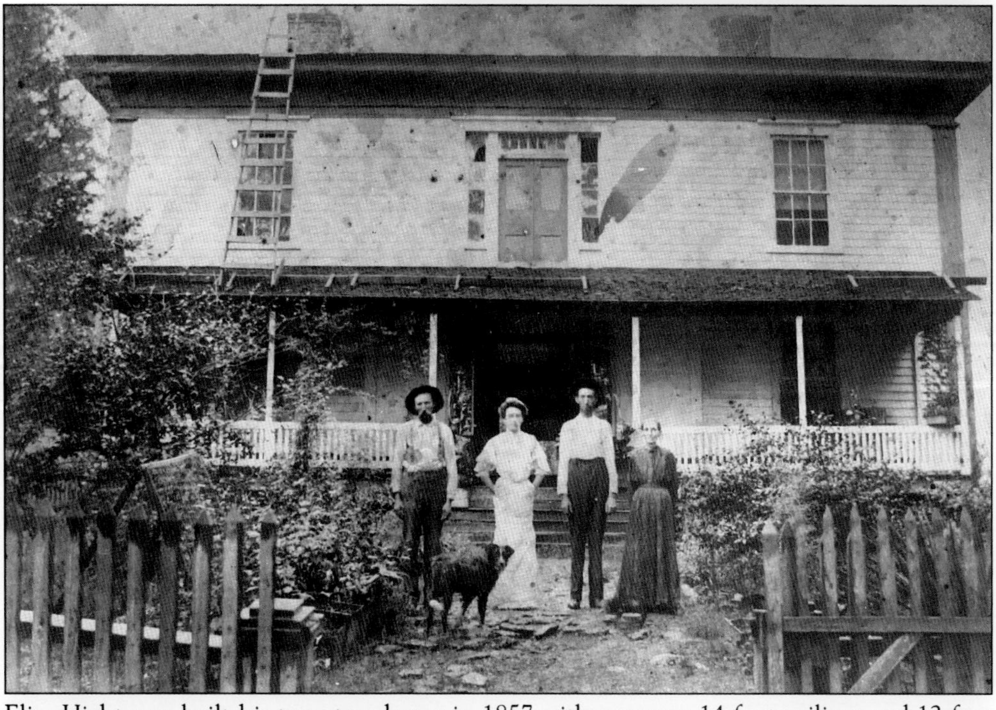

Elias Hightower built his two-story home in 1857 with generous 14-foot ceilings and 12-foot wide halls and raised his 11 children here. In this c. 1907 picture, the Carter family, descendants of Hightower, pose in front of their home, which still stands today and is occupied by the present owner, Ben Cochran.

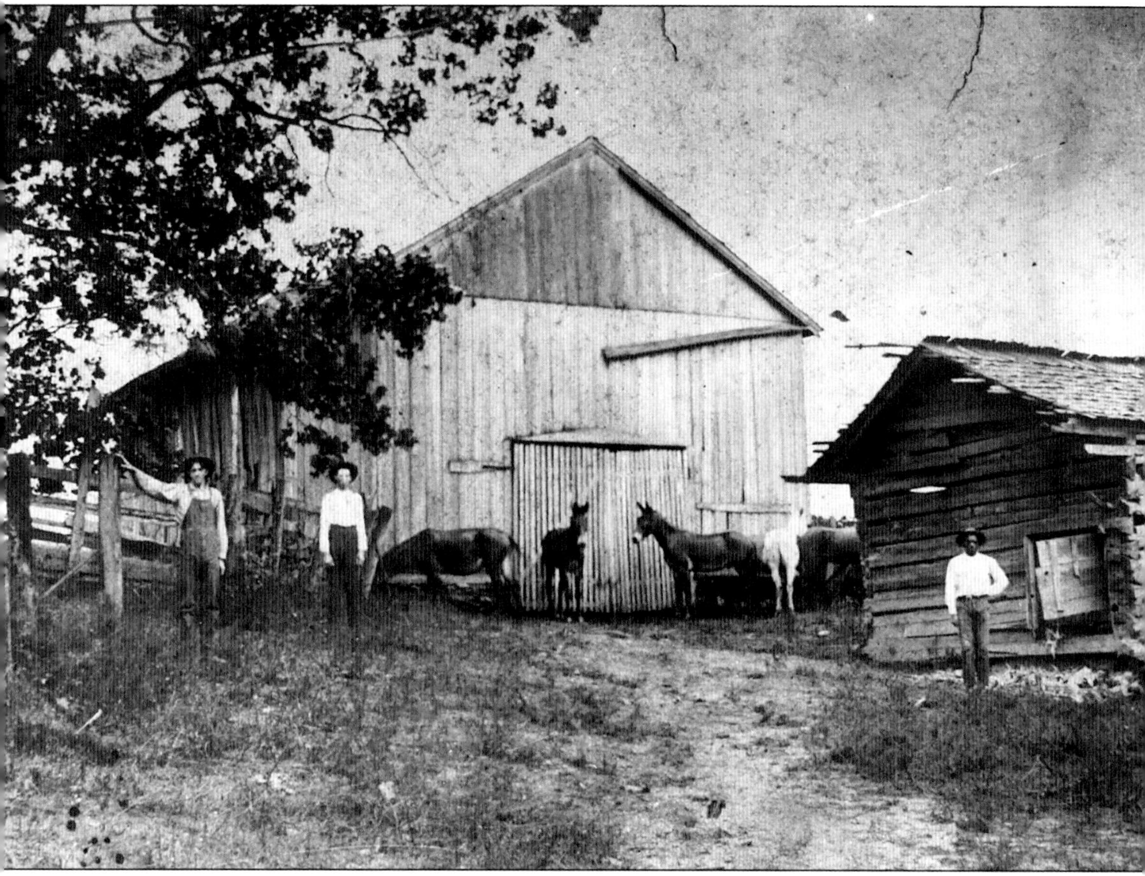

Robert W. Bullock, Charlie Carter, and farmhand George Hart stand in front of the Hightower barn and corn crib in this c. 1900 view. The place survived a visit from Union troops in 1864. Hightower's hogs had been driven into the hills for protection, as the story goes, but one old sow wandered back down just as the Yankees arrived. The troops killed the hog, baked cornbread from the ample supplies of corn meal, and enjoyed a sumptuous supper. Possibly mellowed from the meal, the Yankees spared the Hightower home. Today farm buildings still stand on the same site. Behind the barn, Elias Hightower, members of his family, and slaves are buried in the family cemetery in a grove of oaks, reached by crossing fields.

Two

The Dreadful Conflict

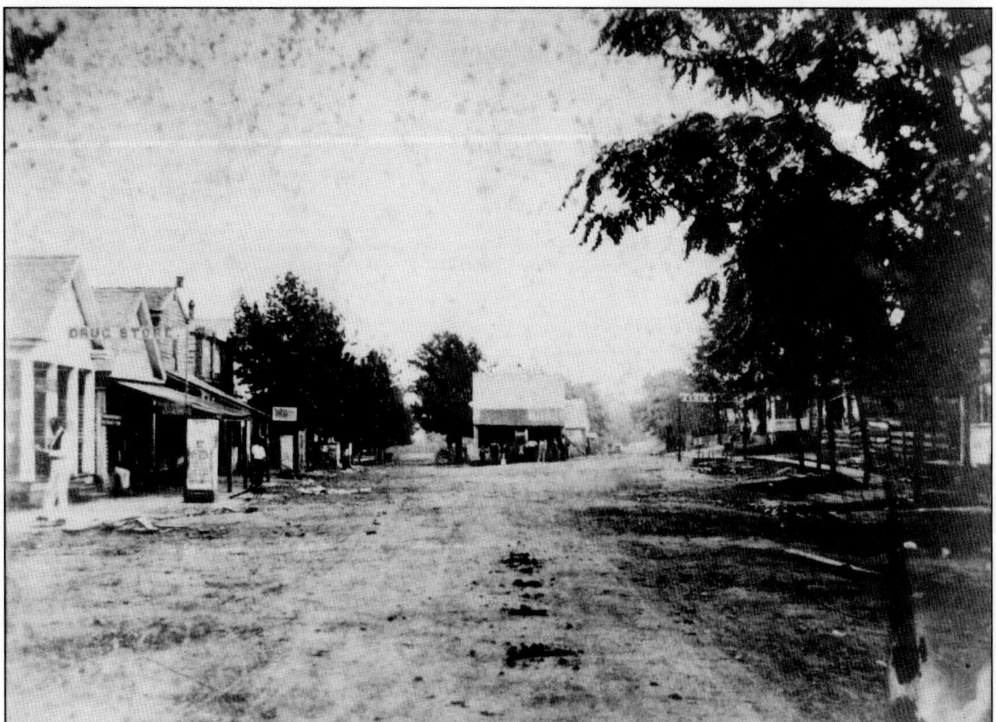

An early view of Cedartown's Main Street looking north presents a grim appearance, possibly showing the town while it was still recovering from the Civil War a few years earlier. In the 1870s a disastrous fire destroyed the wooden buildings shown here on the west side of Main Street. They were replaced by the brick masonry structures seen today. Boardwalks helped citizens in rainy weather, but rain turned the road to a quagmire which mired wagons and pedestrians alike. The drugstore on the left backed on Warehouse Street and may have been operated by a Dr. Reese, an early druggist.

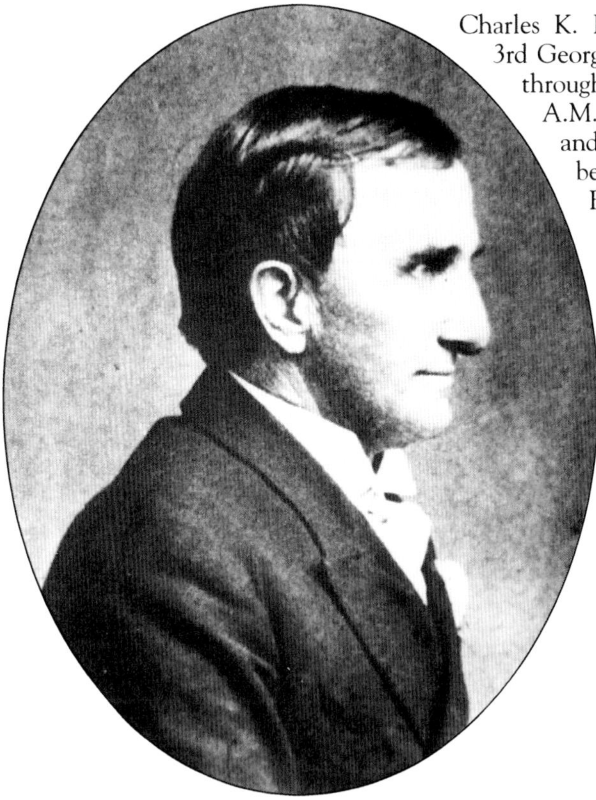

Charles K. Henderson enlisted in Company F, 3rd Georgia, and saw action in several battles throughout the war. He earned A.B. and A.M. degrees from Mercer University and ministered to several congregations before being called to Cedartown's First Baptist Church in 1876. He wrote a history of Polk County which was published serially in the Cedartown *Standard*, starting in 1897.

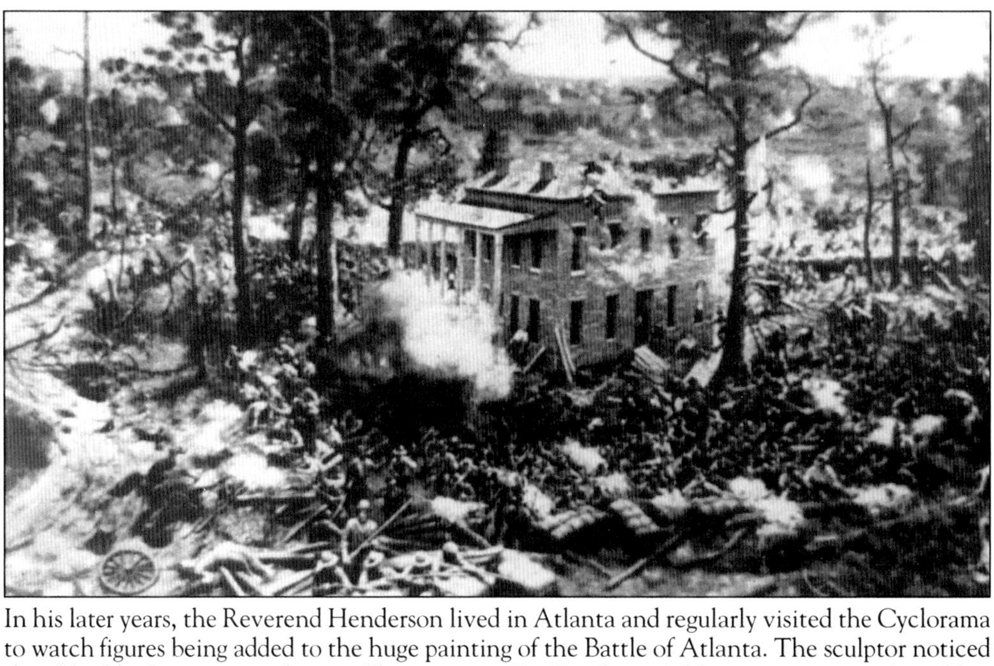

In his later years, the Reverend Henderson lived in Atlanta and regularly visited the Cyclorama to watch figures being added to the huge painting of the Battle of Atlanta. The sculptor noticed the old soldier's interest and invited him to pose. Dr. Henderson's likeness appears in the soldier standing behind the cotton bales at the bottom of this view, and he was finally able to say that he was in the famous battle—at age 91.

The Confederate Monument commemorates the soldiers, both survivors and battle casualties, who served in the Civil War. The 30-foot marble shaft was made in Marietta by the McNeel Marble Company and erected in 1906 by the United Daughters of the Confederacy. Almost 600 men enlisted in the four companies raised in Polk County, which had a population of only 6,295 in 1860.

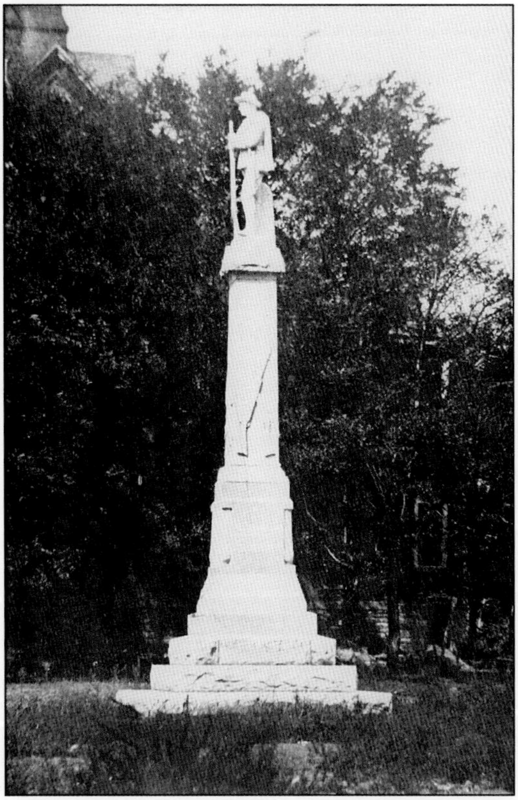

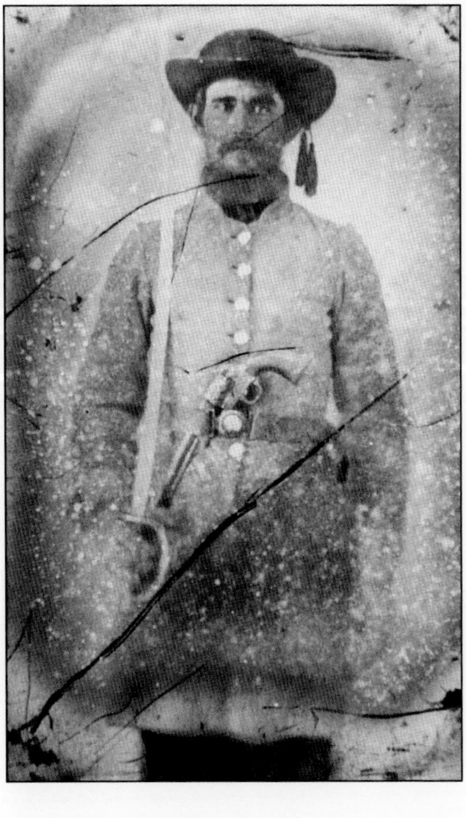

William Madison "Dock" Trippe wears the uniform of a cavalryman in Company C, Phillips Legion, Georgia Cavalry. In 1863, when Trippe returned home for a brief leave, he was married. The photograph, an ambrotype, probably dates from the time of his marriage. He was the grandfather of W.D. Trippe Jr., a noted Cedartown citizen.

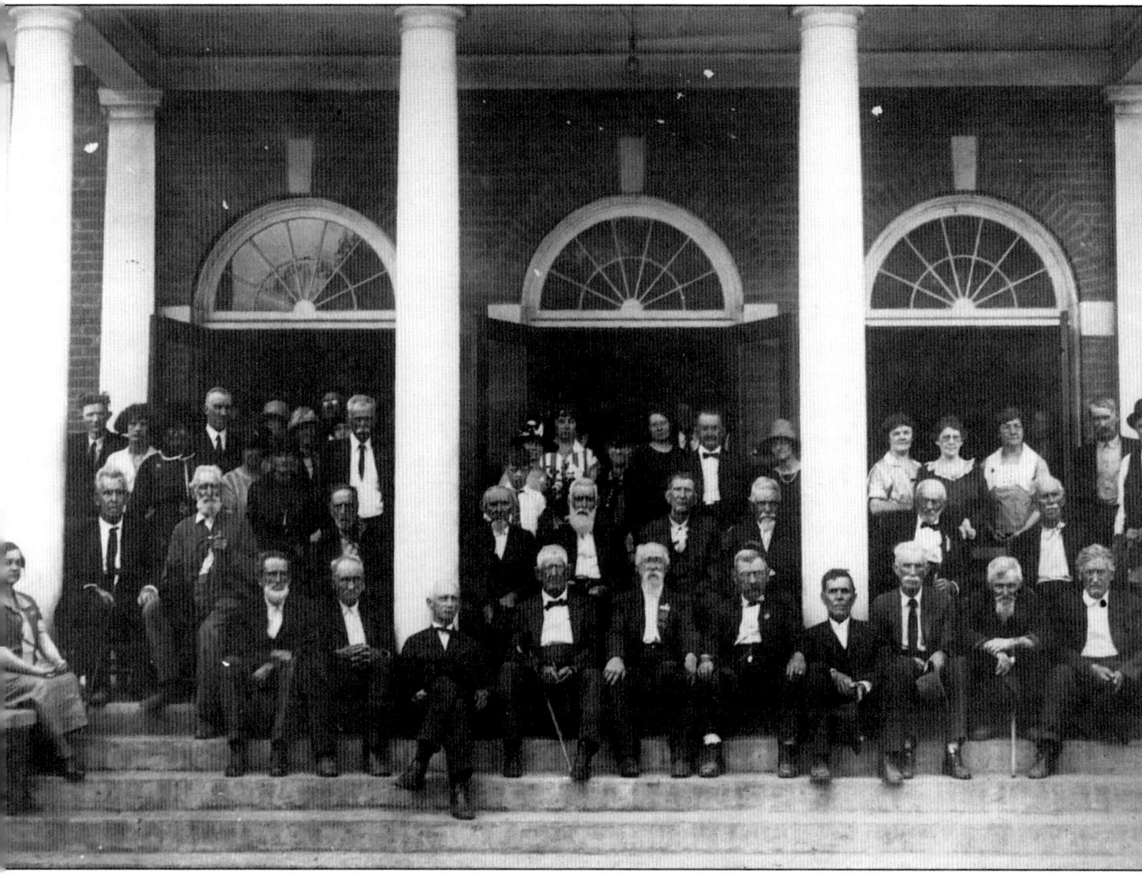

W.M. Trippe survived the war, and years later joined other Confederate veterans in this 1922 reunion in front of the Rockmart City Hall, now the police station. Trippe is seated in the front center with a cane. Polk County sent four companies of regular troops to the war. Raised by J. Waddell, the 20th Regt., Georgia Volunteer Infantry, Company D was called the Toombs' Rangers and was comprised of 117 men. The 21st Regt., Georgia Volunteer Infantry, Company D, called the Cedartown Guards and raised by Colonel J.J. Morrison, served under Captain S.A. Borders and was made up of 151 men (Seaborn Jones served as captain until the unit was mustered into service, when he was promoted to lieutenant colonel and served at battalion level). Colonel J.J. Morrison also raised the 1st Regt., Georgia Volunteer Cavalry, Company A, which served under Captain J.C. Crabb and comprised of 122 men. Lastly, Phillip's Legion, Georgia Infantry, Company D, or simply Polk Rifles, served under Captain H.F. Wimberly and was 187 men strong.

In 1862, William Riley Brock enlisted in Bartow County's Company K, 18th Georgia, and left for the war from his home in Van Wert. After fighting in several major engagements and being wounded, he returned to settle in the Friendship community. Using thread which they dyed with roots, bark, leaves, berries, and even weeds, a ladies aid society cut and sewed shirts and trousers to outfit the new soldiers.

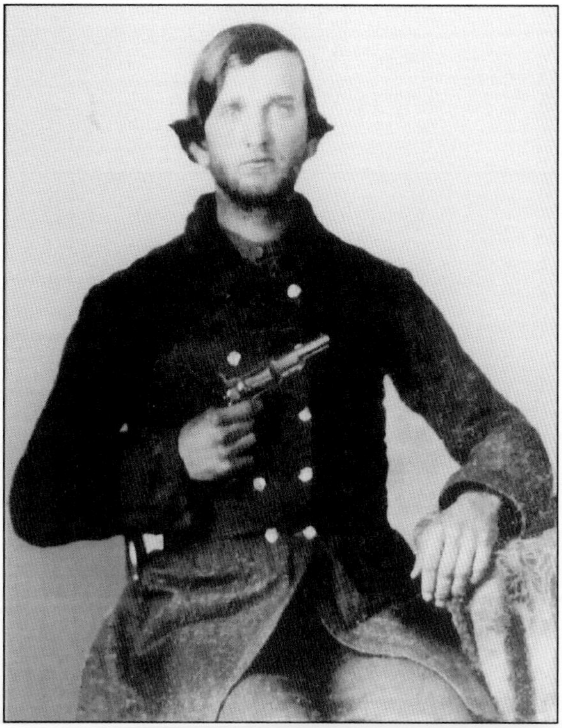

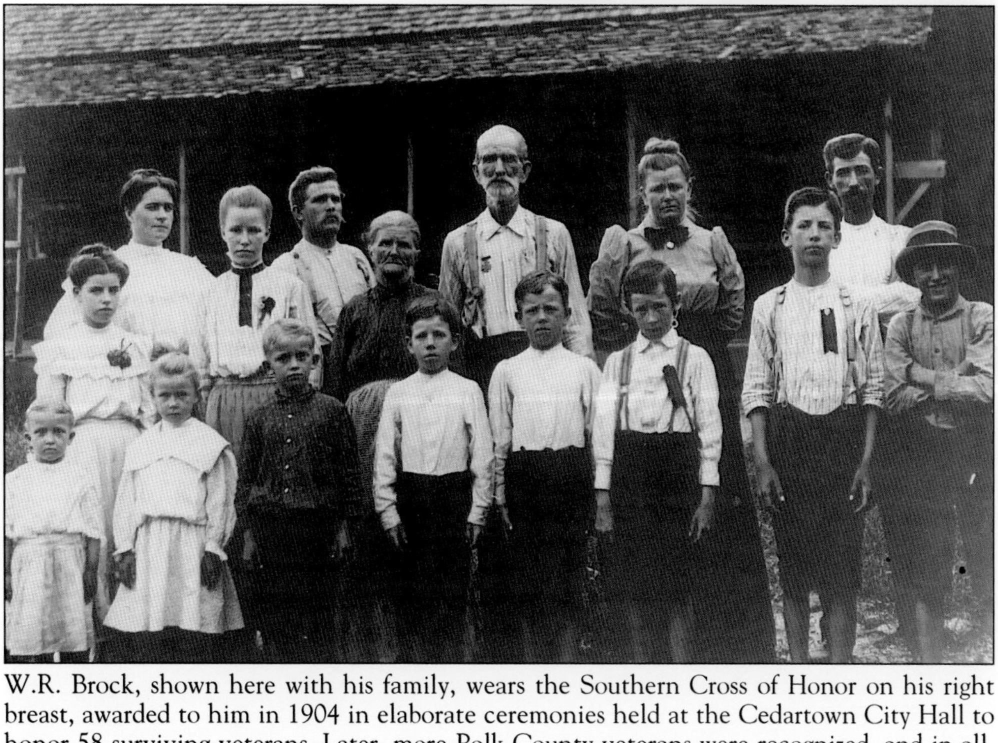

W.R. Brock, shown here with his family, wears the Southern Cross of Honor on his right breast, awarded to him in 1904 in elaborate ceremonies held at the Cedartown City Hall to honor 58 surviving veterans. Later, more Polk County veterans were recognized, and in all, 227 medals were awarded. The children in this image are wearing their Sunday best—which did not include shoes.

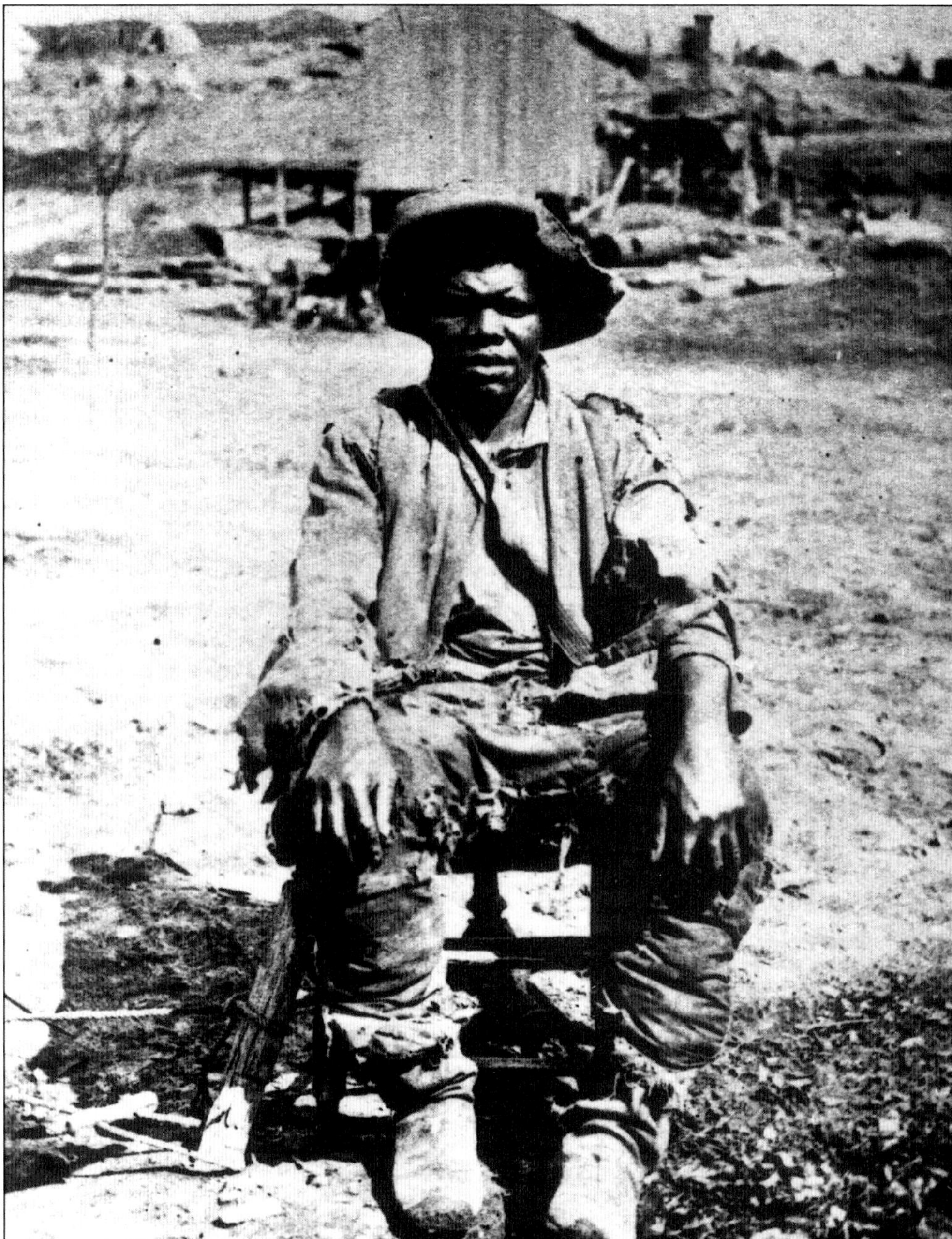

In 1860, the white population of Polk County was 6,295 with 1,171 slaves. In 1864, Hubbard Prior was laboring as one of Haden Prior's (Pryor) slaves, just one of 117 slaves on the largest plantation in Polk County. Sherman's forces were threatening to invade from the north, and the countryside was in chaos. The 22-year-old Hubbard Prior took the occasion to escape from bondage, leaving his mother, wife, and three children at the Prior plantation. He made his way north to Chattanooga and joined Company A, 44th U.S. Colored Infantry, in March. This image of the fugitive slave in rags, as well as the later image in his new uniform, was made by a photographer accompanying the Union army. (Courtesy National Archives.)

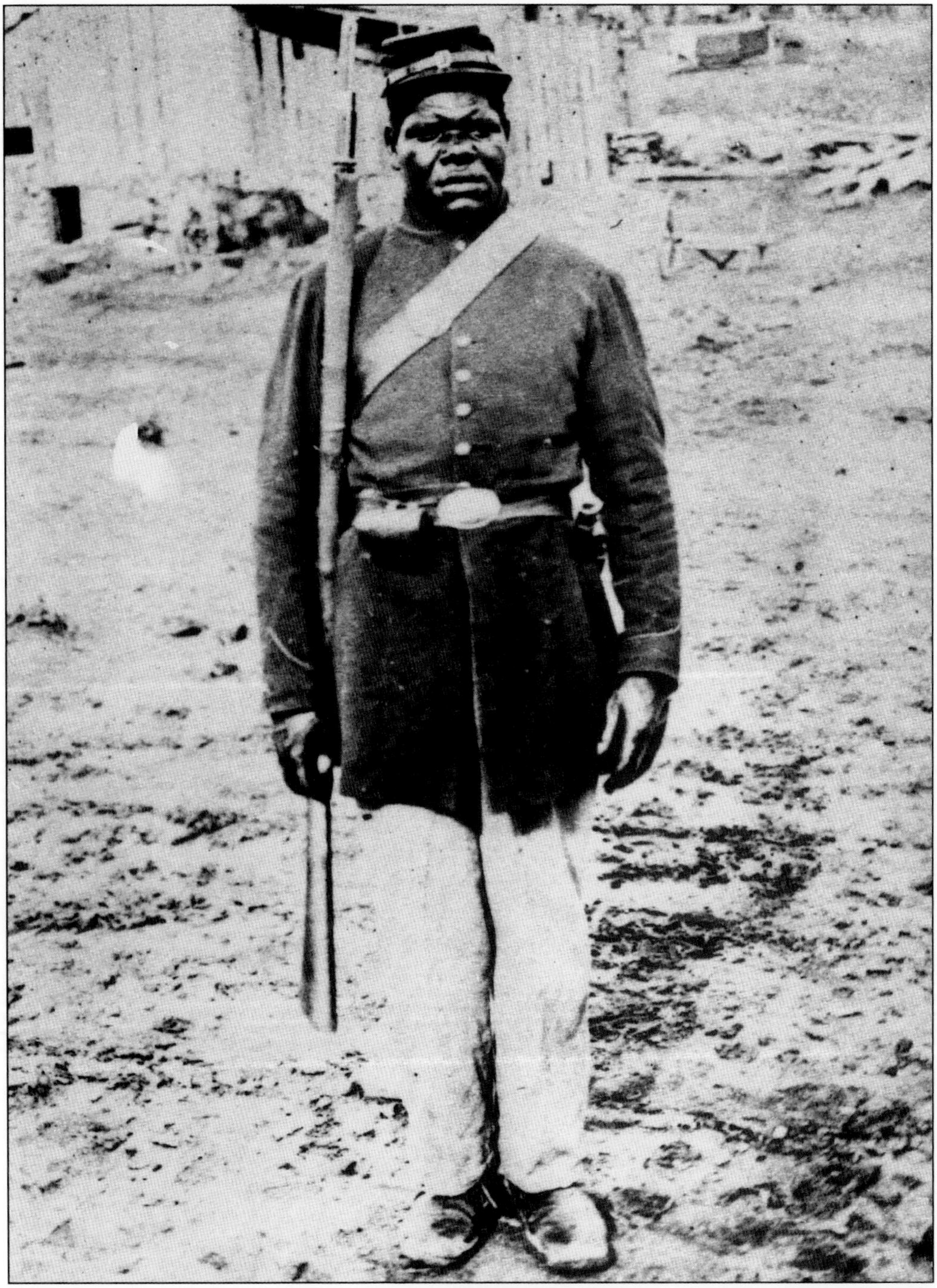

Prior's unit marched south, and on October 13, 1864, engaged the Confederates in a skirmish at Dalton. He was taken prisoner, and when the war ended, was released near Griffin, Georgia. Traveling at night to avoid detection by vengeful ex-Confederates, he walked on to Rome, Georgia, and found refuge in a Union camp. After his wartime service, Prior returned to Polk County to become a tenant farmer. Eventually, he moved with his wife and children to Calvert, Texas, where he died in 1890. (Courtesy National Archives.)

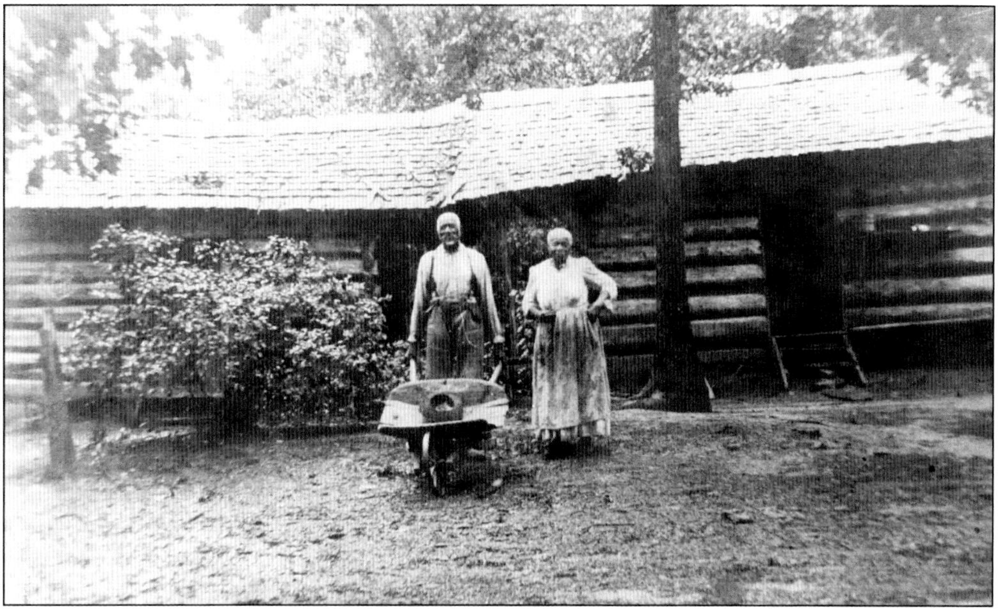

"Uncle" Jerry and his wife, Celia, served the Hightowers as slaves, and after emancipation, had little choice but to continue as tenant farmers, staying for their remaining years. The old couple held a beloved place in the family, and when they died, they were buried in the family cemetery behind the Hightower home. Before the war, Elias Hightower owned 11 slaves.

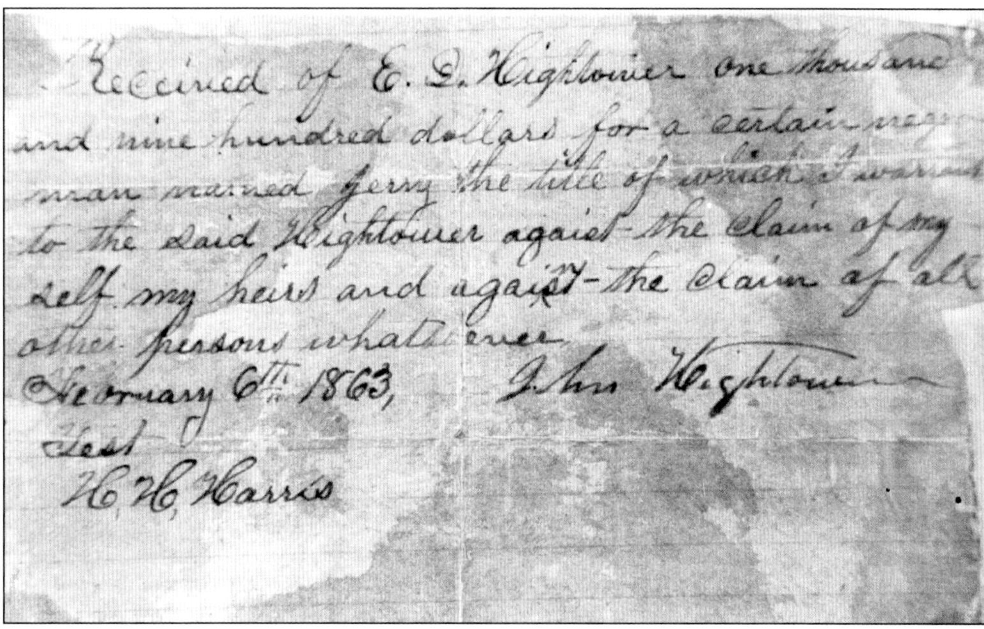

Received of E. D. Hightower one thousand and nine hundred dollars for a certain negro man named Jerry the title of which I warrant to the said Hightower against the claim of my self my heirs and against the claim of all other persons whatever

February 6th 1863, John Hightower

Test

H. H. Harris

Elias Hightower, it is said, anticipated the emancipation of slaves and purchased slaves from family members to take the financial loss on himself. This bill of sale records that E.D. Hightower paid $1,900 to John Hightower for "a negro man named Jerry" in 1863. The price of $1,900 paid for one slave seems extremely generous; an able-bodied field hand would have sold for $1,200 at the time.

McAllen Batts "McB" Wiggins, shown in this 1898 image with his wife, Nancy, enlisted in Company K, 13th Alabama, in 1861 and served until the surrender. He was wounded on the first day in the battle of Gettysburg, and for the remainder of his life carried the scar, said to be a hole in his wrist big enough to drop a coin through. After the war, the couple moved to Polk County to rebuild their shattered lives.

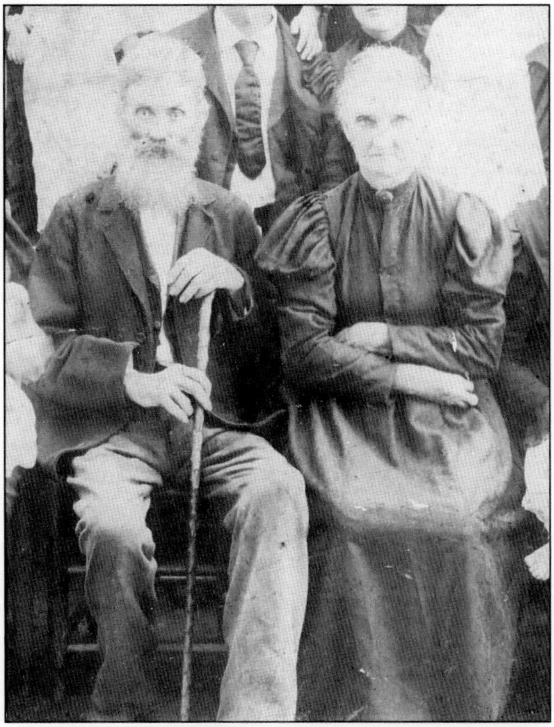

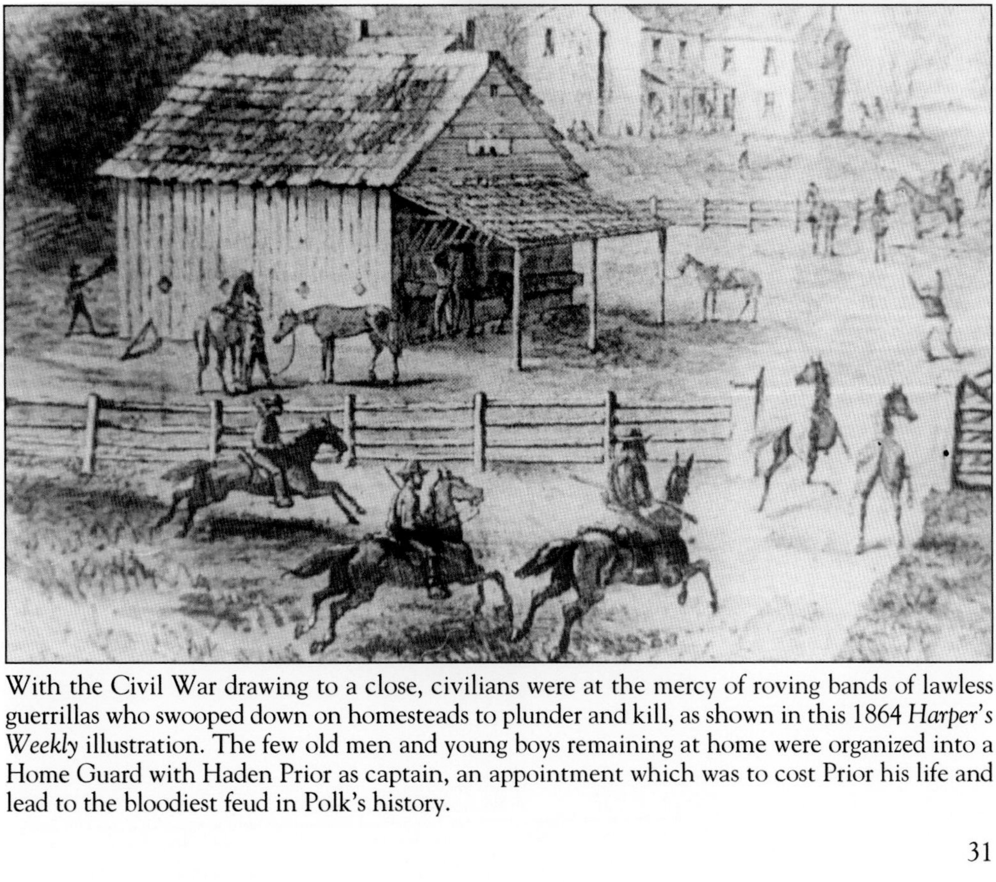

With the Civil War drawing to a close, civilians were at the mercy of roving bands of lawless guerrillas who swooped down on homesteads to plunder and kill, as shown in this 1864 *Harper's Weekly* illustration. The few old men and young boys remaining at home were organized into a Home Guard with Haden Prior as captain, an appointment which was to cost Prior his life and lead to the bloodiest feud in Polk's history.

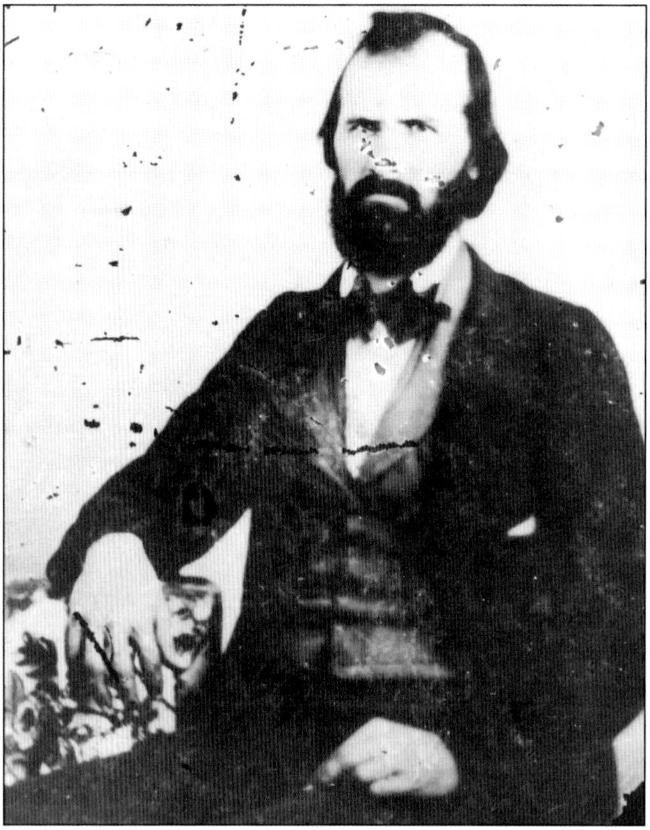

Haden Prior, son of Asa Prior, maintained the Prior plantation, the most prosperous in the county. Seen here at 53, he and his Home Guard arrested Jack Colquitt's gang for raiding Cedar Valley farmers. In revenge for the arrest, the gang killed Haden Prior on April 6, 1865. Haden's son, John Prior, in a rage, tracked down six gang members and killed them where he found them. The "Polk County Avenger" was never charged with the killings.

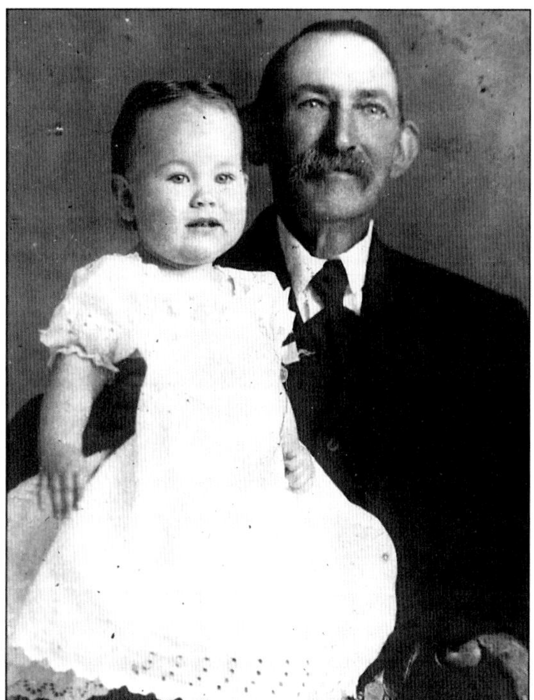

Many years after earning his reputation as an avenging killer, John Prior moved West with his daughter to live in Roseburg, Oregon. There he lived peacefully and enjoyed his life with an adoring granddaughter, Georgia Matilda Davis, shown in this *c.* 1909 image with John Prior. He died peacefully in 1910.

Three

The Industrial Period

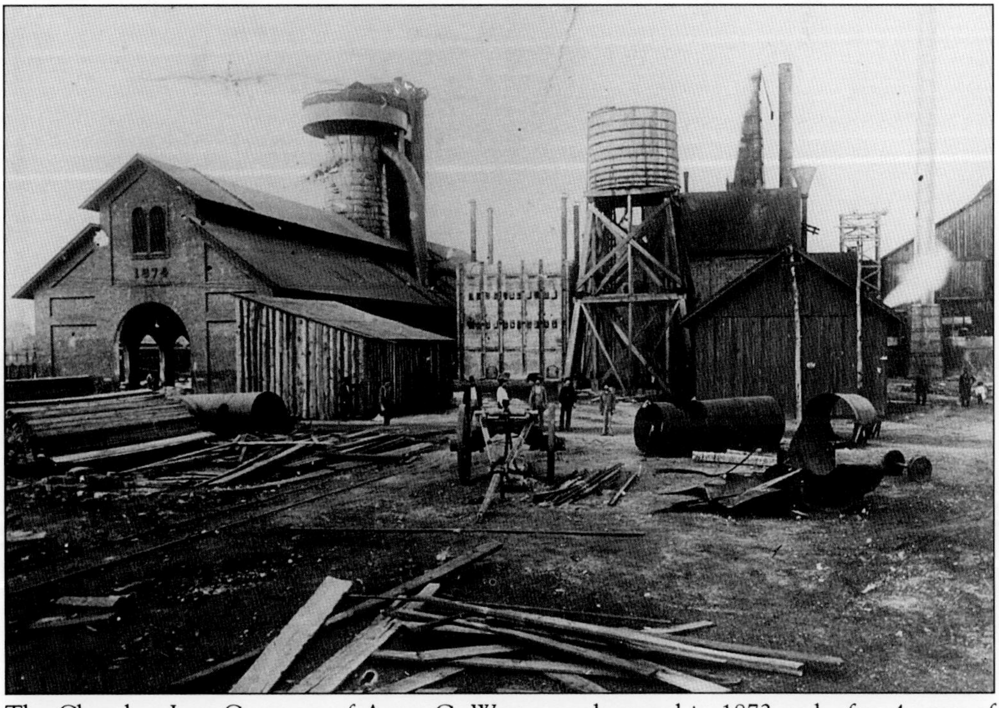

The Cherokee Iron Company of Amos G. West was chartered in 1873 and, after 4 years of construction, started producing 50 tons daily. Every ton of pig iron required over 2 tons of iron ore, almost a ton of limestone, and over a ton of charcoal, all of which had to be transported by wagon for two years before the Cherokee Railroad was completed to Cedartown. Every year the furnace operated, colliers had to cut 15 square miles of mature timberland into cordwood for charcoaling. The iron furnace of the Cherokee Iron Company is shown here c. 1890 during rebuilding to increase capacity to 75 tons daily. On the left is the casting house and 75-foot blast furnace, ringed by wrought iron bands holding the outer shell of cast-iron plates. Behind the water tank are the engine-rooms housing the 500-horsepower blast-air blower and coal-fired boilers.

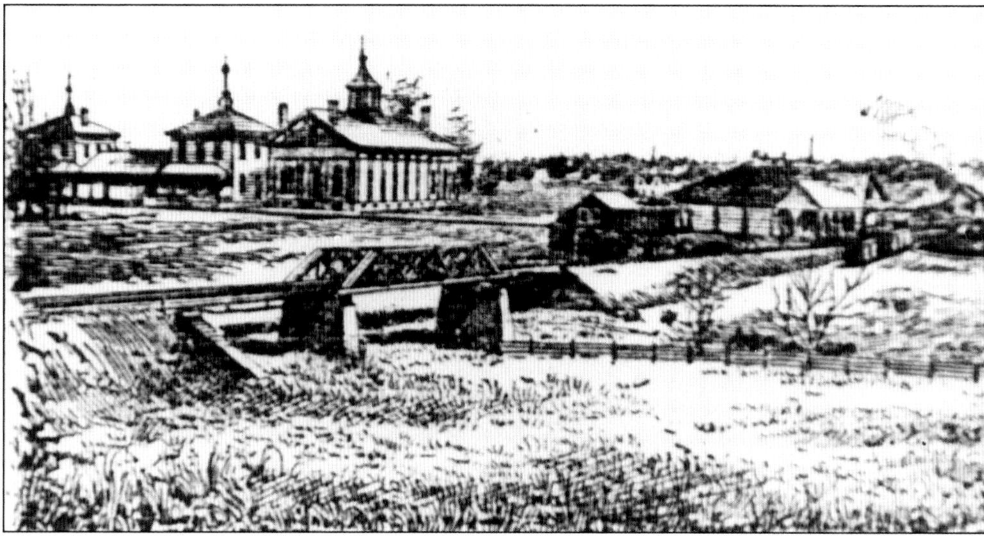

Numerous buildings sprawl along the east bank of Cedar Creek in 1887. Above the bridge is the company store where townspeople were invited to shop. On the left stands the new depot of the narrow-gauge Cherokee Railroad, later the East & West Railroad of Alabama, and on the right are the roundhouse and repair shops, which remained busy until the early 1900s, when the Seaboard Air Line acquired the railroad.

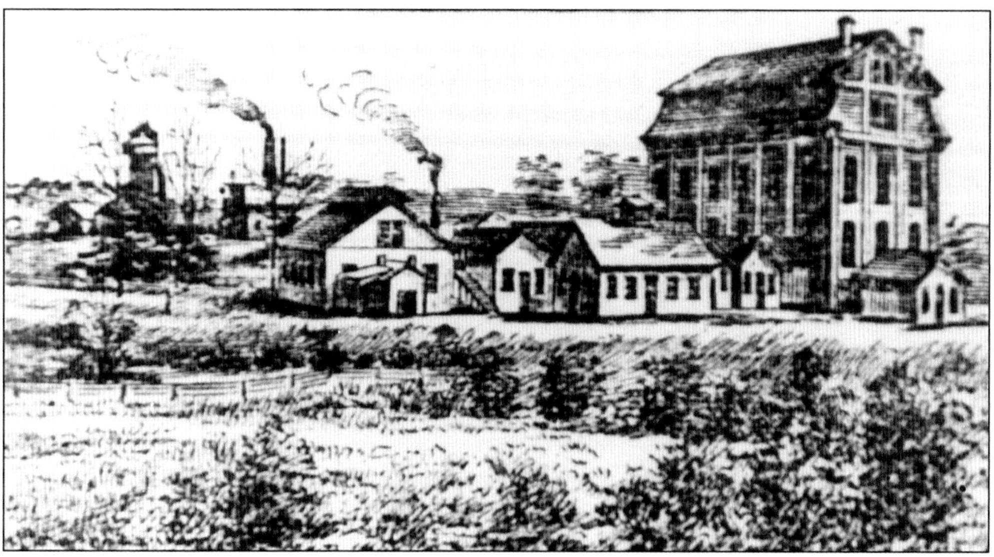

The Cherokee Iron Company's gristmill stood four stories high and for many years was the tallest structure in town. A sizable dam was built on Cedar Creek to supply waterpower to the mill and machine shops. About 60 laborers in two shifts heaved and sweated day and night, as the furnace could not be shut down. Many of the workers were convicted criminals and each trailed a ball and chain.

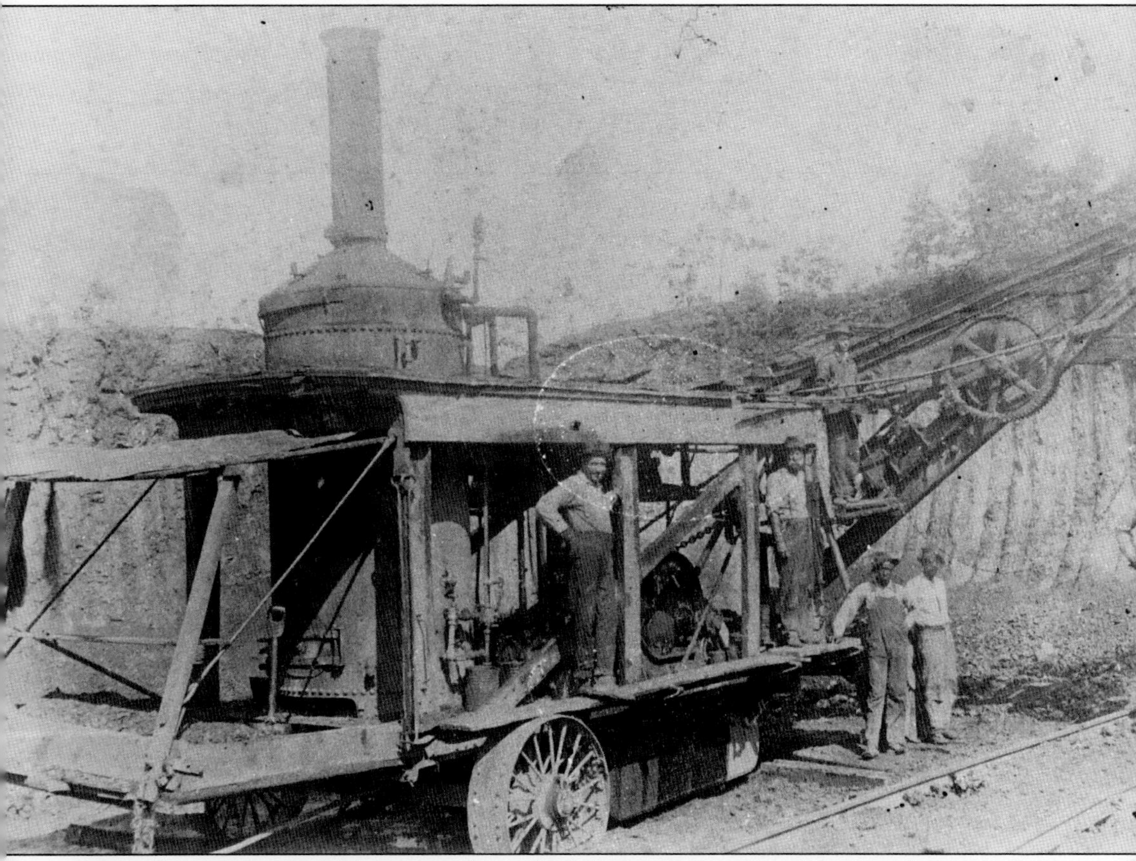

In the late 1800s, chained convicts labored in the iron ore pits with pick and shovel. Later, steam shovels were used in the county's many mines. The brown hematite ore for the iron furnaces at Etna and Cedartown was first shipped by wagon and later by rail. Over a 30-year period the Grady Mine alone produced 1,000,000 tons of the brown hematite ore, one-third of the total Georgia production.

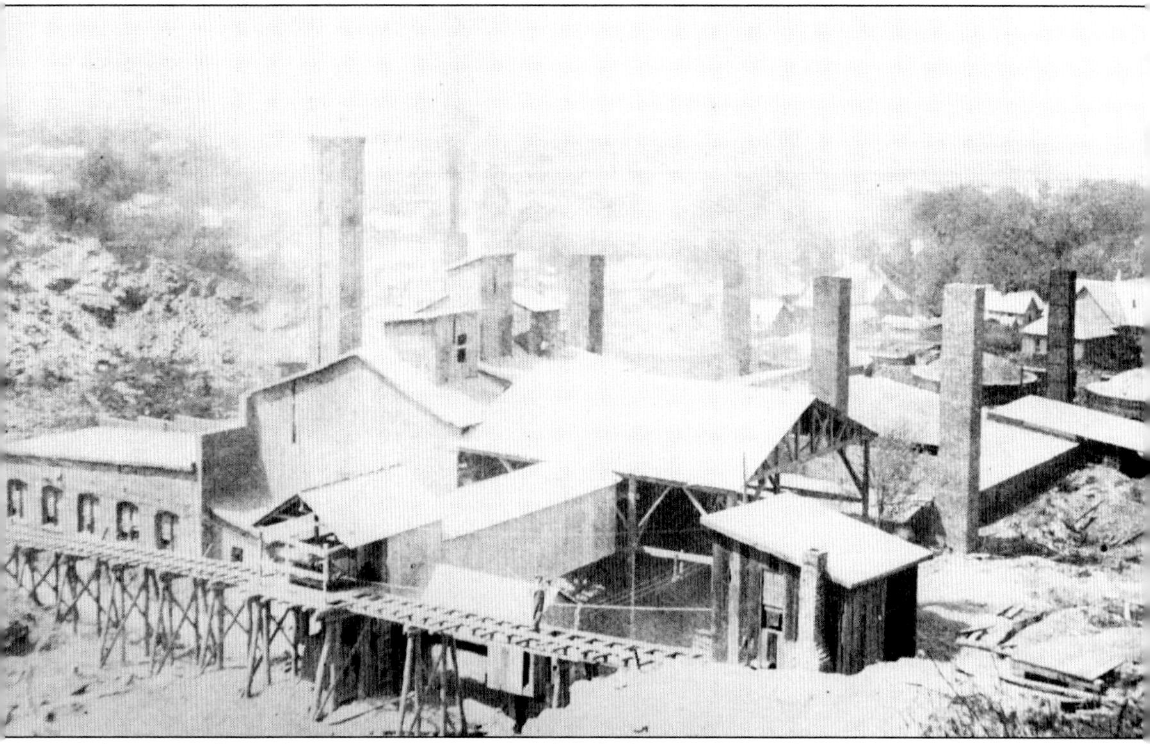

The Monarch Brick Company was organized with the intention of producing slate and using the waste in brick manufacturing. By the time the brick plant was built in 1900, the demand for slate was declining rapidly, and the company never produced any slate. Monarch was soon reorganized, becoming the Rockmart Shale Brick and Slate Company. For about 20 years the brick plant manufactured a vitrified paving brick, using, in part, weathered slate or shale. (Courtesy Georgia Department of Archives and History.)

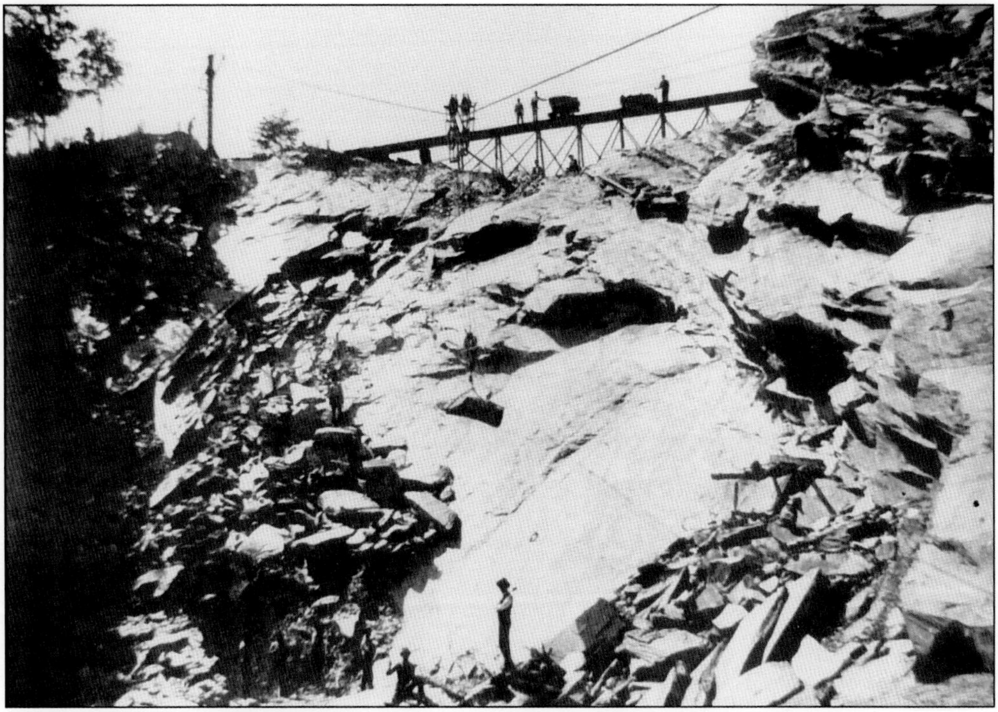

Quarry workers in the old Dever quarry pause while a block of slate is hoisted over 100 feet and loaded onto a narrow-gauge rail buggy for transport to the splitting sheds in this *c.* 1918 image. According to legend, slate was accidentally discovered when a Blance family member was staking out a cow. In 1850, Joseph G. Blance recognized the value of the nearly black slate vein and started a quarry.

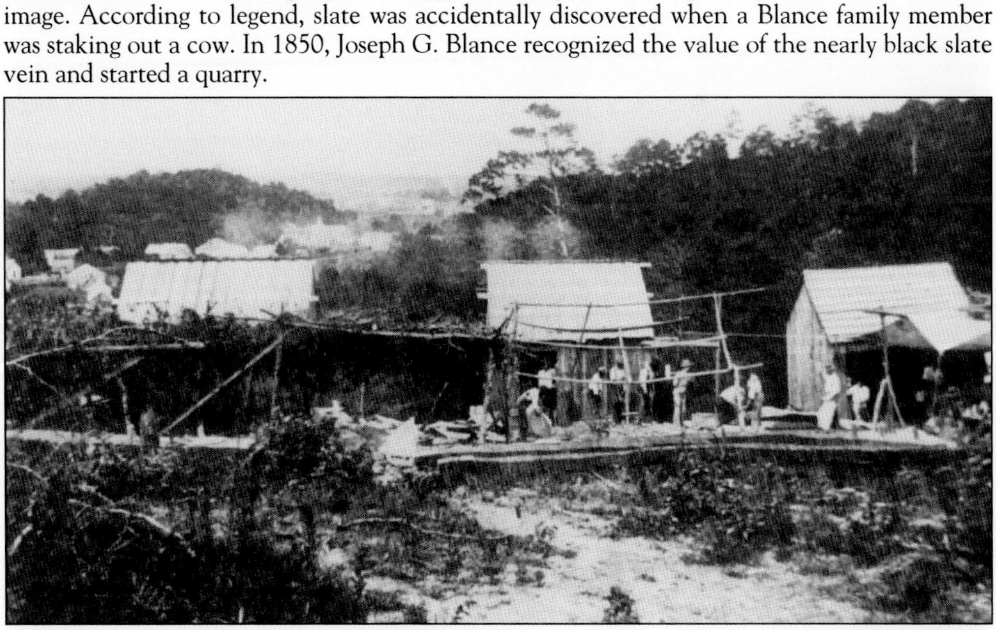

Slate-splitting shanties were organized with three skilled craftsmen: block-maker, splitter, and dresser. Each shanty daily produced over 50 square feet of roofing slate, or about 3,000 pounds, which was packed into burlap bags and loaded in wagons for shipment to Rome and Cartersville. The skilled slate workers who came from northern Wales to work the quarries settled in Rockmart.

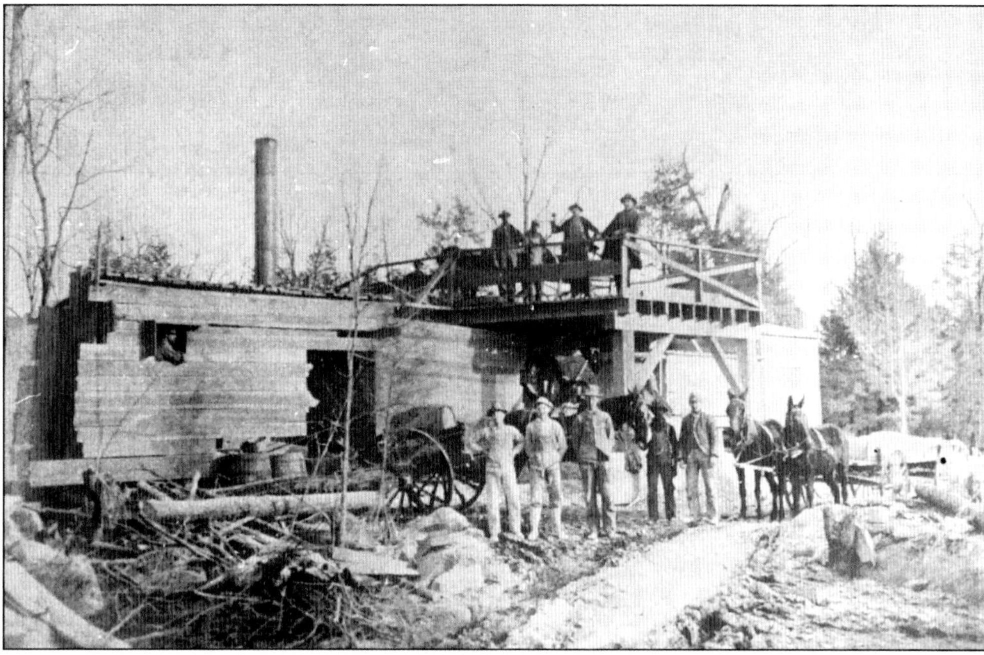

In this 1902 picture, workers pause during the construction of a concrete powerhouse for the Southern States Portland Cement Company. Innovations in power generation in this plant attracted visitors from as far away as Europe to learn more of this "model power plant of the world." The company started in late 1903 and continued in operation for 50 years before being sold to the Marquette Cement Company.

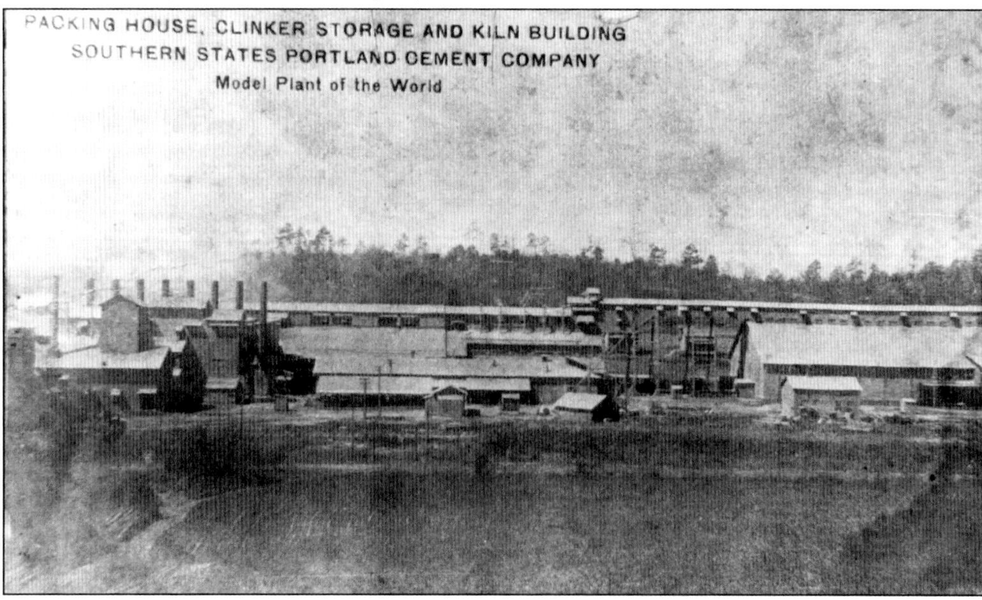

The Southern States Portland Cement Company was organized by J.F. Vandeventer, but start-up and financial problems caused Dan Simon to be brought in as superintendent. It was located 4 miles north of Rockmart in Aragon, at a site having ample deposits of limestone and shale needed for cement production. The weathered slate or shale and limestone were ground and roasted to make Portland cement.

Milton Hendrick takes a break from shoveling coal to pose for this photograph in front of the boiler which he operated in the early 1900s at the Southern States Portland Cement Company. The photographer was J.A. Morris of Cartersville. (Courtesy Georgia Department of Archives and History.)

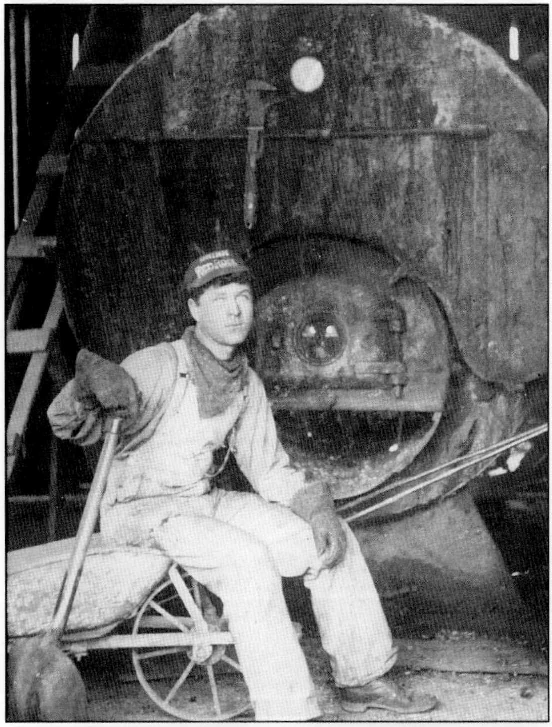

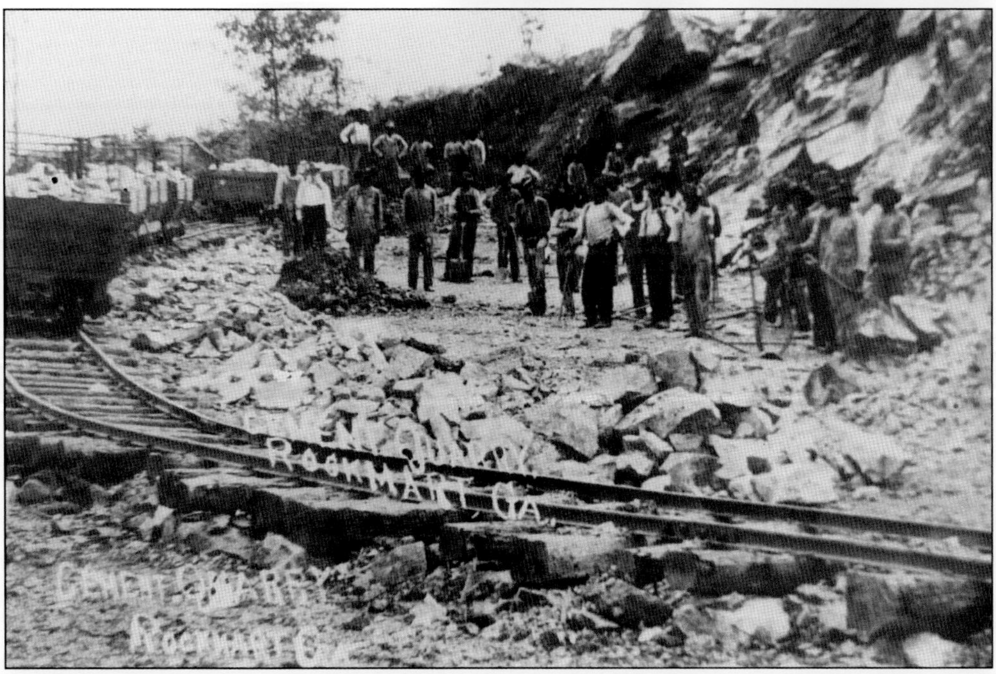

In the first step of cement making, workers dynamited limestone from its bed and broke the rocks into smaller pieces with sledgehammers. The pieces were loaded into cars and transported to a crusher, where the rocks were reduced to a size of 2 or 3 inches. Narrow-gauge steam locomotives, or "dinkies," pulled the cars of stone to the cement plant, probably the Southern States Portland Cement Company.

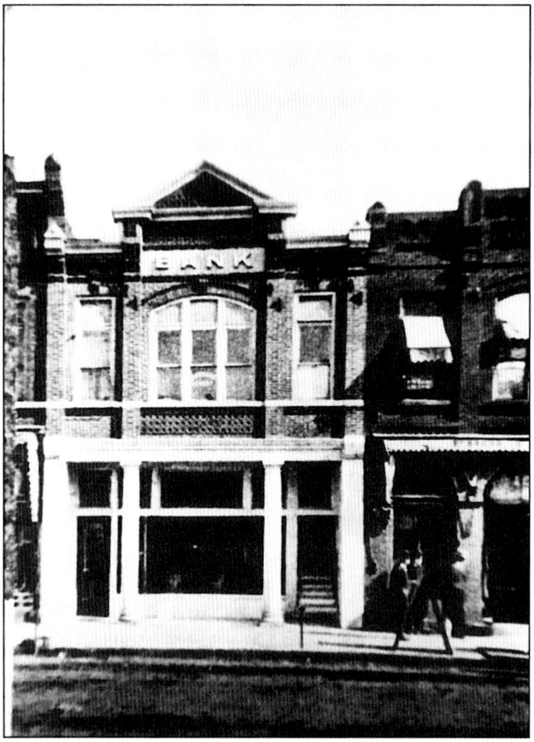

Hardwick & Company opened this branch office of their Dalton bank in 1883. The Clay Brothers, S.L. and H.B., made the bricks and erected the building pictured about 1887. The bank management bragged that their new "vault and safe are both fire and burglar proof, Hall's latest patent." J.O. Hardwick, the bank manager, was also the treasurer of the Cherokee Land and Improvement Company.

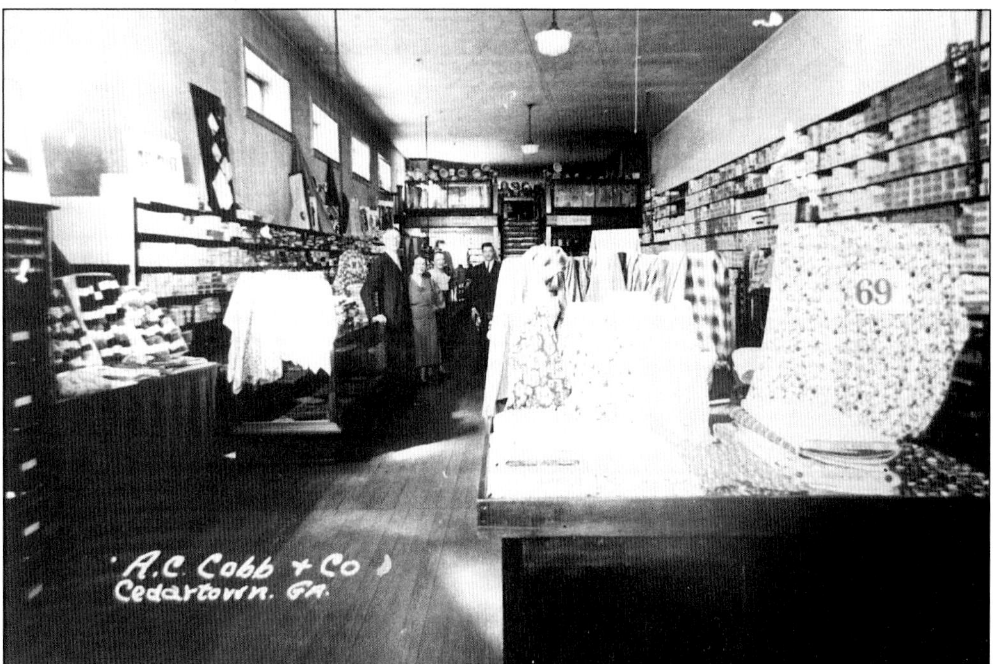

Augustus Cohen Cobb organized his company, A.C. Cobb & Company, in 1893. In 1906, the store moved to the corner of Main Street and West Avenue and for years was known as "Cobb's Corner." Pictured here *c.* 1930, the establishment had nine departments selling a variety of clothing for women and children.

William Bradford and John C. Allen opened Bradford Drugstore in 1875, which later became the Hunt Drugstore, shown here *c.* 1913. The stairway to the right led upstairs to Hunt Jewelry, a business which purchased the pharmacy in 1918 and relocated to that street-level shop.

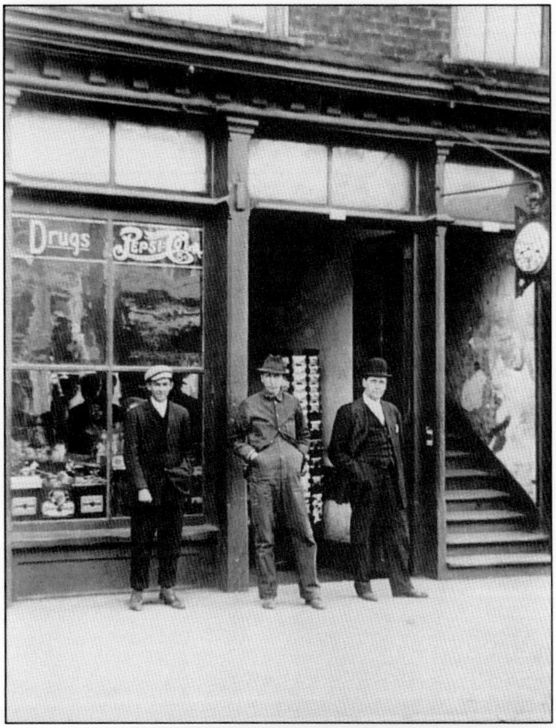

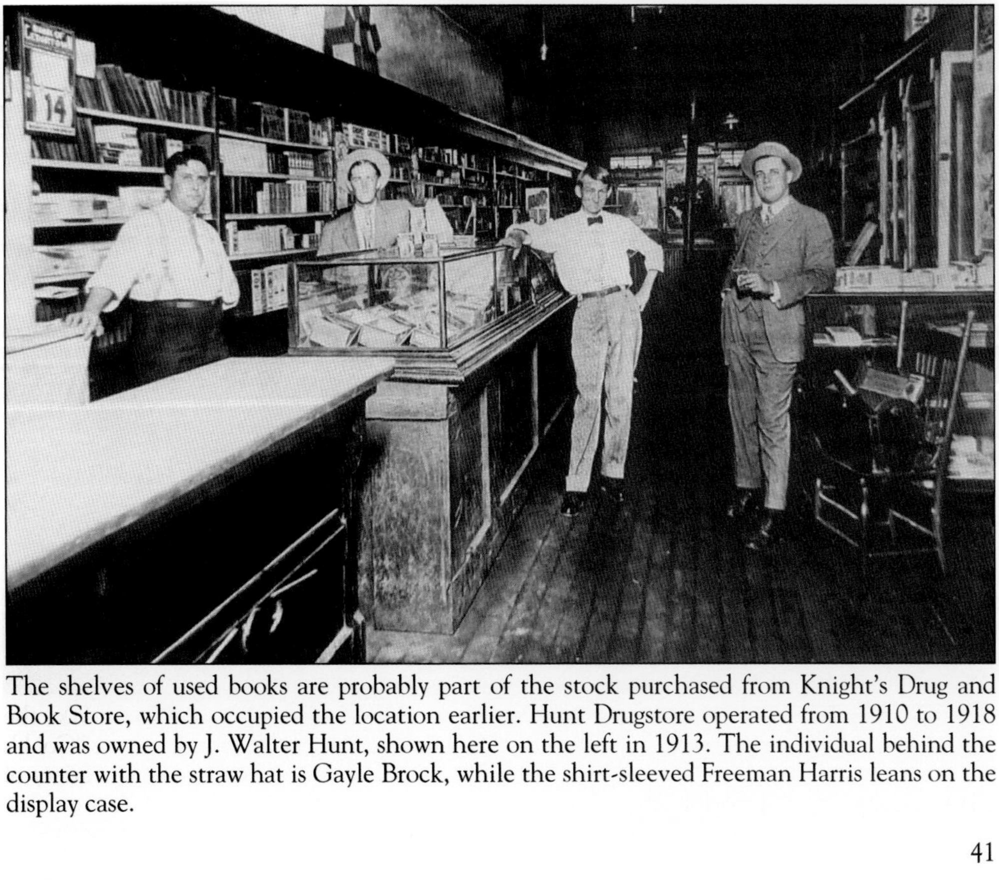

The shelves of used books are probably part of the stock purchased from Knight's Drug and Book Store, which occupied the location earlier. Hunt Drugstore operated from 1910 to 1918 and was owned by J. Walter Hunt, shown here on the left in 1913. The individual behind the counter with the straw hat is Gayle Brock, while the shirt-sleeved Freeman Harris leans on the display case.

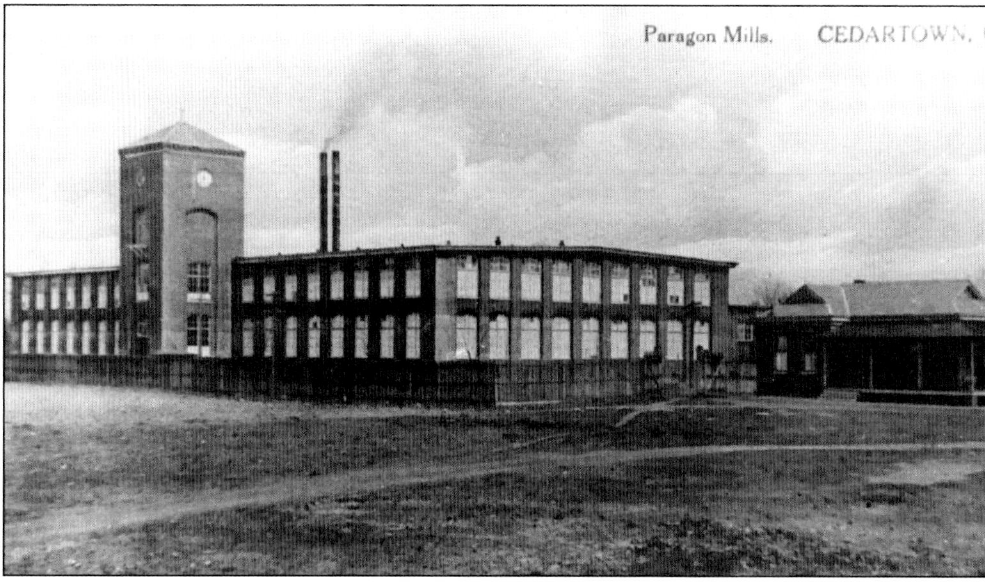

William Parker built the Paragon Mill *c.* 1897, but before it could begin operations, Charles Adamson bought the mill. Combined with his Cedartown Cotton Manufacturing Company, it became the Cedartown Cotton Company. Later, after additions, the complex became the Cedartown Cotton & Export Company, making yarns for the hosiery and plush trade.

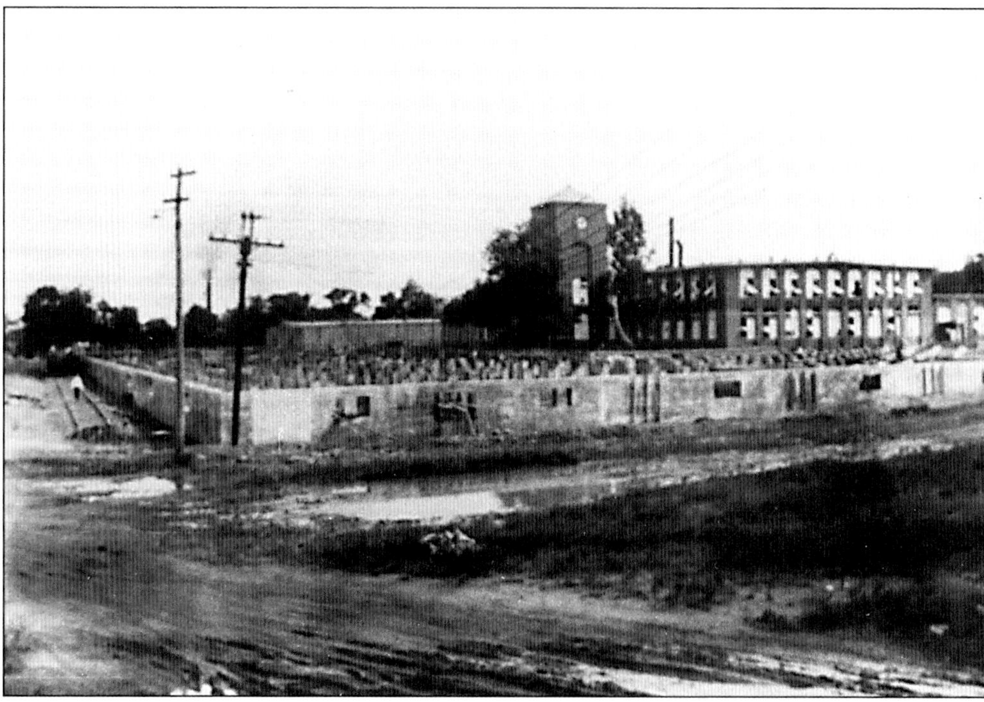

After Charles Adamson sold his Cedartown Cotton & Export Company to the Goodyear Tire & Rubber Company in 1925, this new building, shown under construction in 1926, was erected by Goodyear. While piles were driven, concrete poured, and old machinery was replaced, the mill continued operating without interruption. The plant was named the Clearwater Mill, after the sparkling waters of the Big Spring.

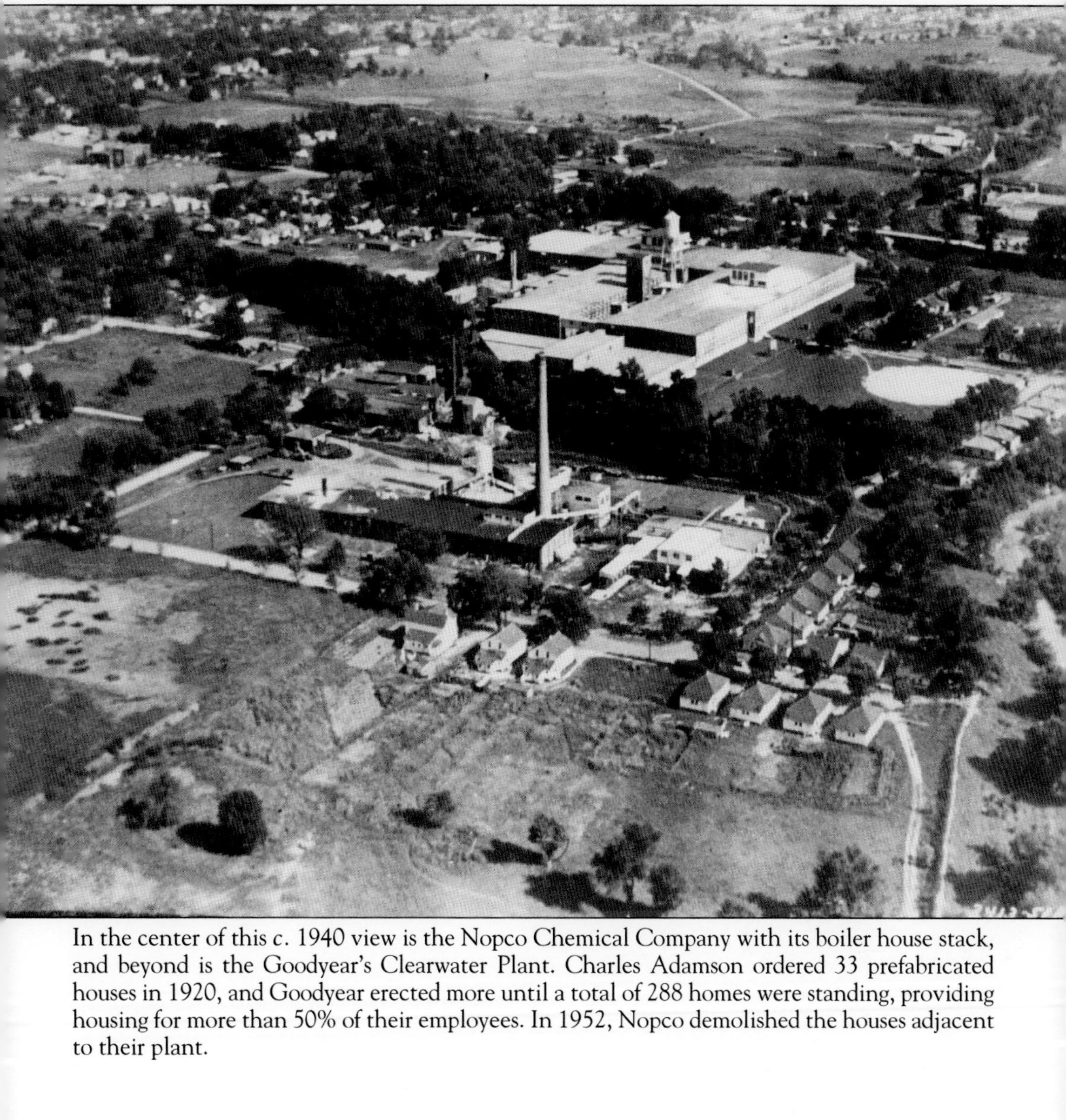

In the center of this *c.* 1940 view is the Nopco Chemical Company with its boiler house stack, and beyond is the Goodyear's Clearwater Plant. Charles Adamson ordered 33 prefabricated houses in 1920, and Goodyear erected more until a total of 288 homes were standing, providing housing for more than 50% of their employees. In 1952, Nopco demolished the houses adjacent to their plant.

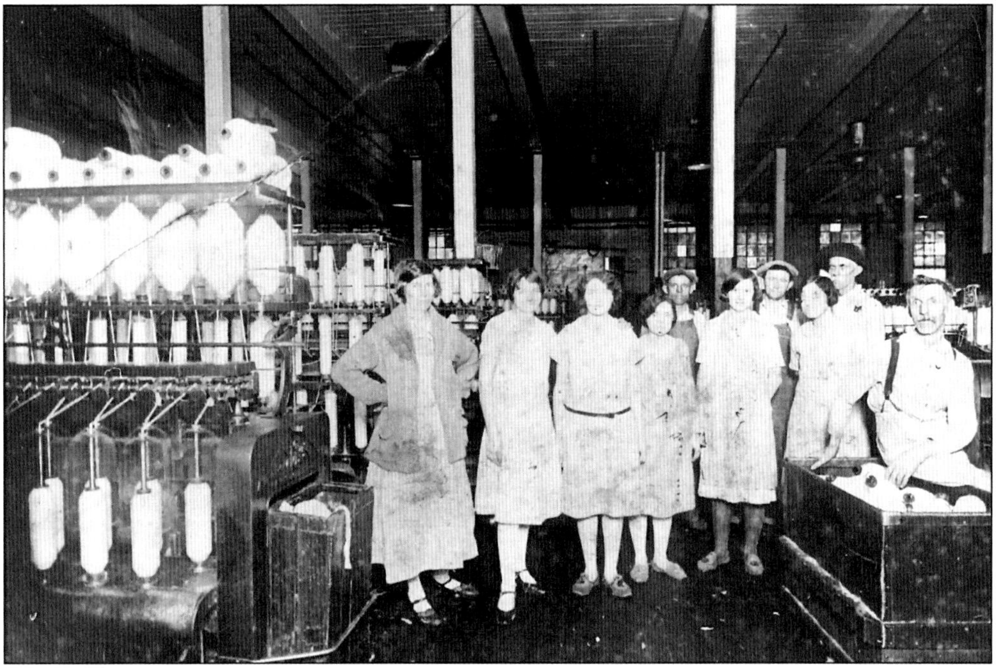

In 1926, the Goodyear Tire & Rubber Company acquired and greatly expanded Adamson's mill, and then in 1930, built a large modern mill in Rockmart. After another decade, Polk County became 11th in manufacturing employment out of Georgia's 159 counties. Textile mill work was light enough for women, and at the turn of the century, even children as young as eight years old were employed by one factory in Polk County.

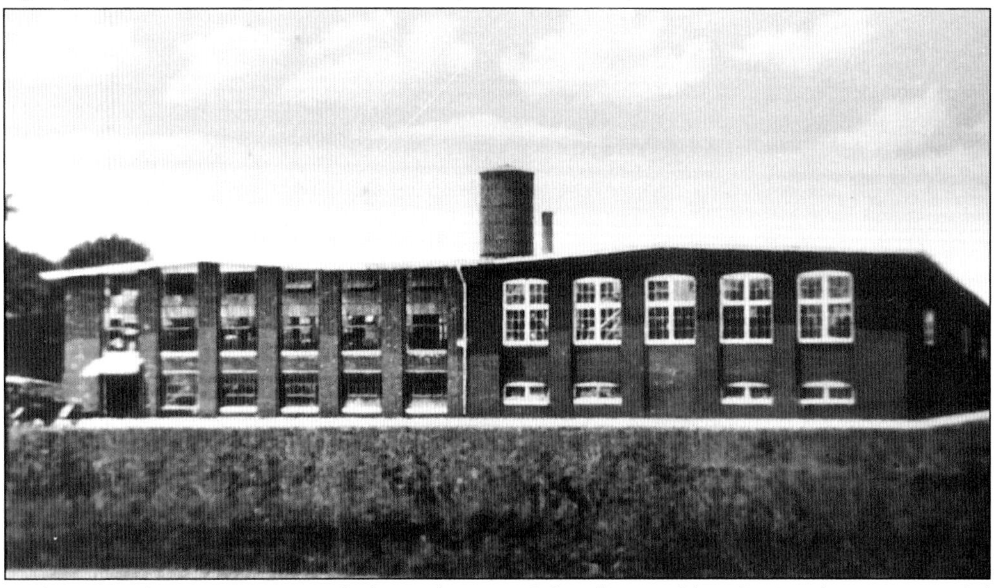

Built in 1900 by James E. Houseal, the Cedartown Oil Mill was sold to the Southern Cotton Oil Company, remaining under the management of Houseal for another 11 years. The United States Finishing Company took over in the 1920s and produced textiles until 1937. The company was acquired by the National Oil Company (Nopco), which at one time manufactured over 350 different chemicals.

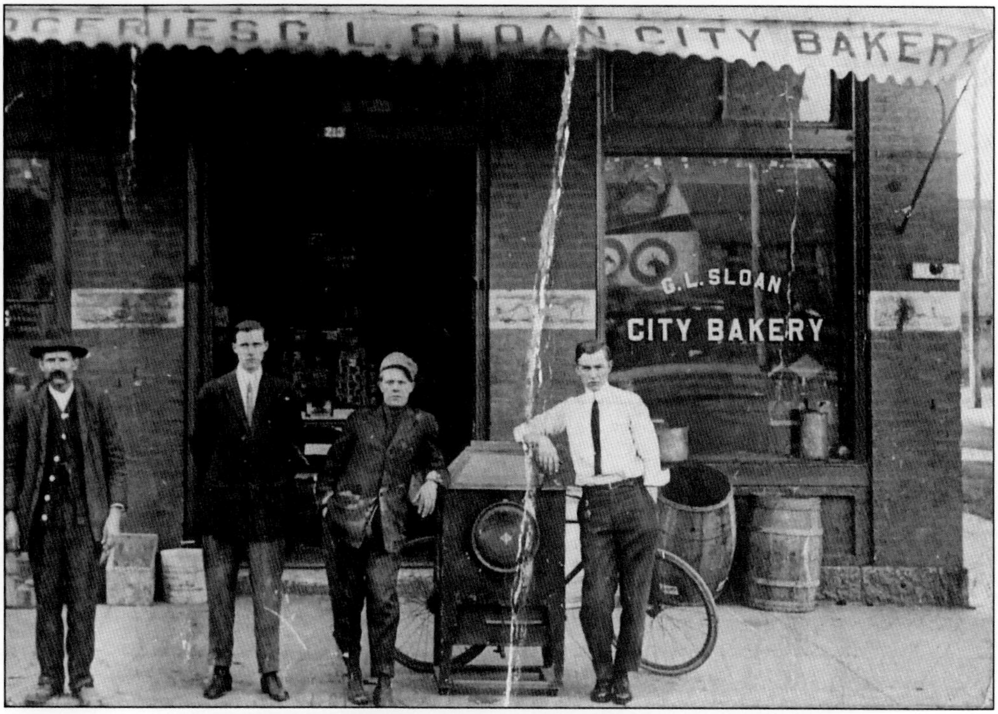

This picture and the individuals standing at the curb are not identified. In 1900, a bakery was located on the corner of Grace and Main Streets, which may have been the City Bakery of G.L. Sloan shown here. The curious device in the center of the picture is thought to be a crank-operated peanut roaster.

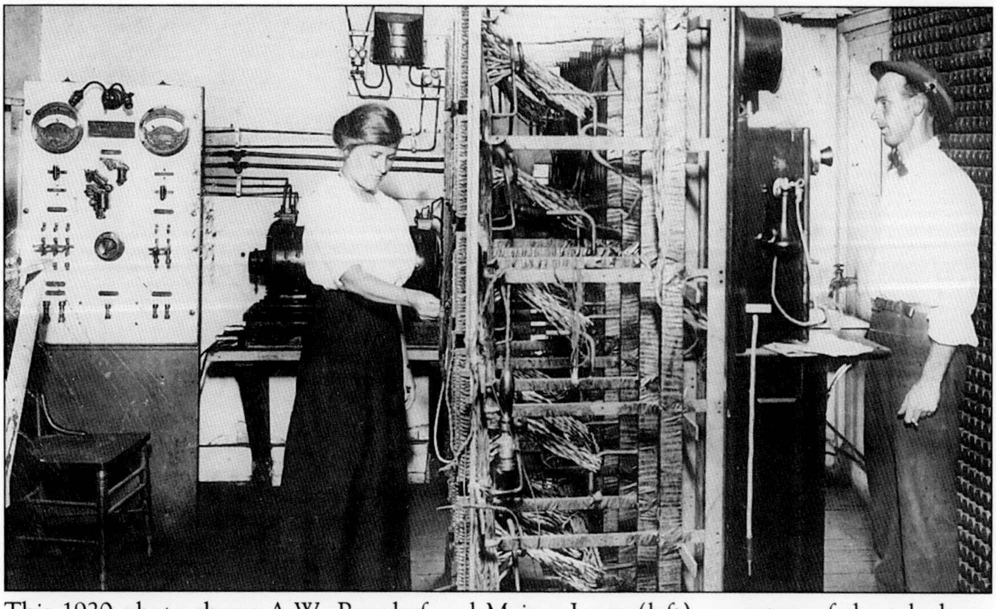
This 1920 photo shows A.W. Burgdorf and Maime Jones (left), operators of the telephone exchange which was located upstairs in the 300 block of Main Street. When the system was first installed, there were 12 telephones. The citizens protested that the wire stringing was sure to attract lightning.

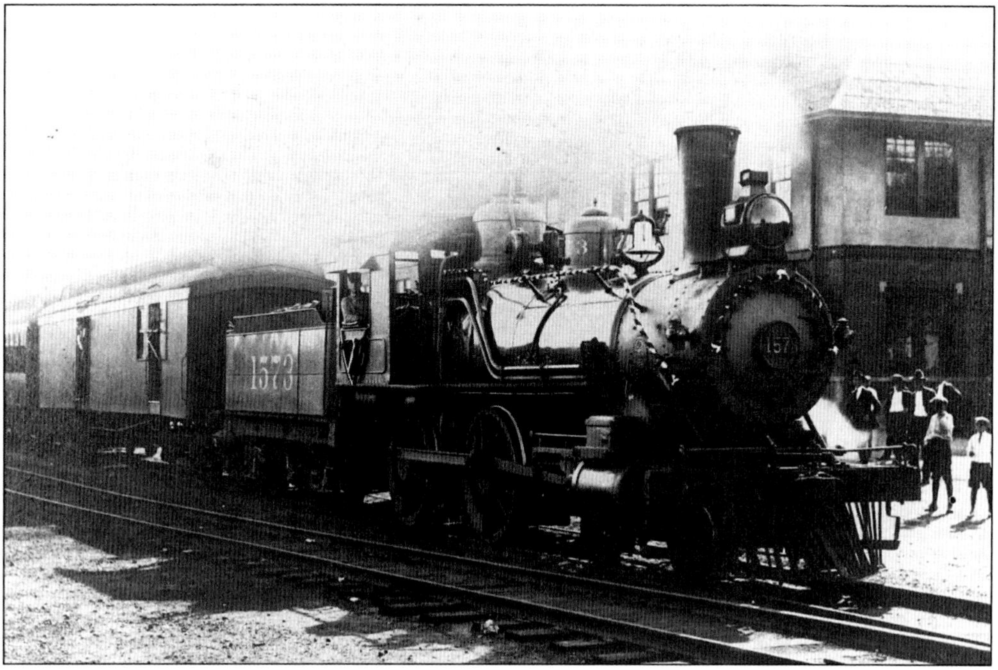

Two youngsters gaze in awe as the passenger train's locomotive of the Central of Georgia, with engineer Clarence B. Turner at the throttle, leaves Cedartown steaming north to Chattanooga, c. 1918. The Central of Georgia acquired the Chattanooga, Rome & Southern Railroad in 1901 and made Cedartown a repair center with a large roundhouse and repair shops, altogether employing over 125 men.

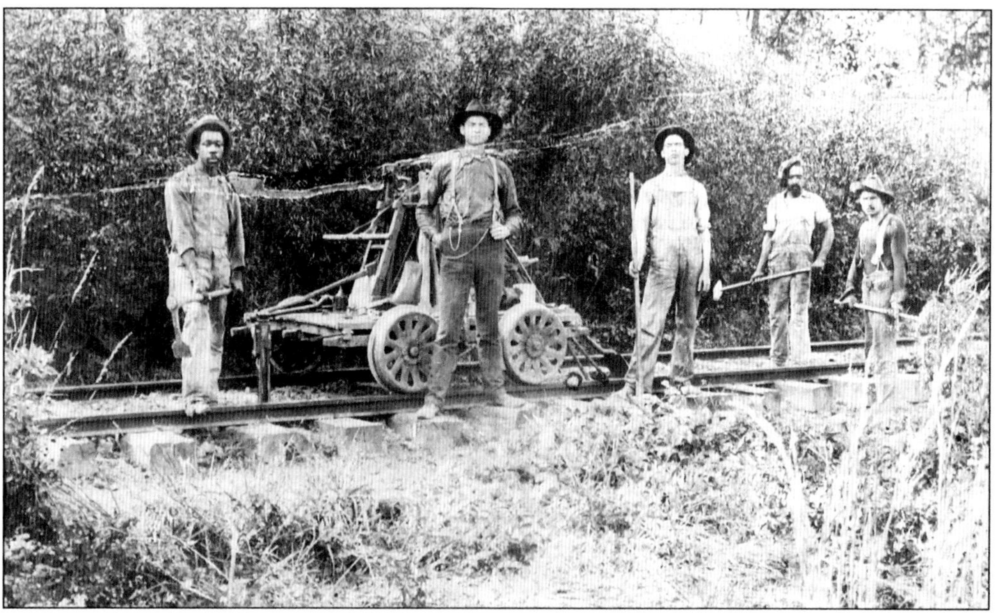

Track workers on the Seaboard Air Line Railroad pause to pose after their ride out to a job site in 1905. They appear to be about to tamp up the track and spike it down. The foreman, John Thomas Barrett, stands in front of their hand-propelled car. (Courtesy Georgia Department of Archives and History.)

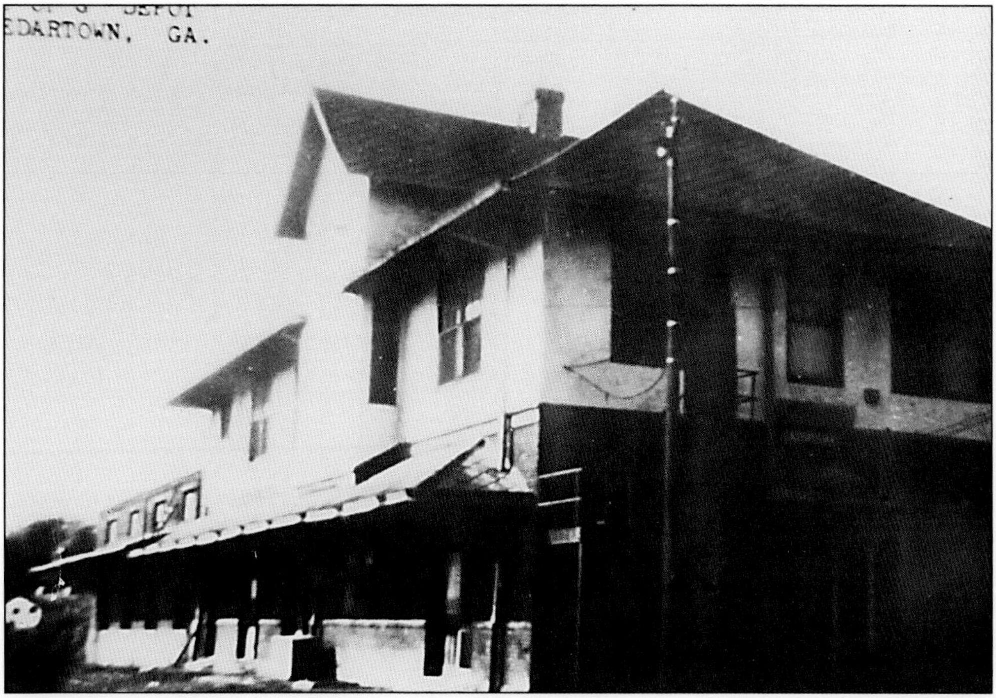

The Central of Georgia was built north-south through the county in 1887, one of four railroads which would traverse the county. The depot shown here was on the eastern edge of Cedartown. The railroad crossed the East & West Railroad south of Cedartown. The latter railroad was built by Amos West when he extended his Cherokee Railroad in 1879 from Rockmart to his iron furnace.

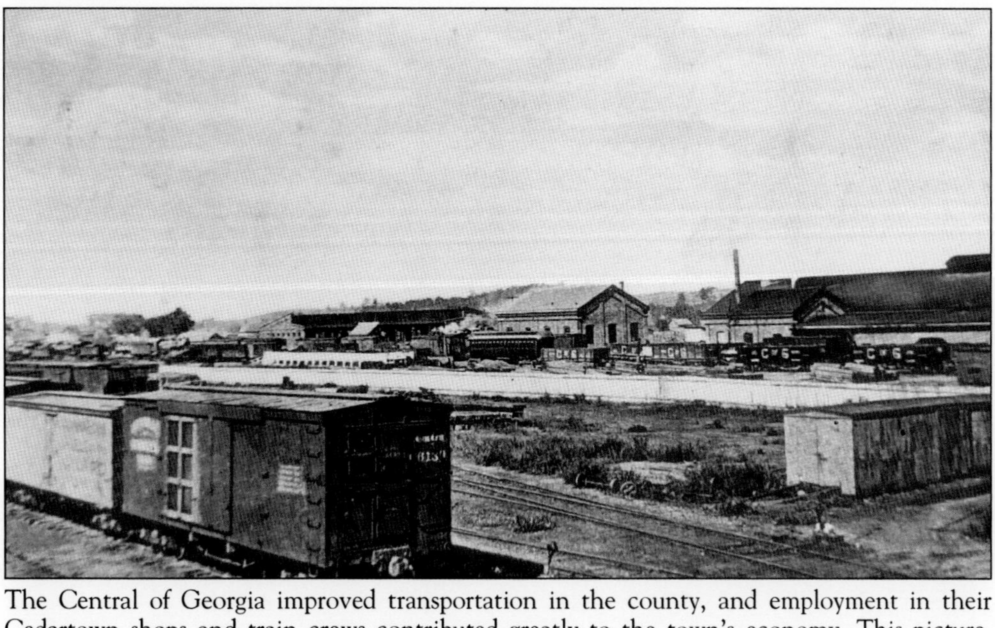

The Central of Georgia improved transportation in the county, and employment in their Cedartown shops and train crews contributed greatly to the town's economy. This picture, taken about 1920, shows the train yard in its heyday. The wooden freight cars in the foreground were gradually replaced with longer steel cars.

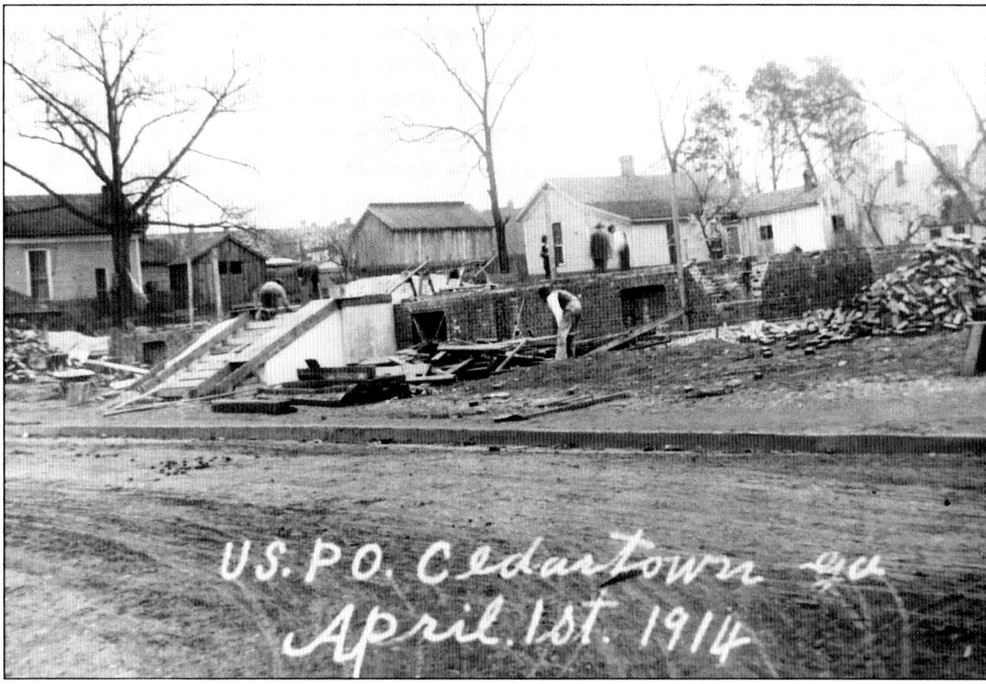

Erected on the south side of West Avenue in 1914, this brick building was designed by Arthur Wenderoth. The post office was ready for occupancy the first of 1915, and with the level of postal receipts qualifying the city, free mail delivery was to start then.

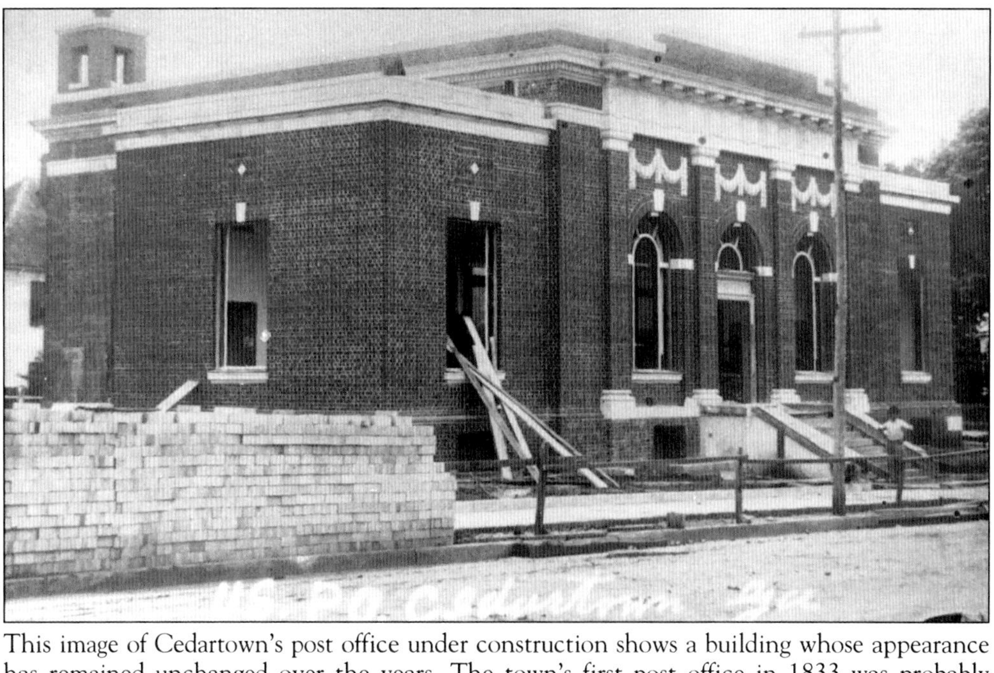

This image of Cedartown's post office under construction shows a building whose appearance has remained unchanged over the years. The town's first post office in 1833 was probably located in the store of the postmaster, John Witcher, and the second in L.H. Walthall's store during his five-year term, probably located in an area of Lime Branch known for a time as Walthall.

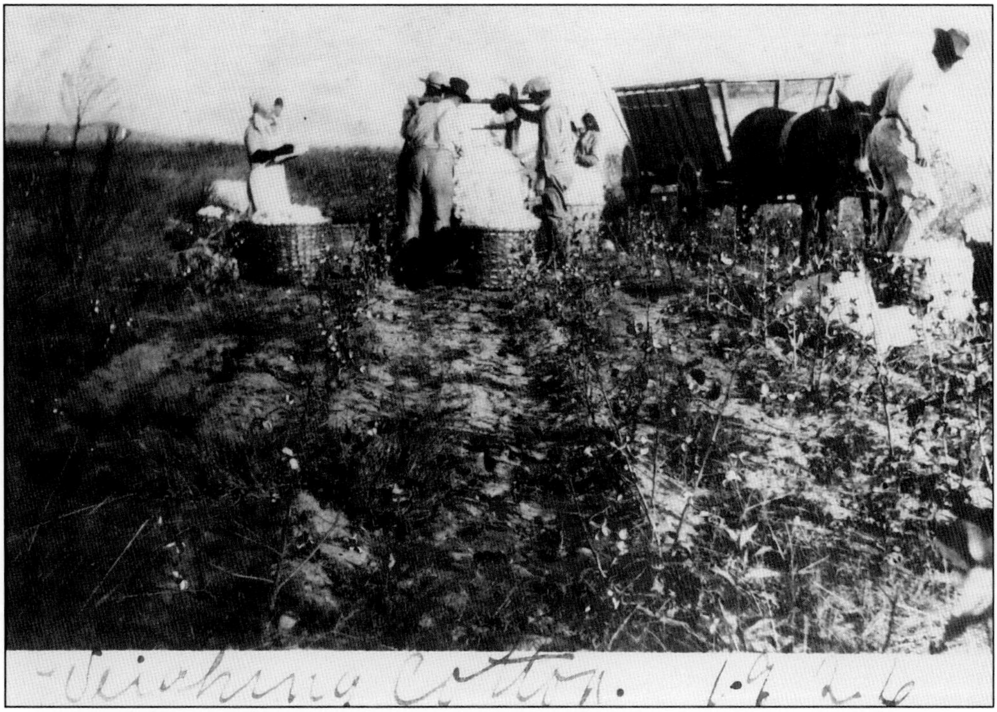

In this 1926 picture, field hands pick cotton and carry their filled baskets to be weighed. Before the Great Depression struck in 1929, cotton was recovering from dramatic price declines and the threat of the boll weevil. In addition to cotton, farmers also raised corn, wheat, oats, and hay on more than 2,000 farms in Polk County, mostly on tenant farms.

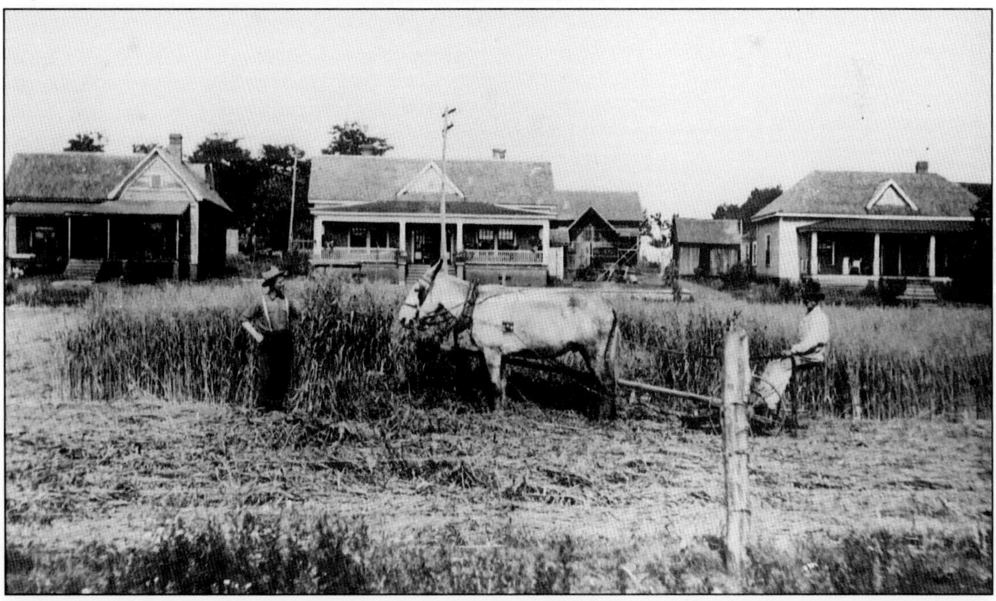

This scene shows a farmer mowing hay in the early 1900s on Marshall Street, an area now occupied by homes. Rev. Randolph W. Hamrick's home stands between two other houses. Until the mid-1900s, tractors and motorized farm equipment were rare; oxen, mules, and horses provided the horsepower. (Courtesy Georgia Department of Archives and History.)

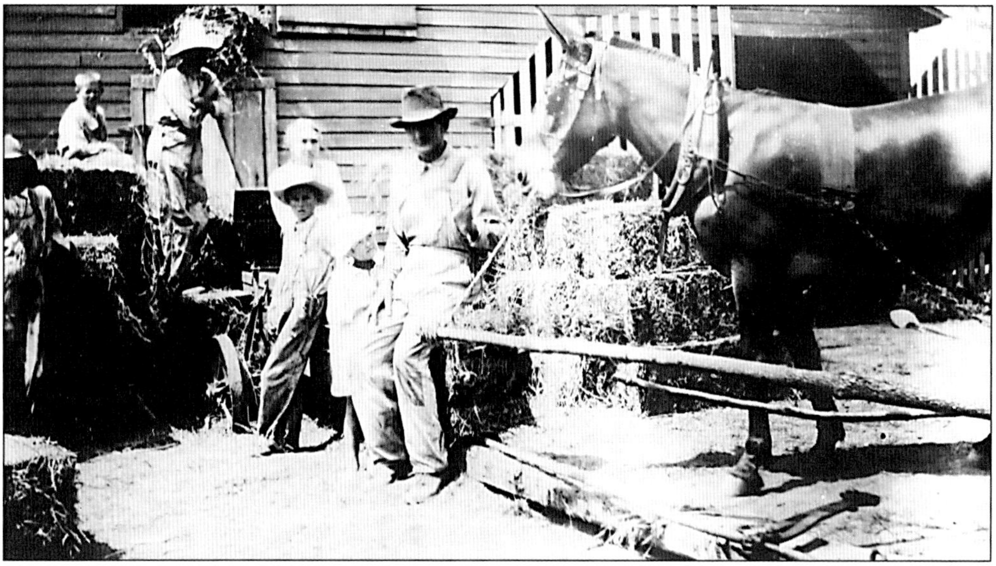

On his farm on Cave Spring Road near Cedartown, Frank Lyon is seated in front of the mule while he and his hands bail hay. His bareheaded wife stands to the rear. (Courtesy Georgia Department of Archives and History.)

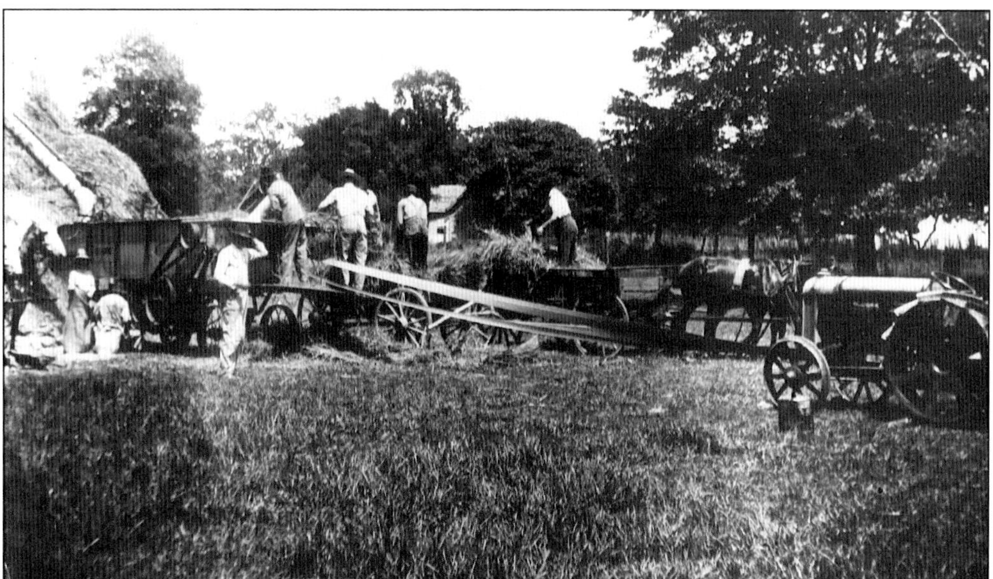

Frank Lyon stands in front of the wheat-threshing machine powered by a tractor and leather belt *c.* 1924. (Courtesy Georgia Department of Archives and History.)

Four

Cedar Valley: Cedartown

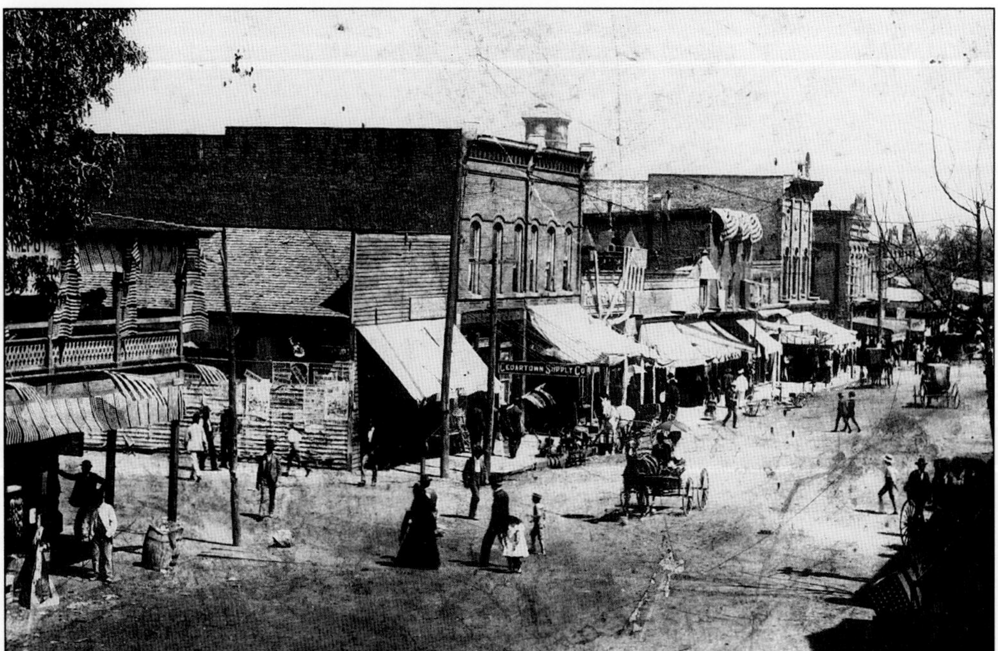

In this 1899 photograph, Cedartown was a bustling and prosperous community. Flags and bunting decorated the buildings for the Fourth of July celebration. The town had to be rebuilt after the Civil War when the courthouse and 65 buildings were burned by Union troops. In the 1870s, the west side of Main Street was destroyed by fire, and the wooden buildings were replaced with brick and masonry structures. The original layout of the town called for stores and businesses to be located on a square around the courthouse, but by the 1870s, Main Street was growing as the commercial district, and the few businesses on the square relocated.

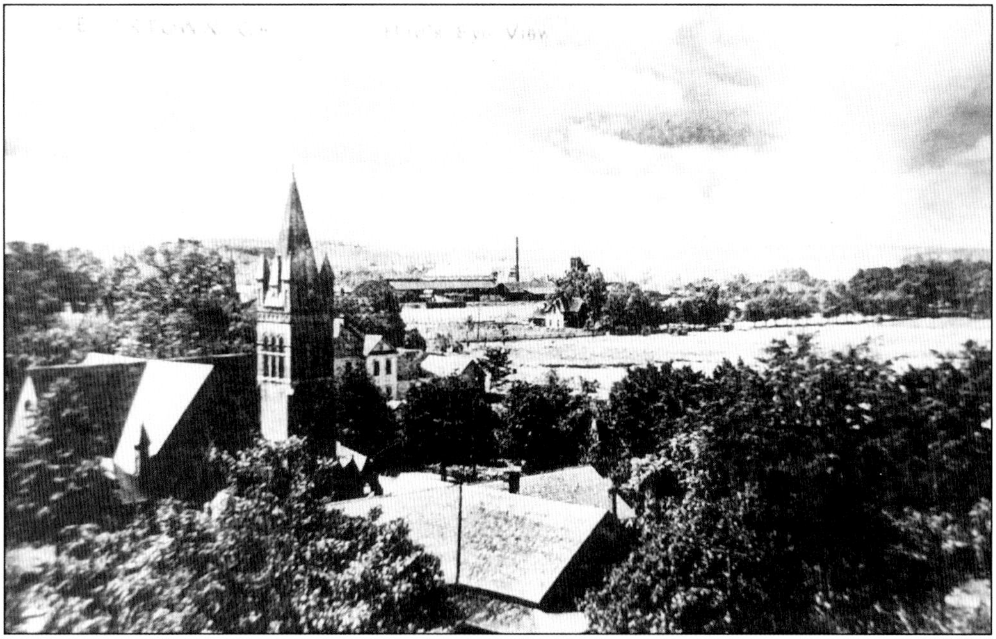

This bird's eye view of southwest Cedartown was taken from the courthouse clock tower. The First Baptist Church in the foreground was built in 1891 on the corner of Grace and College Streets and served the congregation until 1955, when a new church was built. In the distance West Avenue runs along the edge of open fields; the 75-foot-high smokestack of the Cherokee Iron Company rises in the center.

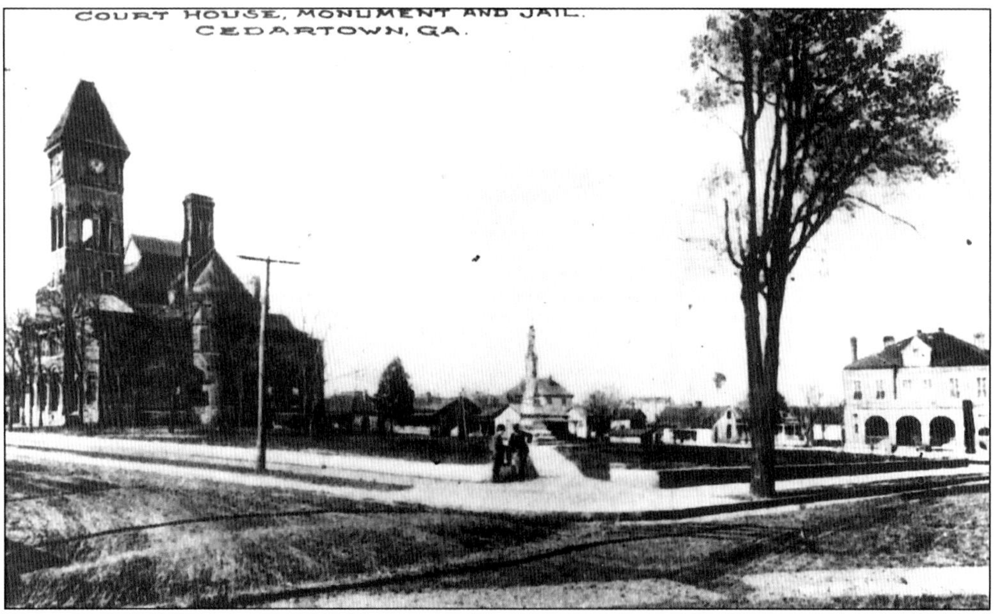

In 1852, Asa Prior sold 19 acres to the County for $1,200 to be used as a courthouse site and town square, specifying that citizens retained the right of access to the Big Spring. After Polk County was formed from Paulding County, court was held in the Woodland Academy until a new courthouse could be built in 1852. The building, shown here with the Confederate monument and jail, was built in 1889.

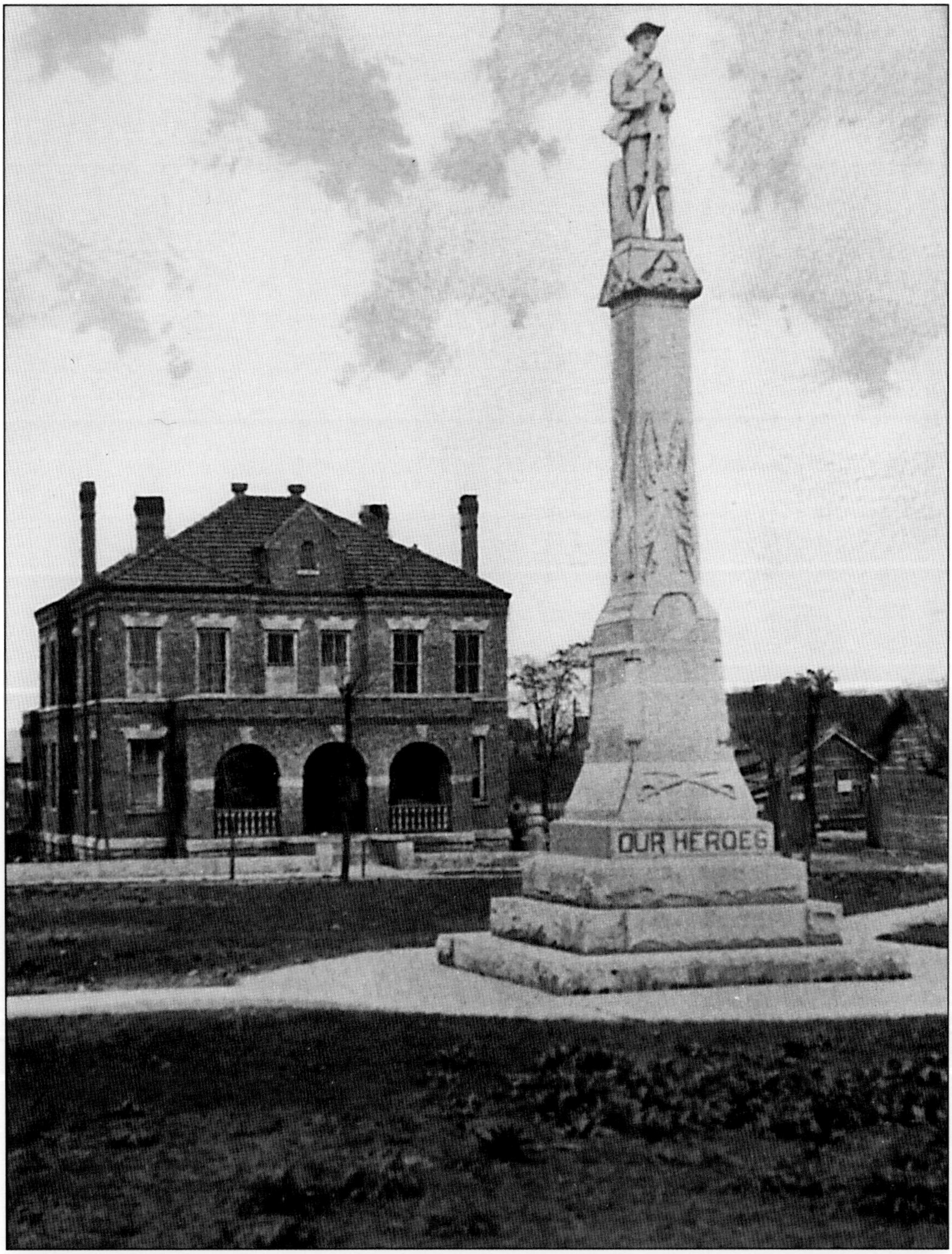

Construction of the two-story brick jail, measuring 36 by 46 feet, started in August 1874. The first floor had four rooms and served as the jailer's residence. At one time, the jail was called the "Hotel de Dempsey" after a long-serving sheriff. The upper floor had two rooms, each divided into three cells. Curiously, half the cells were to be iron and half wooden. Although it might have been better to build on a higher site, the new jail was considered "an ornament to the town." One old-timer remembers that a gallows was built in a hallway, where the last hanging took place in the 1930s. The jail and the spacious town square, once called Hightower Park, did not stand the test of time and disappeared long ago.

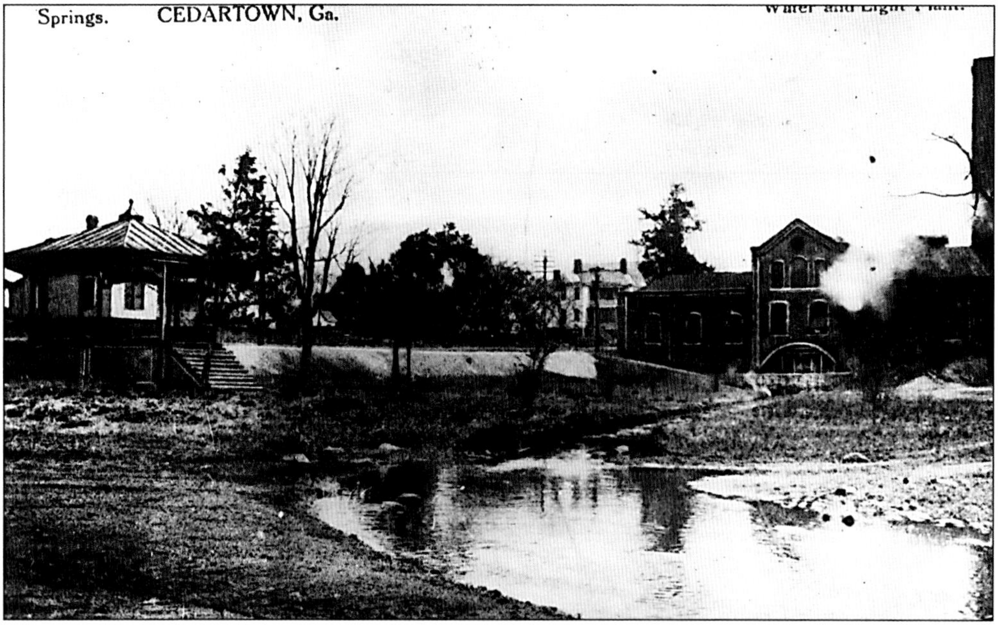

The Water and Light Plant on the right stands above the Big Spring in 1910. The bandstand on the left was the scene of concerts by the Cedartown brass band, famous throughout this section of Georgia and Alabama. The Big Spring wells up from limestone caverns and gives life to the cedars, which thrive on lime. The large cedar trees which once grew around the spring provided the city's namesake.

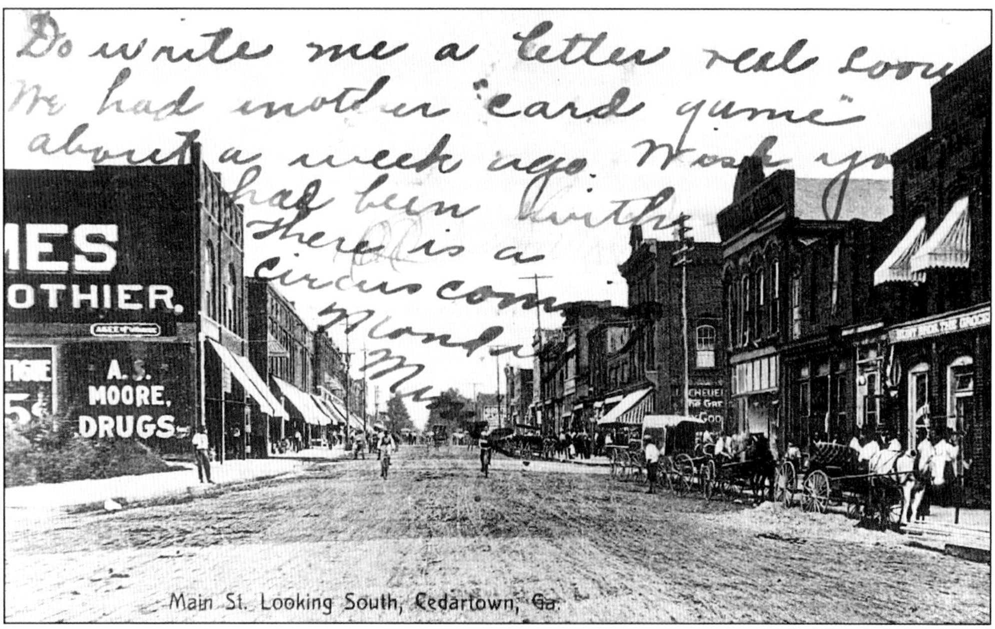

In 1832, when Paulding County was surveyed, much of the land along the southern end of Main Street was owned by Judge Witcher. At that time, the road was anything but straight. The surveyors' notebook explained that "lots 920, 921, 952, 953 include Witcher's farm." Farther south, lot 918 was noted as being "at Judge Witcher's yard & field." The 40-acre lots included both sides of Main Street.

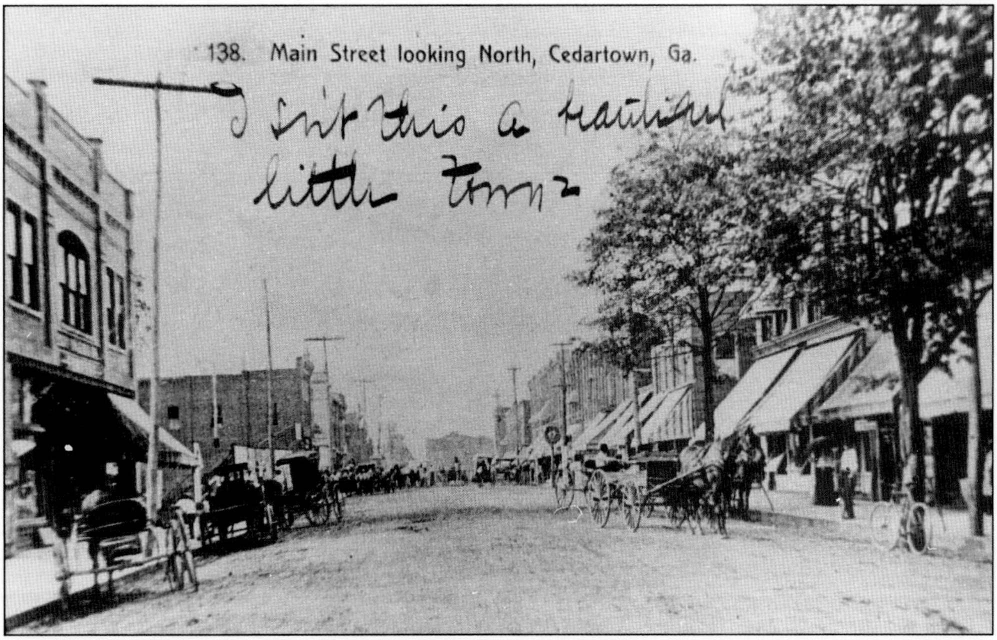

The sender of this postcard noted that the Main Street scene with buggies and wagons was "a beautiful little town," a sentiment still true today. Sidewalks had been installed, but the street was still dirt and would not be paved until 1911. These were still the horse-and-buggy days, although a newfangled automobile can be seen on the left side of the street.

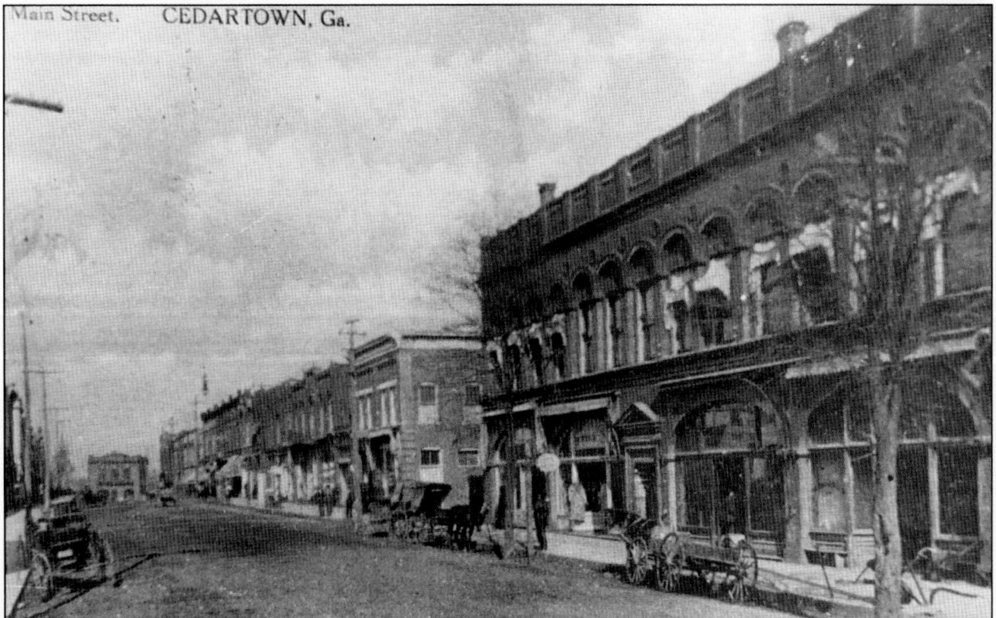

In 1889, Dr. Everard H. Richardson built the two-story block, shown in the foreground, with his drugstore and a furniture store. M.T. Borden operated the furniture business and offered undertaking services, including a fine hearse and an attractive line of coffins and caskets. Dr. Richardson graduated from the Augusta Medical College and became one of the first doctors in town to practice medicine.

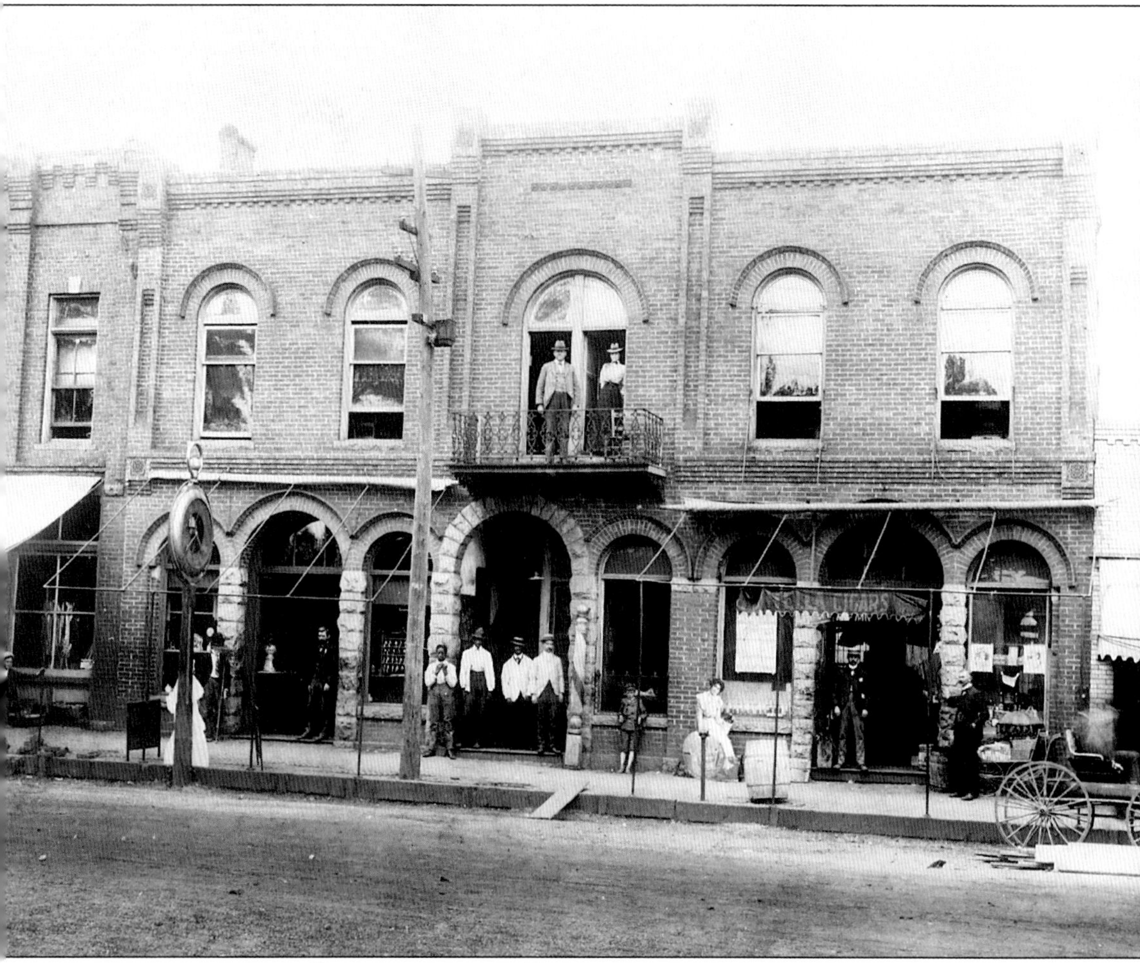

The City started installing concrete sidewalks with granite curbs on Main Street in early 1904—the construction materials appearing in the street may date this image. The two buildings on the right are believed to be the Cedartown Hotel, built by Col. Ivy Thompson at 224–226 Main Street in 1885 and operated at one time by Mr. and Mrs. Johnson. On the balcony stands J.H. Sanders and his wife, Ora Sewell Sanders. He occupied law offices along with Judge J.K. Davis. Standing in the left doorway is a bearded man believed to be Walt Turner, who opened a jewelry store in that location. (Courtesy Georgia Department of Archives and History.)

Names of some hotels which have disappeared from the scene can still be recalled by some: the Harris House (named after the senator and located on Main Street near the depot), the Booz House, and the Wright Hotel. The two hotels that advertised in this March 28, 1878 issue of the *Cedartown Express* have not only disappeared, but have been forgotten, possibly due to a short life.

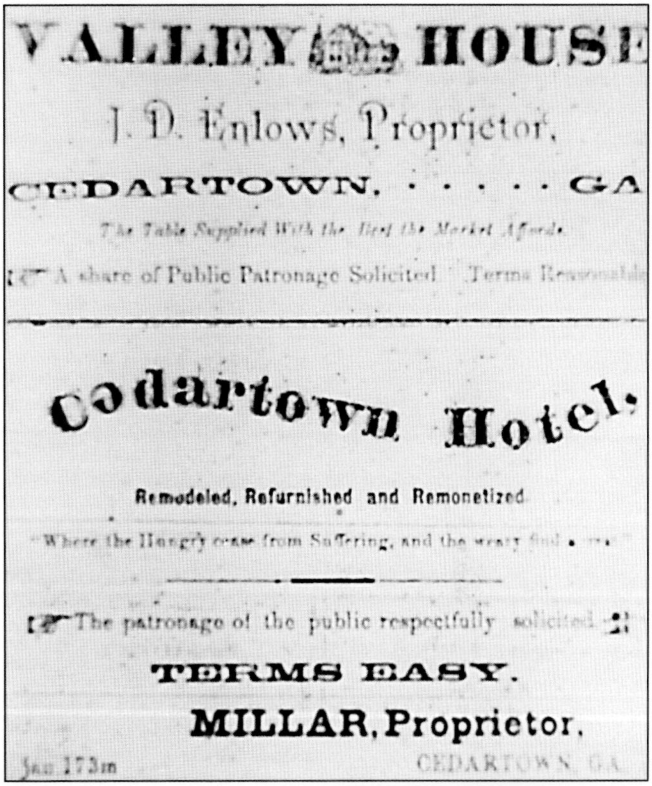

VALLEY HOUSE

J. D. Enlows, Proprietor.

CEDARTOWN, ... GA

The Table Supplied With the Best the Market Affords.

A share of Public Patronage Solicited. Terms Reasonable

Cedartown Hotel.

Remodeled, Refurnished and Remonetized

Where the Hungry cease from Suffering, and the weary find rest.

The patronage of the public respectfully solicited.

TERMS EASY.

MILLAR, Proprietor.

Jan 17 3m CEDARTOWN, GA

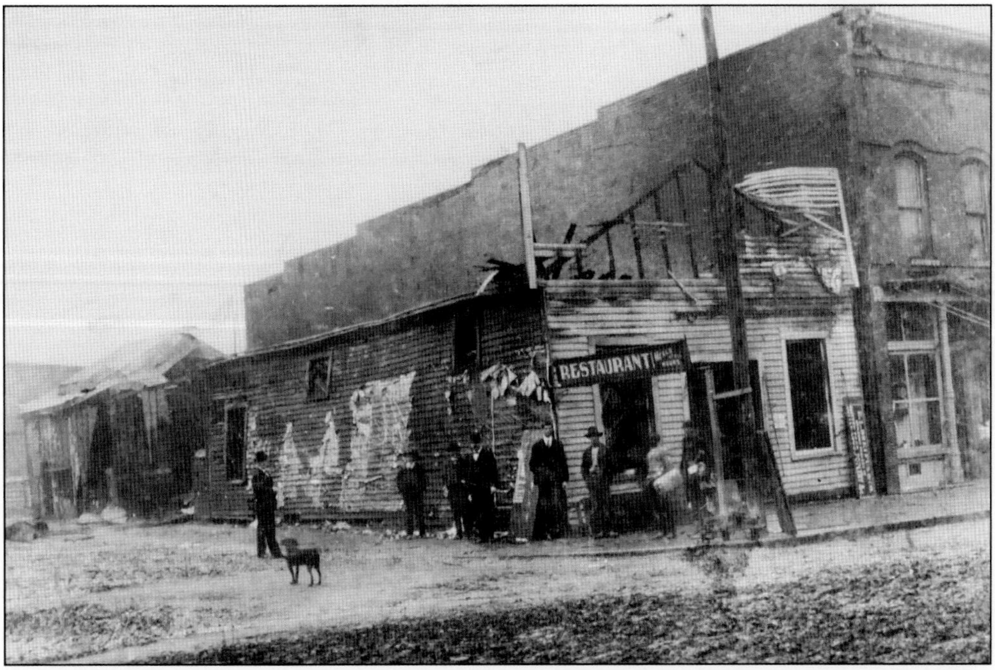

Fire completely destroyed this restaurant at the corner of West Avenue and Main Street on January 19, 1906. The same year, A.C. Cobb & Company moved to this corner, probably after building a new brick structure. (Courtesy Georgia Department of Archives and History.)

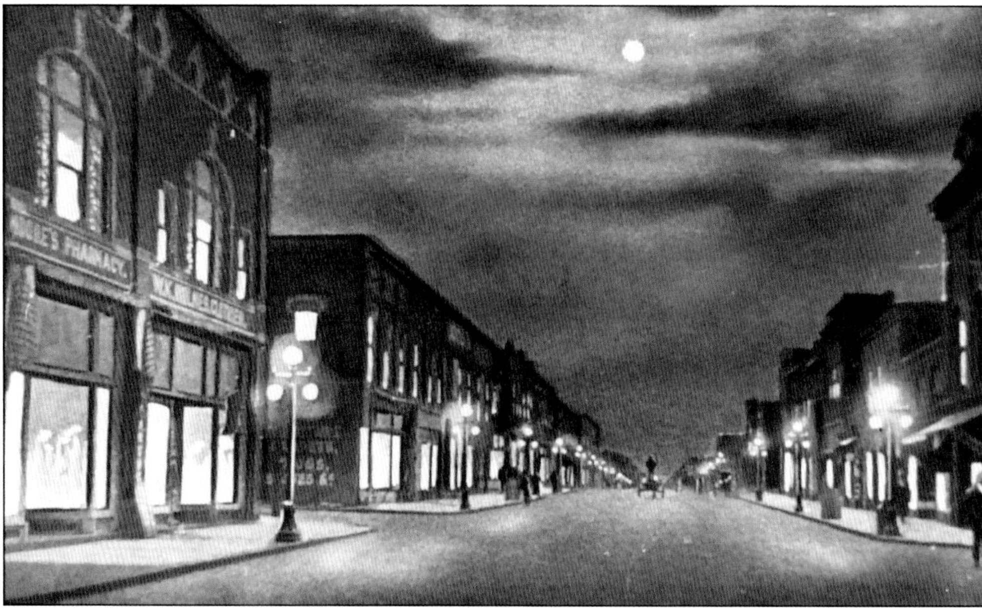

In 1913, the city's Light and Water Company erected poles and lights between the railroad and East Avenue, making this section of Main Street a "Great White Way." According to an incident once described by a Seaboard Railroad conductor, two Birmingham ladies on a trip to Atlanta saw this night scene and, thinking they had arrived in Atlanta, tried to disembark at the depot.

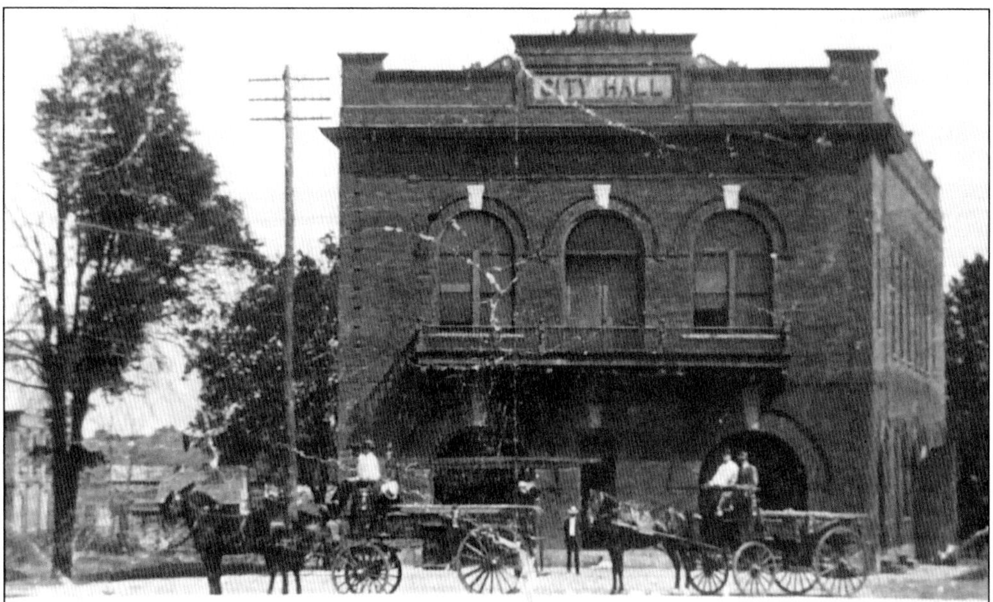

Fire Company Number 1 poses in front of City Hall, where the first floor housed the fire company. A large wooden building stood on this site earlier, the home of the first fire department. The City Hall was constructed in 1901 and was used for the city council, the recorder's office, the fire department, and the city prison. An elegant auditorium, the Lyceum, was located on the second floor.

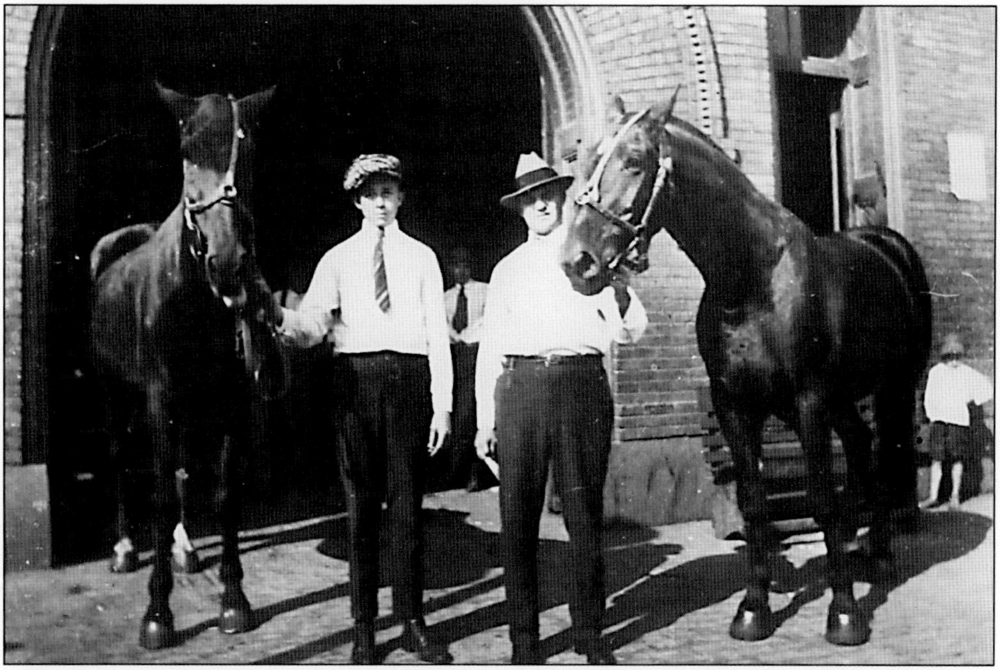

A.W. Bobo, on the left, poses with fire-horses at City Hall. In 1903, Dr. Joseph A. Liddell and George G. Styles were sent to Indianapolis, Indiana, to purchase fire-horses. From a selection of 750, they chose three horses for $180 apiece. One was named "Pat" after an earlier fire-horse, and the other two, who were to draw a large hose wagon, were named in honor of the purchasers: Joe and George.

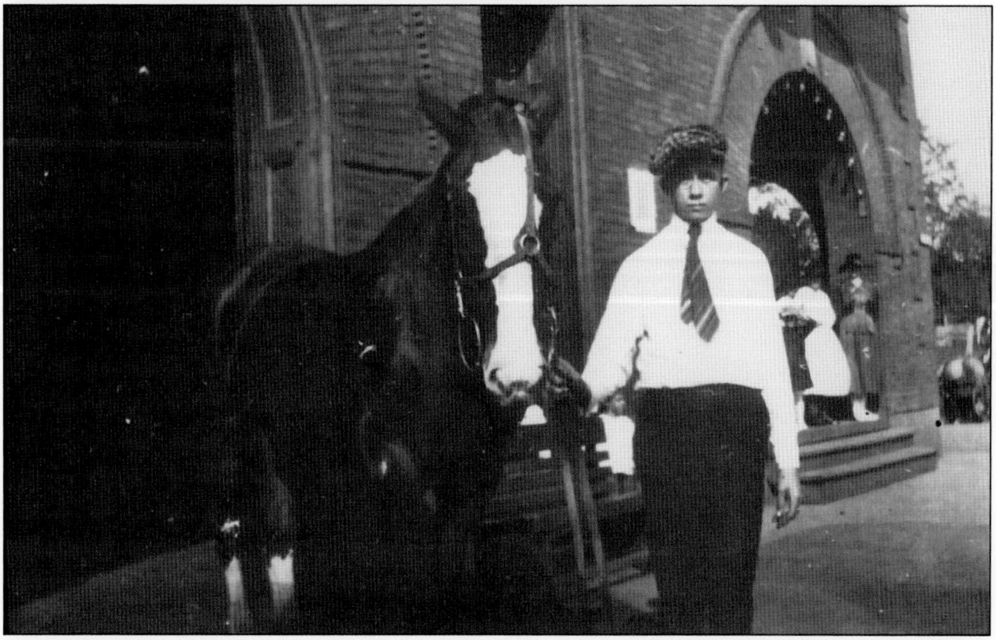

Fire Chief M.D. Russell reported that in 1902 the fire department had answered 15 fire alarms and losses were only $6,699 of the $270,469 value of the endangered property. A.W. Bobo holds the fire-horse, Kimball, used for pulling a fire wagon equipped with hoses and ladders.

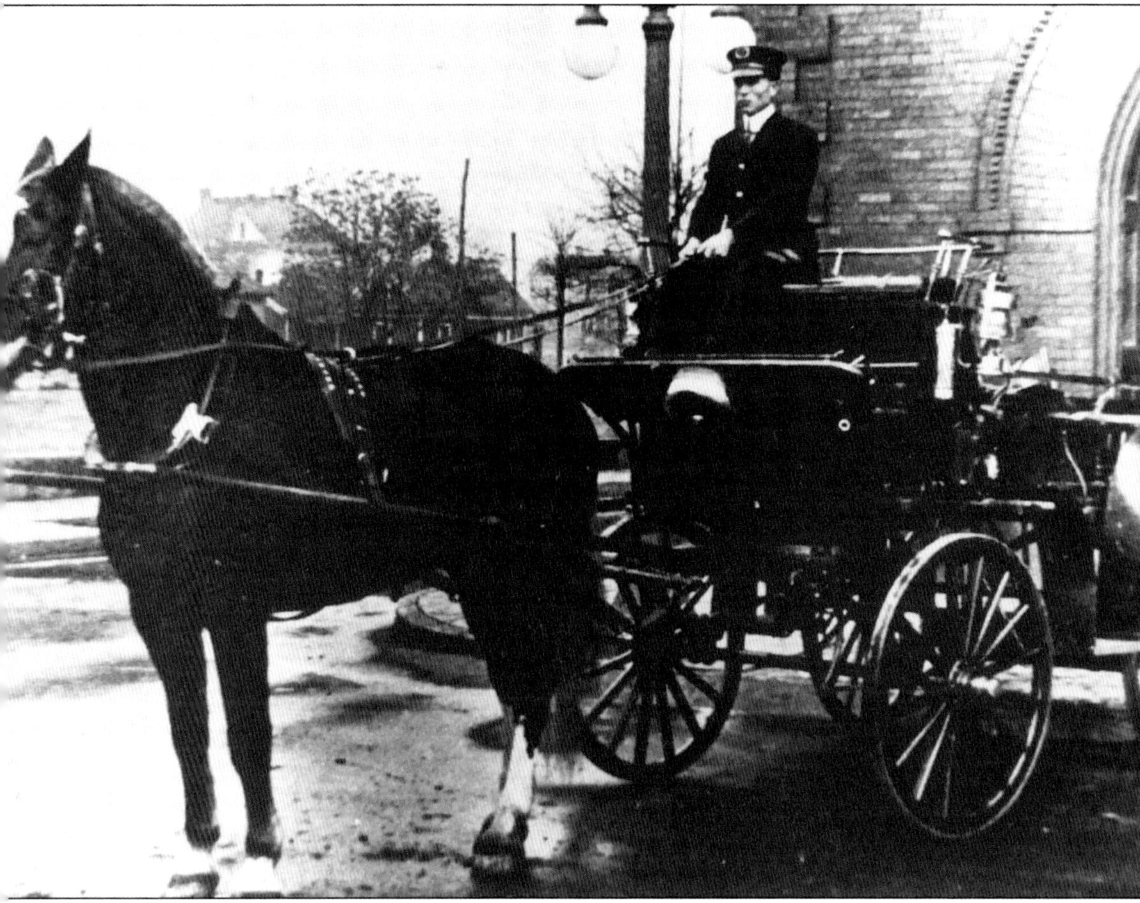

The first fire wagon was purchased in 1898, and five years later two wagons and three horses were purchased for the Cedartown Fire Department. Such wagons were often equipped with ladders and barrels of water. In early days firefighters reported to the fire alarm with their buckets and formed a bucket brigade to douse the fire. Driver Luther Cambron poses in this image with fire-horse Kimball.

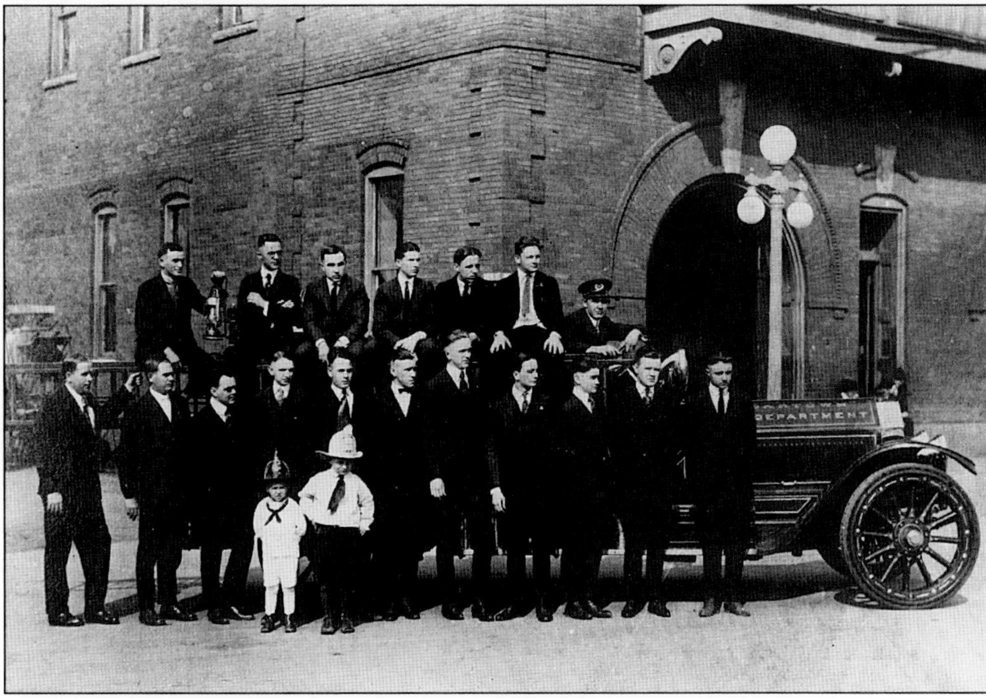

In 1918, the City purchased a new La France pumper, shown here with solid tires. The company of volunteer firemen has two small admirers, and present-day admirers still enjoy the sight of the old fire engine, which has since been retired to a pizza parlor in Portland, Oregon.

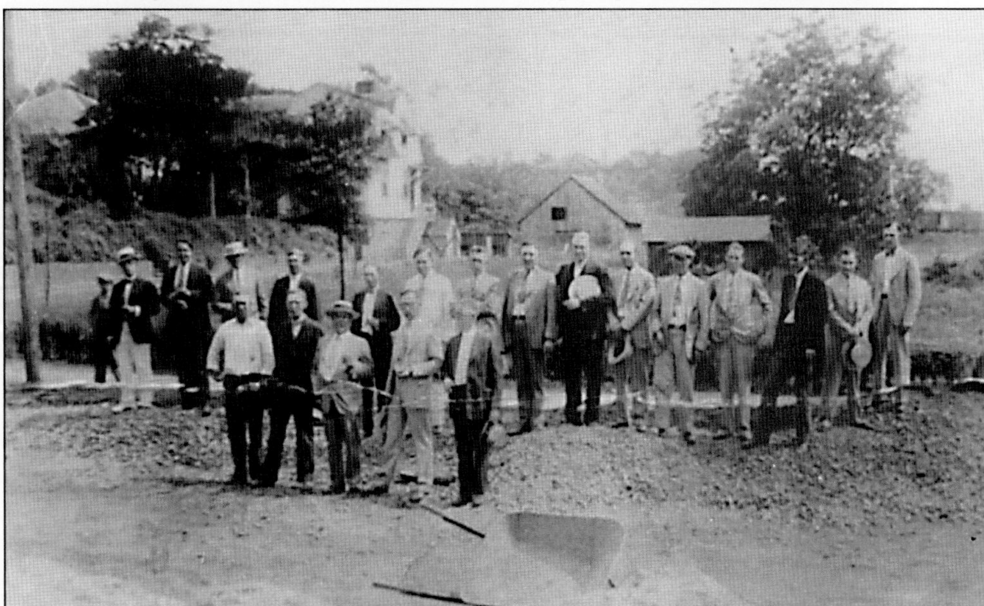

West Avenue was graded and paved for the first time in 1927. Cedartown's first newspaper, the *Record*, noted that in 1875, the Cherokee Iron Company was grading part of this street, making it the "first decent street in town." The first section of Main Street was paved in 1911 and extended from City Hall to the corner of Gibson Street.

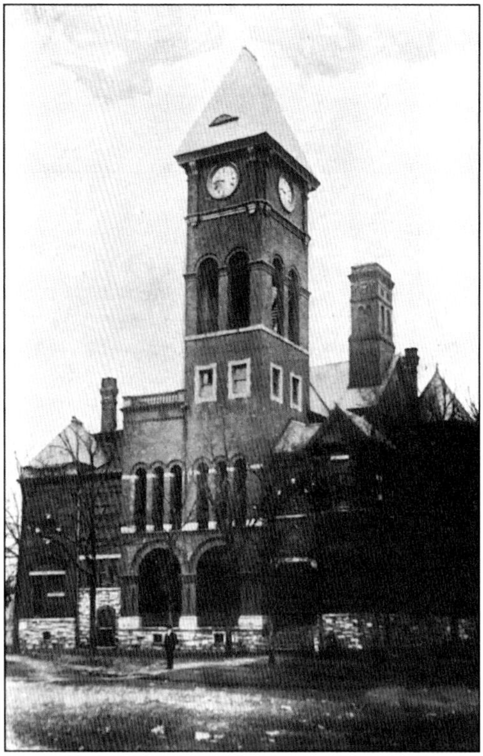

Polk County's third courthouse, built in 1889, included a handsome four-sided clock with shiny blue enamel faces 10 feet in diameter, purchased at the World's Fair in Philadelphia. The clock had two weights which could travel two stories down the tower before the city clock keeper had to rewind it. One weight operated the clock while the other, weighing well over a ton, operated the bell clapper, which itself weighed 150 pounds.

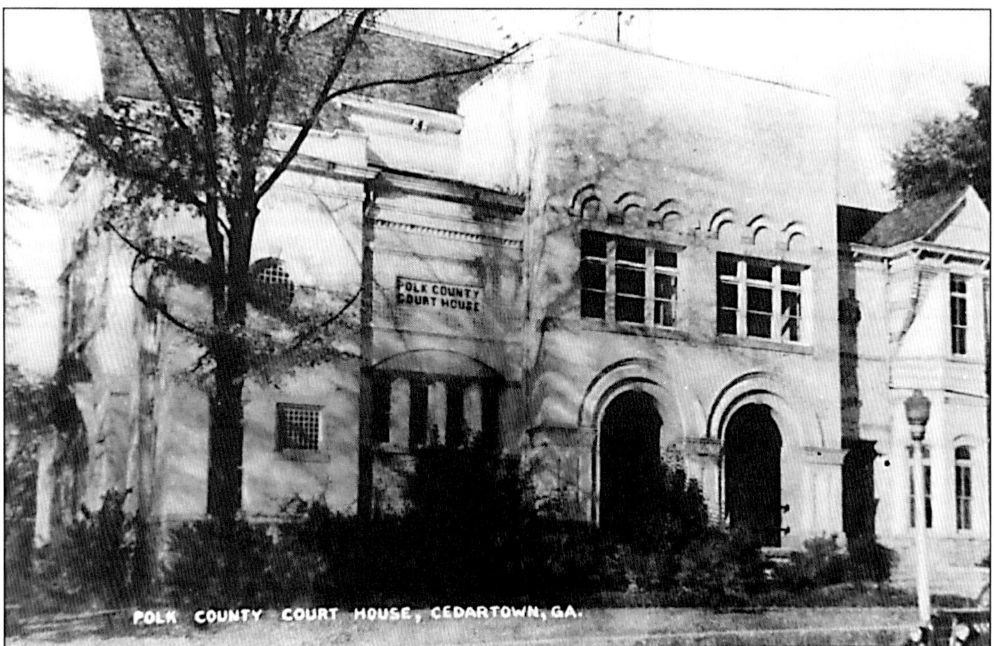

After 50 years of service, the clock tower was removed, and the brick building was painted white. The weight of the massive clock works apparently weakened the courthouse walls and required the clock's removal. Whatever happened to the old clock remains an unsolved mystery to this day.

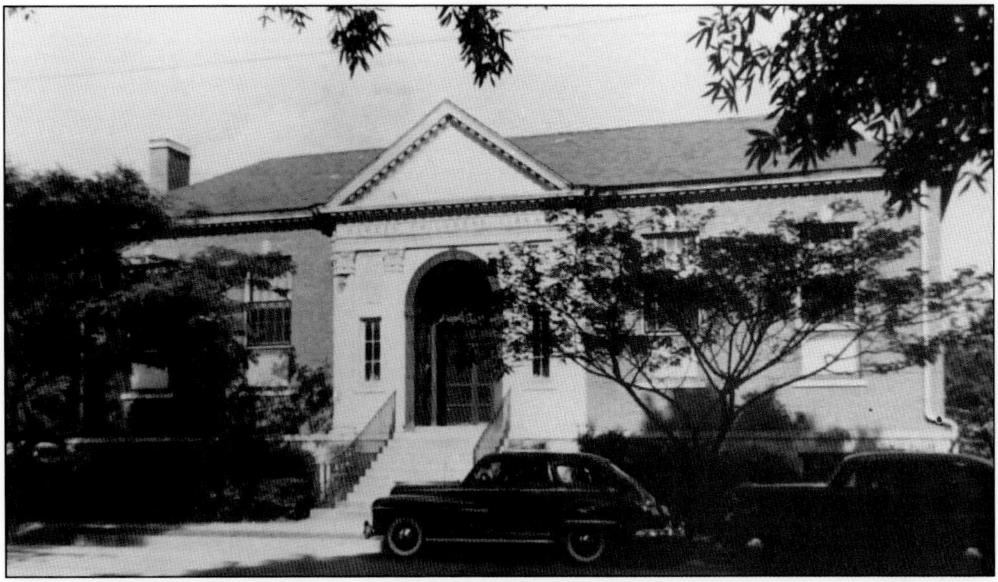

When A.K. Hawkes bequeathed funds for children's libraries, Cedartown was one of five towns selected for a library. To kick off a fund drive, a sumptuous dinner party was given by Charles Adamson. Adamson's company donated the lot for the library site, and the building was designed by Neil Reed, the noted Georgia architect. The Hawkes Children's Library was opened in 1921 to serve adults as well as children. Today, it serves as the museum of the Polk County Historical Society.

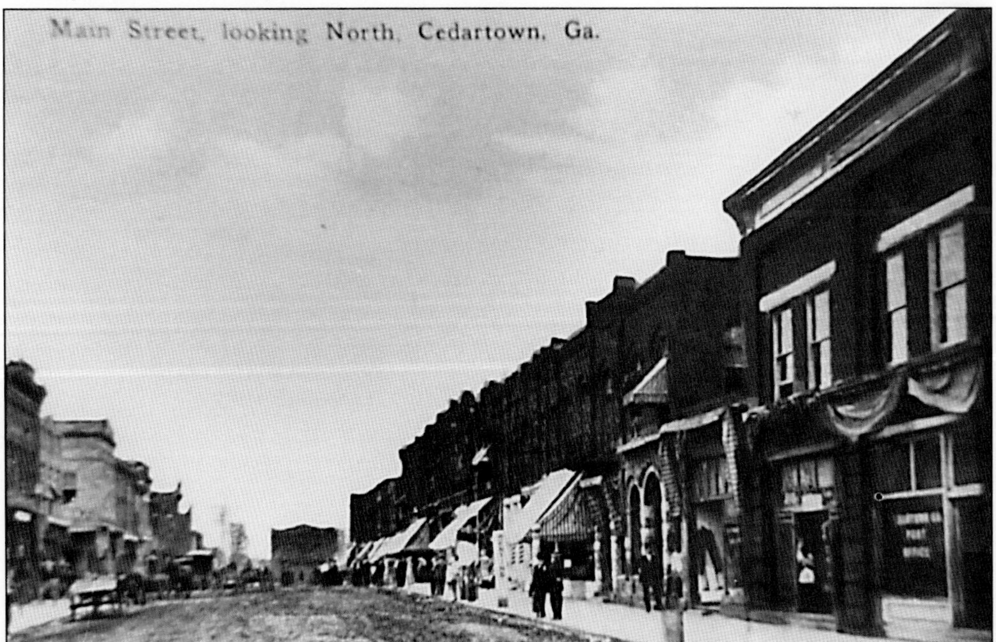

The Cedartown Post Office, in the first building at the right, served until 1914, when a new post office was built on West Avenue. Cedartown's first post office was established in 1833 in the store of the first postmaster, John Witcher. Rockmart's first post office was listed as Clean Town and established the same year, with John Gentry serving as postmaster.

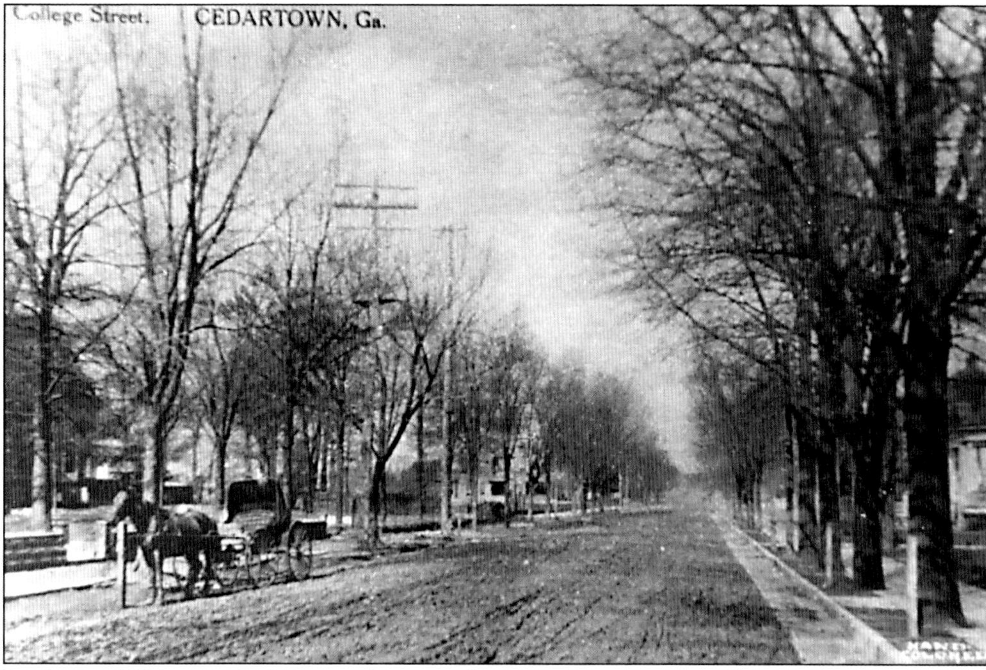

In this *c.* 1910 view looking south on College Street, new sidewalks parallel the unpaved street and hitching posts can be seen, with a horse and wagon tethered to one of them. It was illegal to fasten a horse to a shade tree or fence, according to ordinances listed in the July 18, 1874 *Record.*

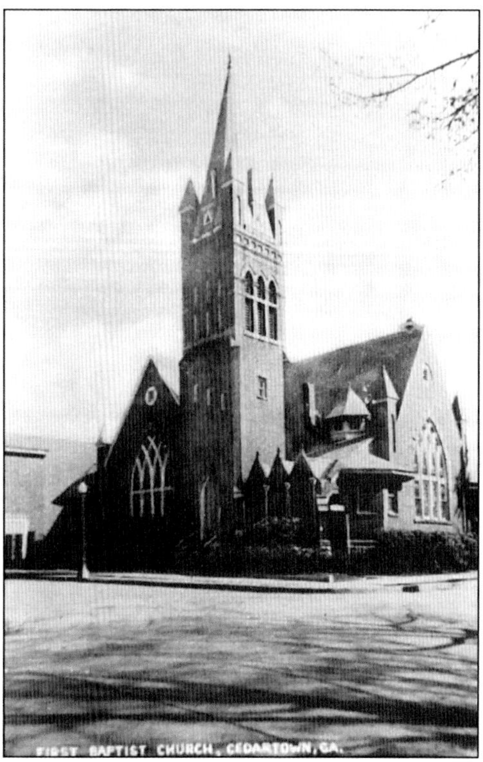

In 1891, the Baptists replaced their 1845 structure with this imposing building on the corner of College and Grace Streets. Sixty-four years later the congregation of the First Baptist Church had outgrown their sanctuary and started construction of a larger church.

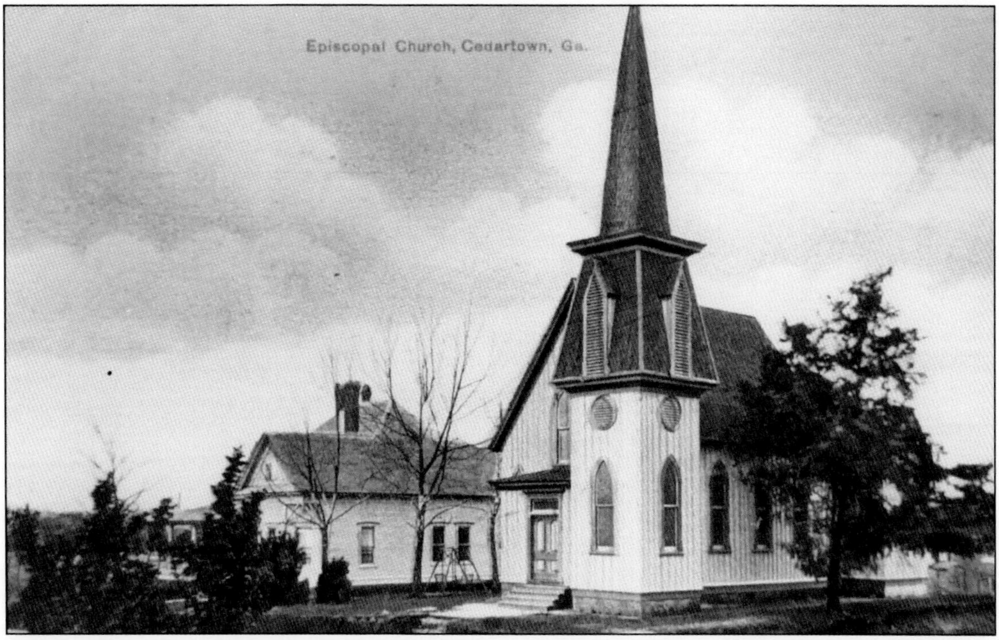

This Carpenter's Gothic style church was completed in 1883 on land donated by Amos G. West. A handful of communicants held their first service about six years earlier in the Presbyterian church, then in rooms above a store, and finally over Mr. West's Cherokee Railroad depot. St. James Episcopal Church was named by Mrs. West after her parish in Manhattan, New York, which provided some retired furnishings.

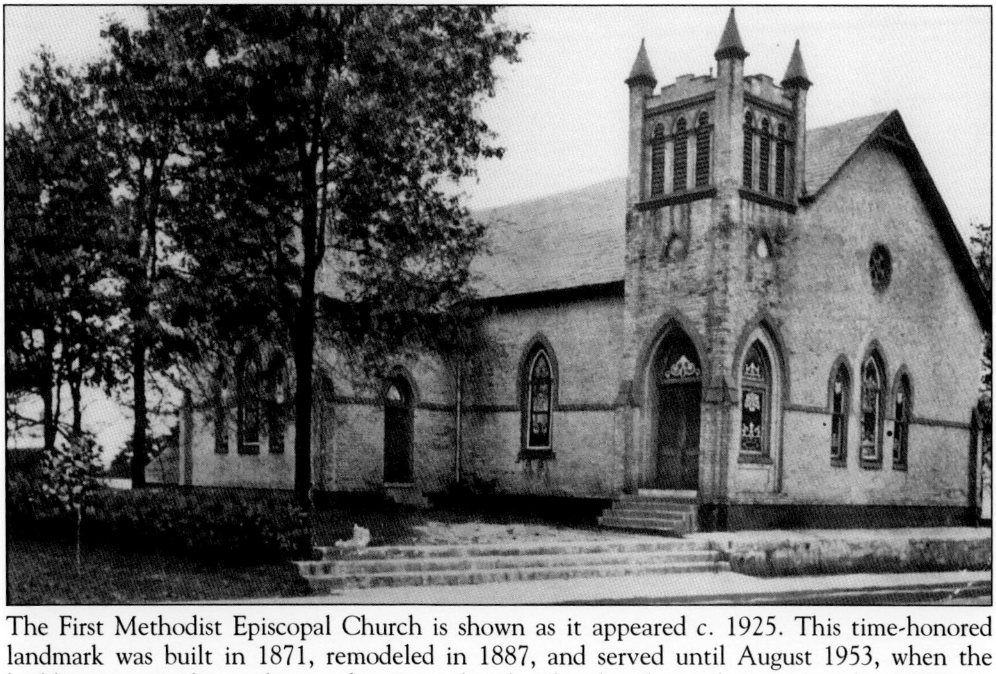

The First Methodist Episcopal Church is shown as it appeared *c.* 1925. This time-honored landmark was built in 1871, remodeled in 1887, and served until August 1953, when the building was razed to make way for a new church. The church was first organized in 1850 in a small log storehouse, and the first church home was erected in 1852. This structure was donated to the black Methodist church in 1871.

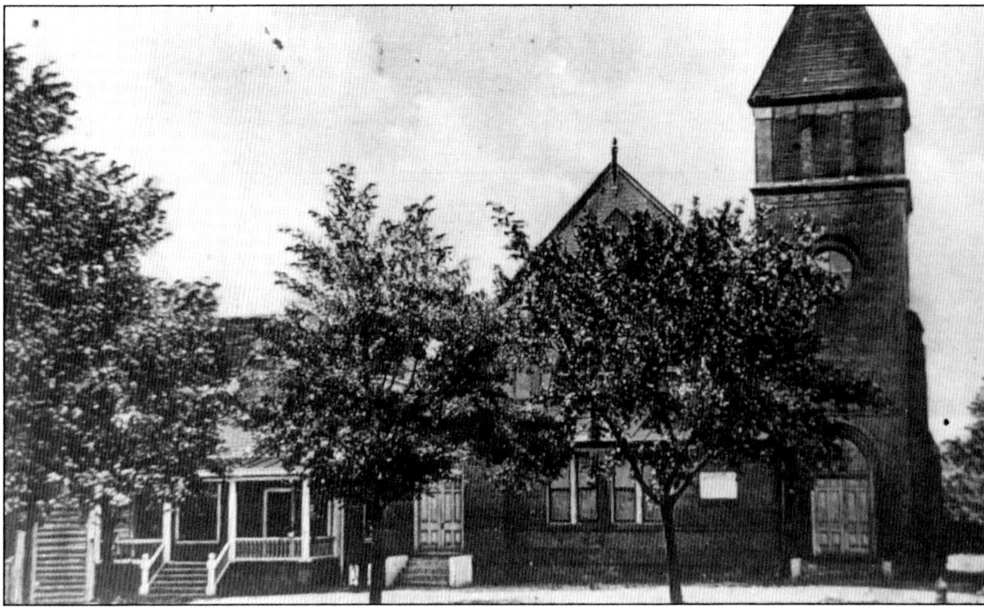

The First Presbyterian Church and manse were located on Herbert Street. The church was first organized about 1853, but faded out until 1873, when the Cedar Valley Presbyterian Church was organized. Renamed a few months later, the church held its first services in the town academy on the Carrollton Road (now Main Street). After 16 years that property was sold to finance the church shown here.

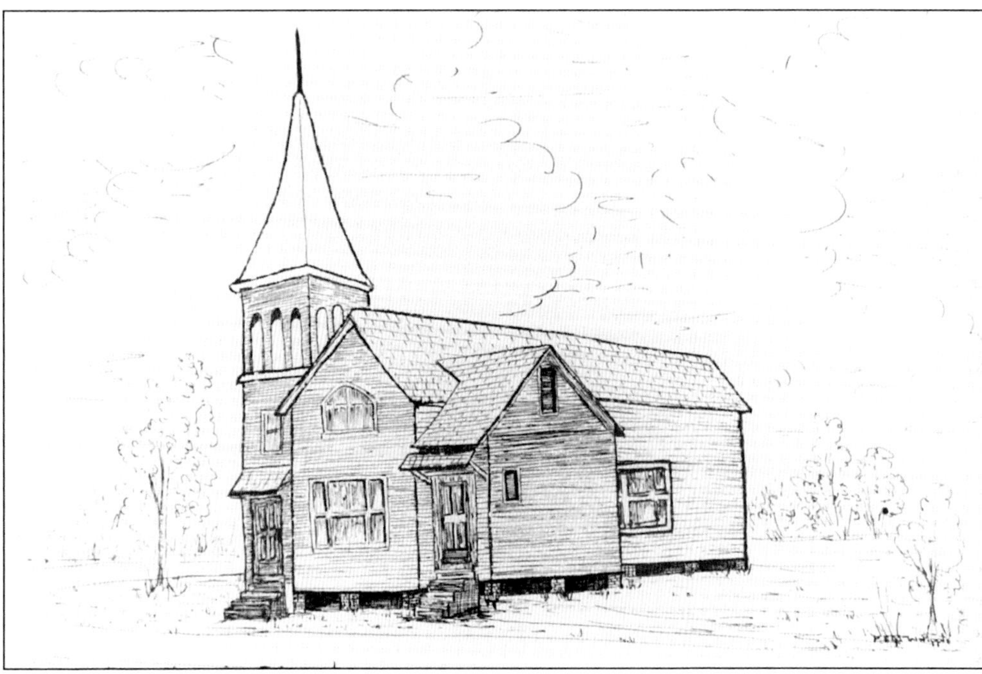

In the early 1900s, one group of Methodists began to hold meetings in an old textile mill building, and then in a private home. In 1914, the McCarty Settlement House was erected to house mission-school activities, which grew until a separate building was needed for worship. This sketch shows the West Avenue Methodist Episcopal Church built in 1918.

Five

Euharlee Valley: Rockmart and Aragon

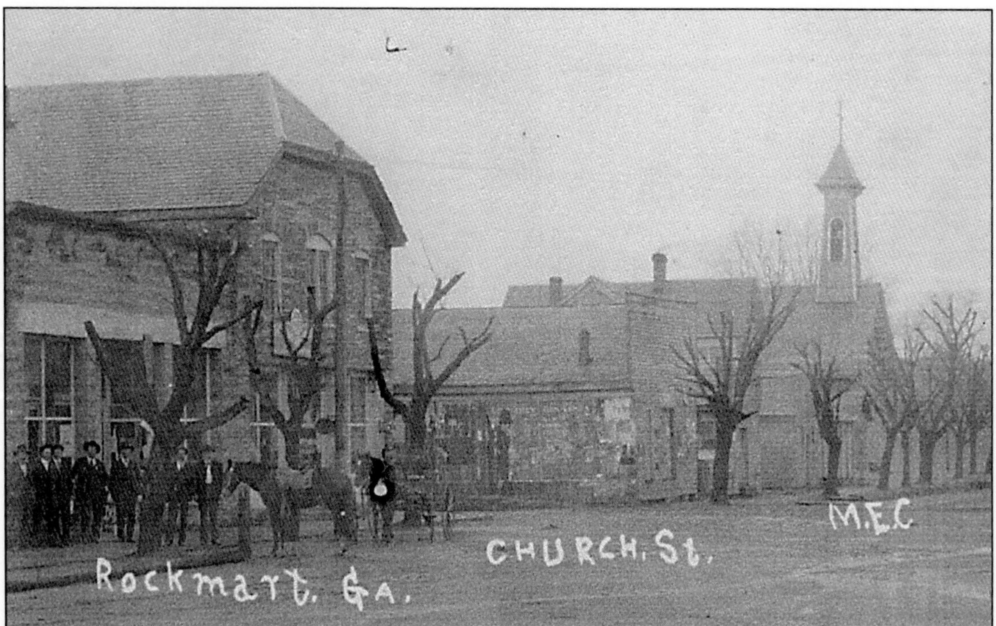

This 1890s picture shows Church Street in Rockmart, with the Methodist Episcopal Church at the far right. The Reverend Ballenger served this church as minister for one year before he started the Piedmont Institute in 1889. The building in the foreground utilized naturally occurring deposits of slate. When Rock Mart was chartered in 1872, the name was chosen anticipating the growth of the slate industry.

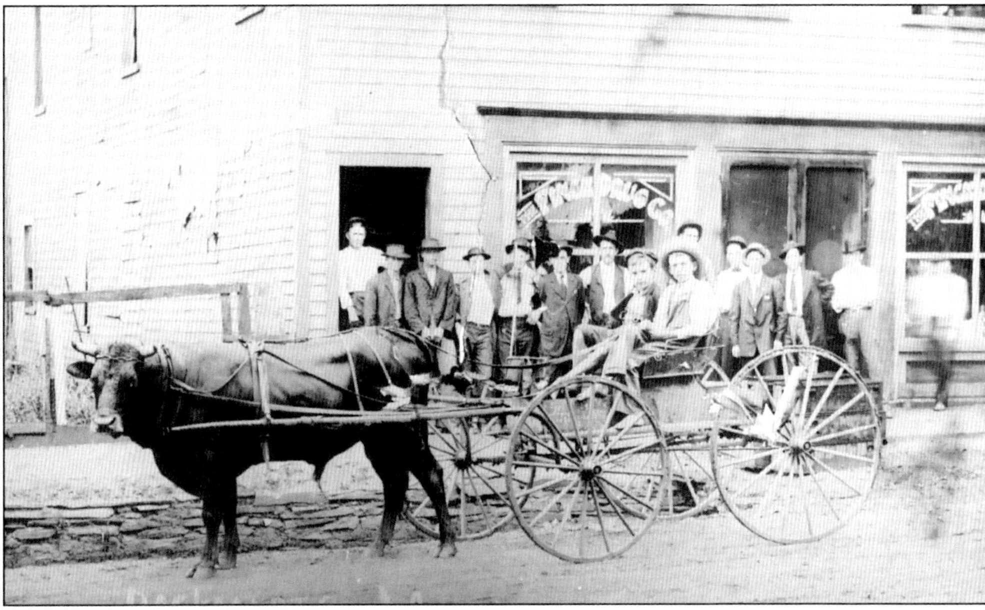

This photograph shows the structure on the site now occupied by the City Drug Company. Standing with a group in front of the Finch Drug Company is Hugh M. McRae Sr., fifth from the left. Next to him is the store owner, J. Arthur Finch. Seated in the buggy pulled by an ox which, at the time, was Rockmart's mascot, are B.F. Denton (on left) and A. Lee. (Courtesy Georgia Department of Archives and History.)

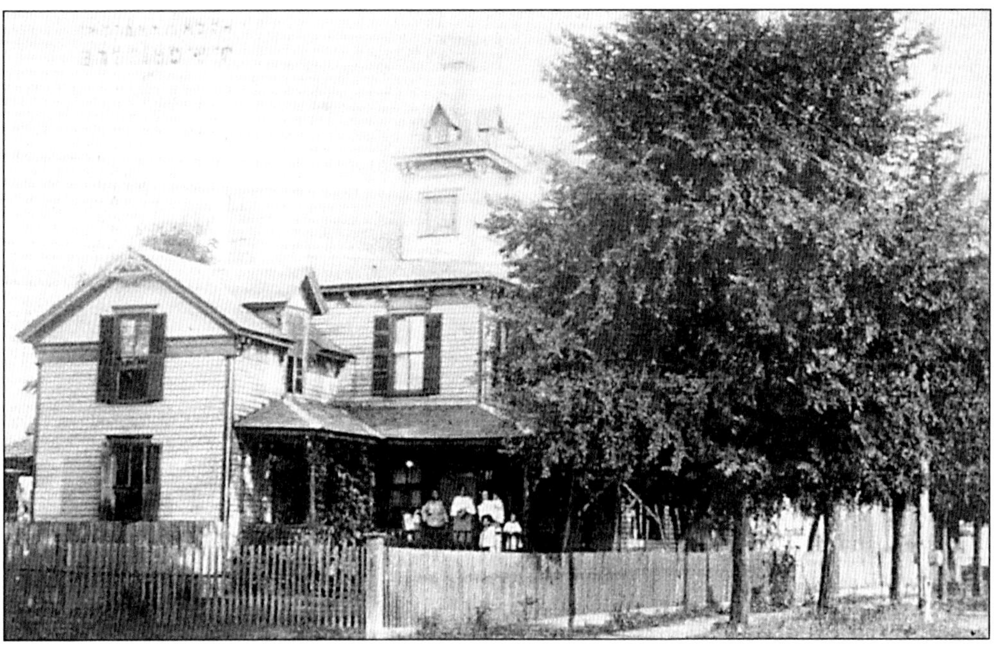

The faint imprint "J.A. Gribble, Rockmart, GA" located in the upper left corner identifies this photograph as taken about the turn of the century by Rockmart's "Nickel Jim" Gribble. The family standing on the porch of their comfortable home is not identified. (Courtesy Bob Basford.)

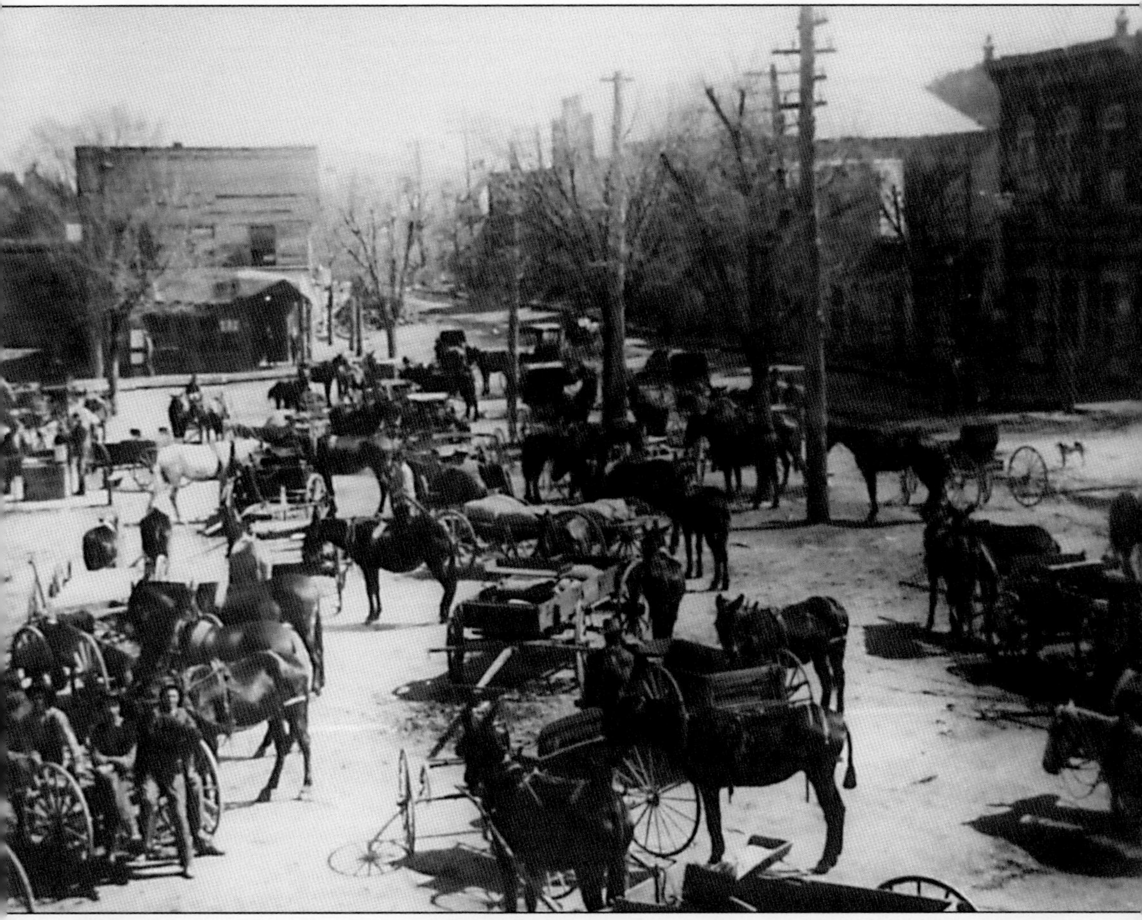

This picture of the Rockmart city square looking north along Marble Street was taken sometime before 1914. The city square was used then as a hitching yard, where farmers parked their wagons and hitched their horses or mules when they came to town. While the animals chomped on hay or fodder, the farmer shopped for needed supplies or traded with other farmers for mules, knives, watches, or anything else.

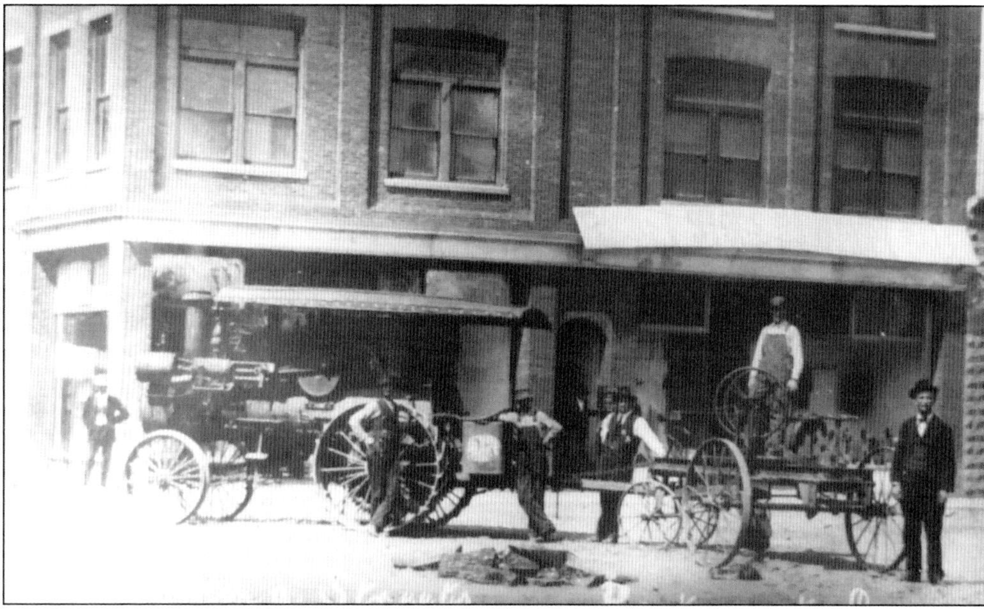

In this 1910 scene, a crew pauses from their work of repairing the street to pose for the photographer. Their equipment includes the latest in vehicle technology, a coal-fired, steam-driven tractor. Rockmart would get their first paved road in 1924, running between the Southern and Seaboard Railroads.

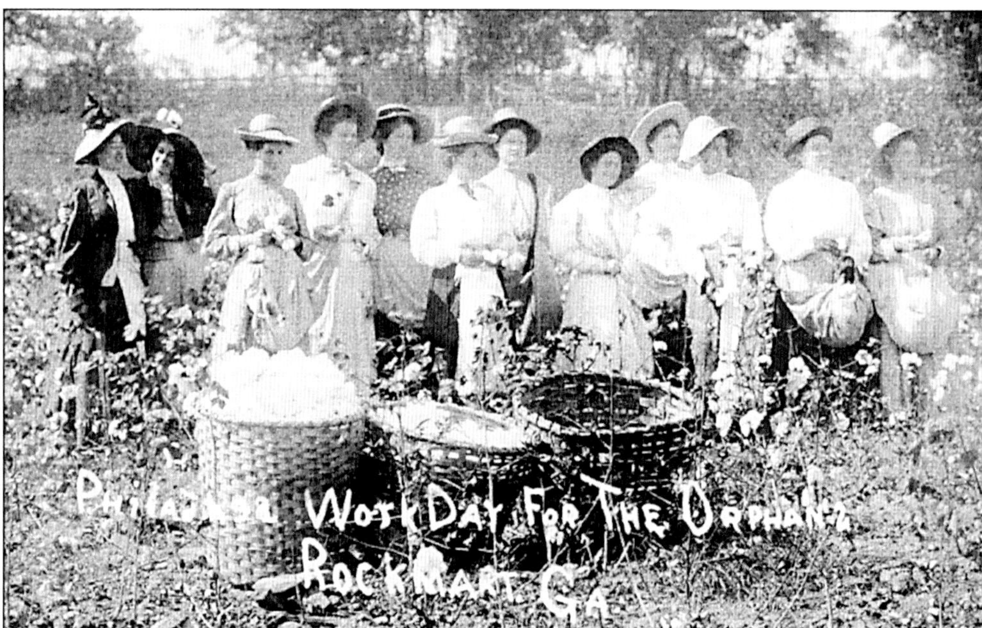

These civic-minded ladies in long skirts and sun bonnets are spending the day picking cotton to benefit orphans. The Philathia Society was a women's service organization of the Rockmart First Methodist Church. (Courtesy Bob Basford.)

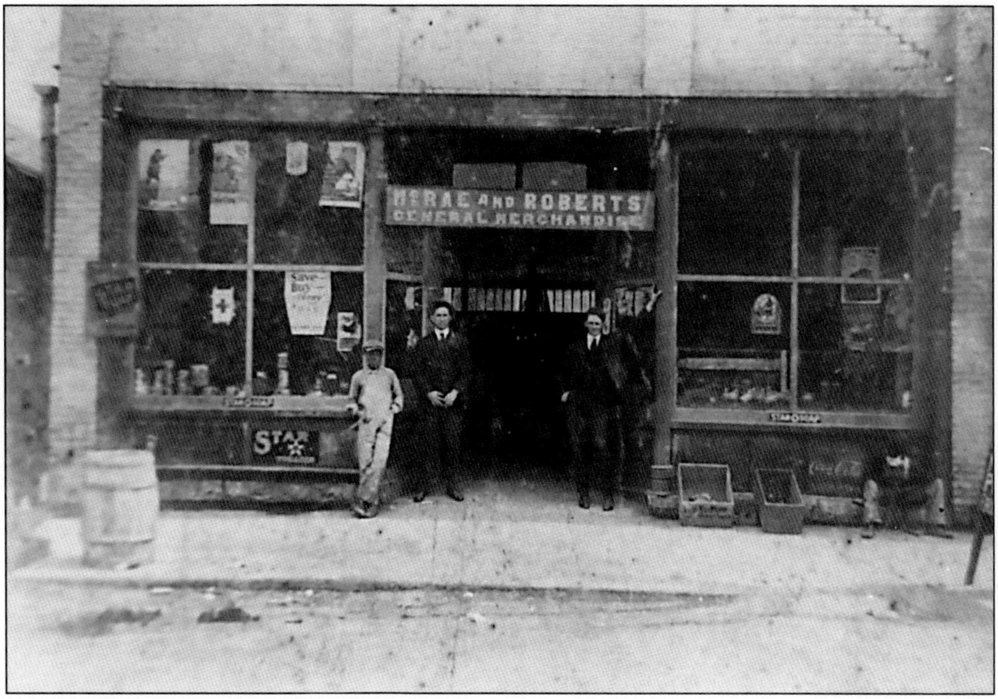

Hugh McRae Sr. stands in the doorway of the McRae and Roberts General Merchandise store in this *c.* 1915 photo. The store was located on Marble Street and served Rockmart citizens for many years.

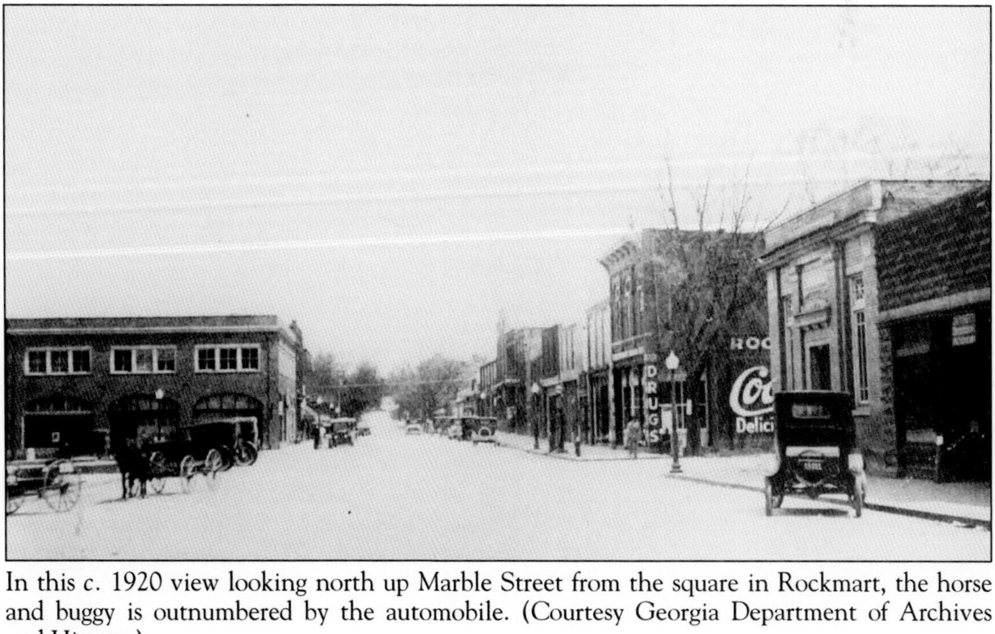

In this *c.* 1920 view looking north up Marble Street from the square in Rockmart, the horse and buggy is outnumbered by the automobile. (Courtesy Georgia Department of Archives and History.)

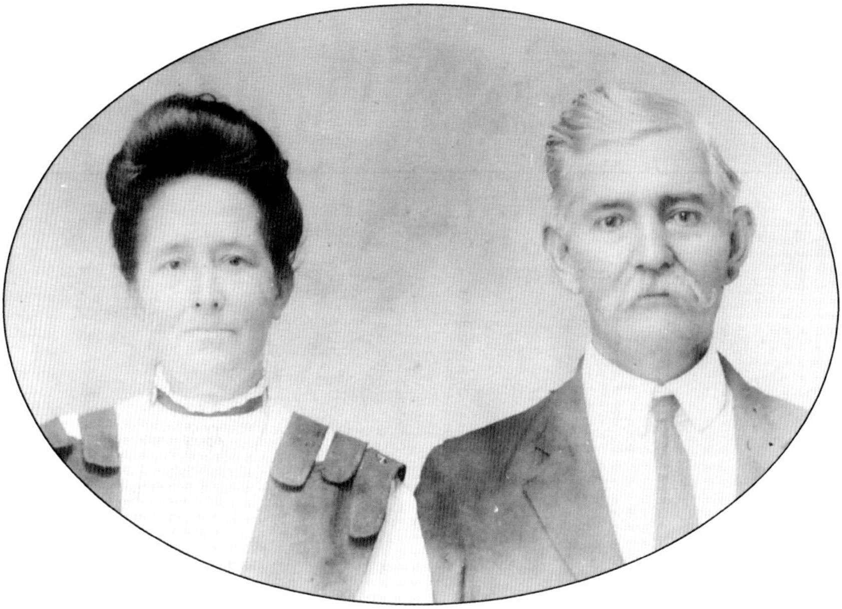

Mr. and Mrs. B.T. McGarity, shown here *c.* 1906, ran the popular Marble Hill Hotel for several years. The landmark hotel provided accommodations for traveling businessmen brought to Rockmart as a result of the railroads and the stone products industries. Local folk also enjoyed the popular rendezvous for the dining and dancing that accompanied various social functions. (Courtesy Georgia Department of Archives and History.)

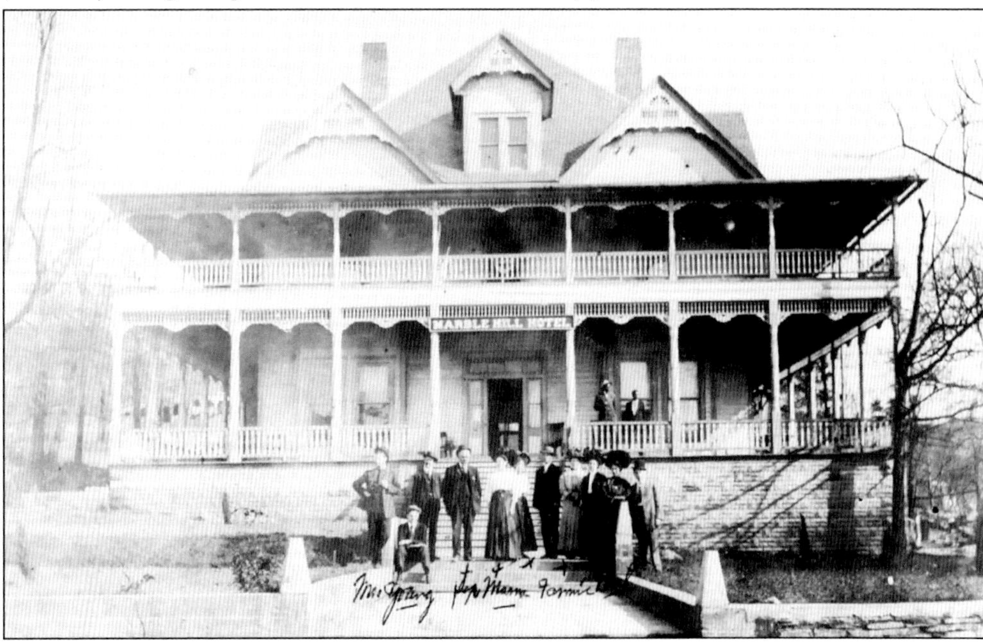

The impressive structure shown here in 1906 stood at the foot of Marble Hill, mistakenly named after the limestone rock found there. The hotel site was solid rock, which had to be cleared by blasting with dynamite. The Marble Hill Hotel lasted well into the 1950s, but sadly, it was eventually demolished for the construction of a much-needed supermarket. (Courtesy Georgia Department of Archives and History.)

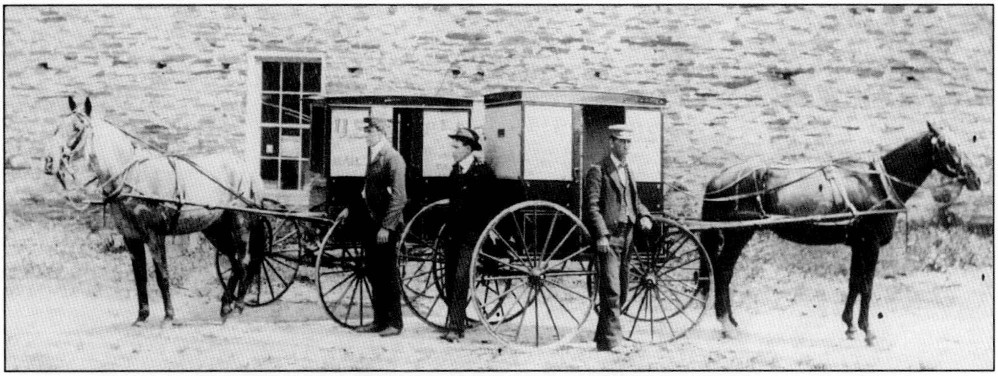

In this 1909 picture, rural mail carriers line up on Church Street next to the building housing the post office at the time. The RFD act went into effect in the late 1890s and provided 25-mile delivery routes for which the carrier was paid $60 per month. (Courtesy Georgia Department of Archives and History.)

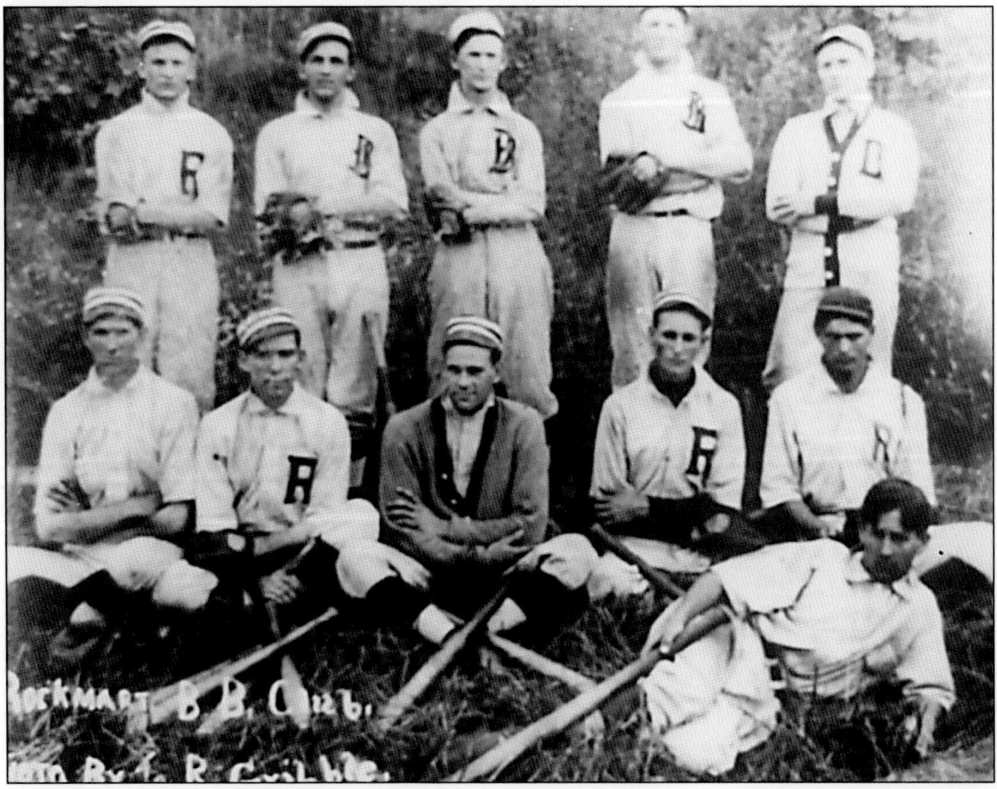

This picture of the 1910 baseball club was taken by Rockmart photographer "Nickel Jim" Gribble. At the turn of the century, many cities had a baseball team and competed with other cities. Over the years, a number of players went on to play for professional teams. The players were Young, Hamrick, Ferguson, McRae, Jenkins, Perryman, Mosely, Calhoun, and Barber. The reclining player is unknown.

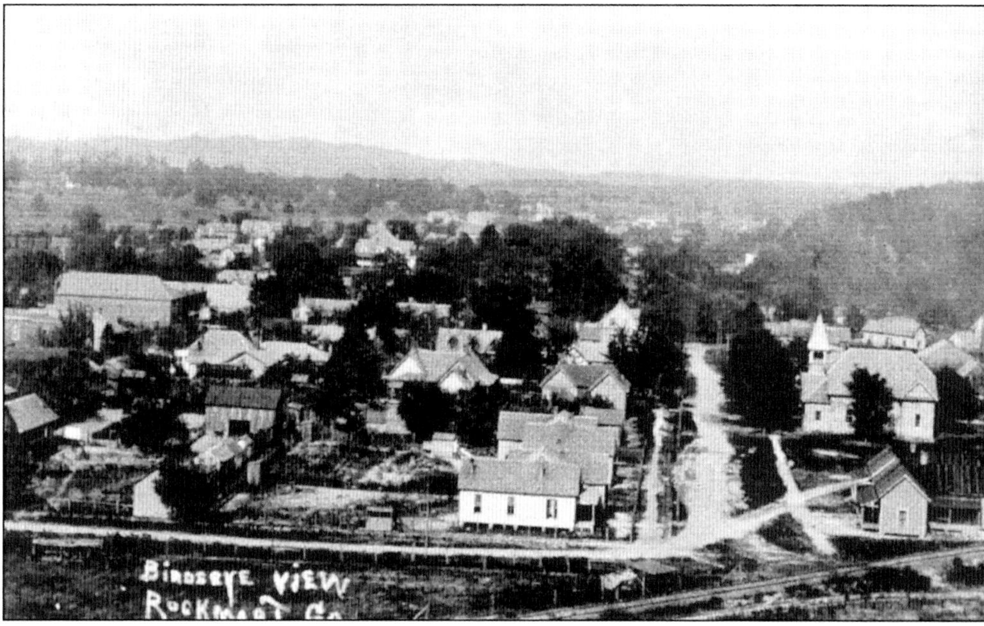

An early panorama view of Rockmart looks north on Slate Street with the Church of Christ on the right. The church and some of the houses are still standing today. Faintly visible in the left center is the distinctive roof of the Marble Hill Hotel. (Courtesy Bob Basford.)

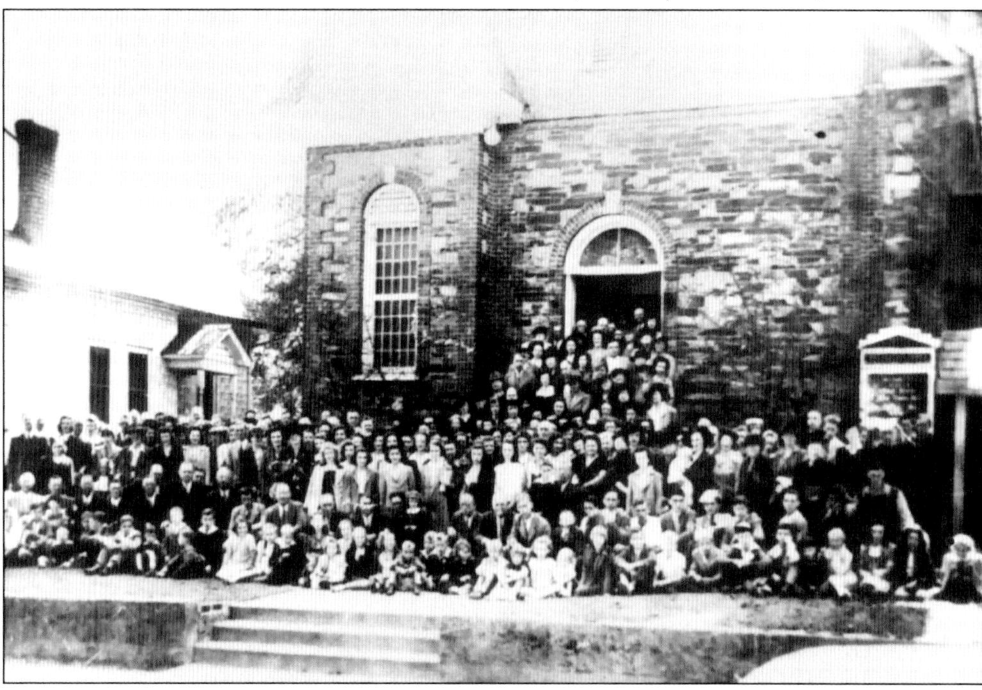

The Rockmart Baptist Church was organized in 1875 and services were held for three years in the old Williams Academy on the west side of Euharlee Creek until a new church could be completed. Land for a second church was donated by the widow of Seaborn Jones for a token payment of one dollar. The building on East Elm Street, now called the Chapel, was constructed in 1891 using native slate and stone.

The First United Methodist Church was organized in 1881 or 1882 with J.T. Gibson as the first pastor. The Methodists held services in the Presbyterian church until their new sanctuary was completed in 1883, on a site presented by Seaborn Jones.

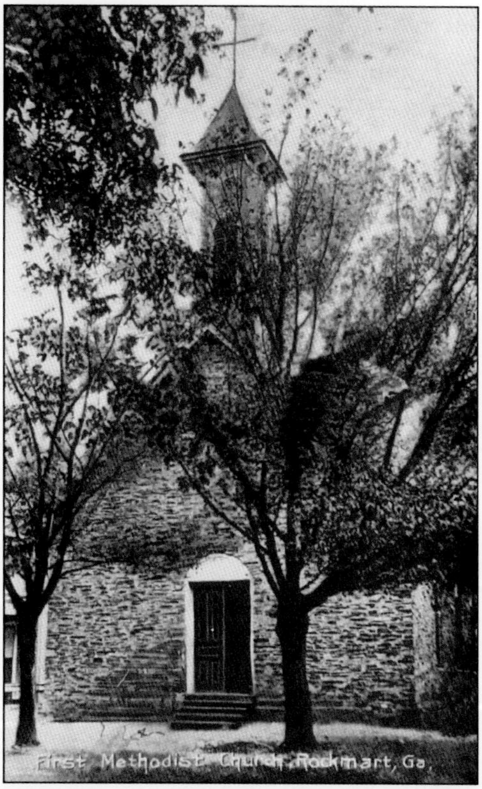

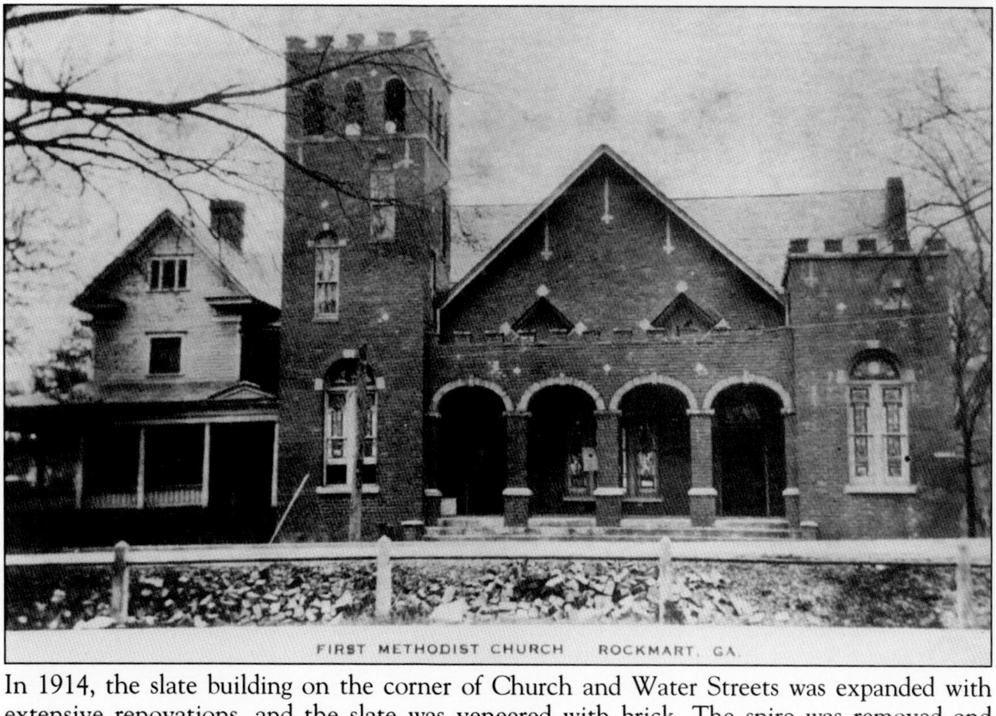

In 1914, the slate building on the corner of Church and Water Streets was expanded with extensive renovations, and the slate was veneered with brick. The spire was removed and replaced with the brick tower shown in this picture.

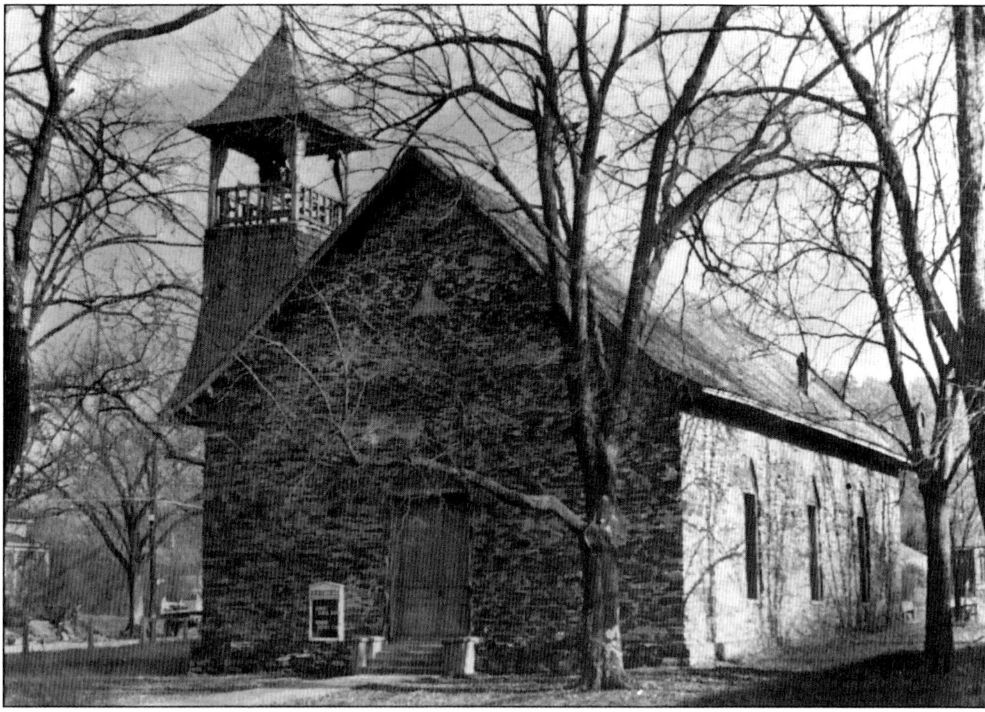

Eight founding members met on May 28, 1871, in the Van Wert Methodist Church to organize the First Presbyterian Church, shown here. In another of his many contributions to Rockmart, Seaborn Jones donated a lot on the corner of Slate and Marble Streets for the church in 1878.

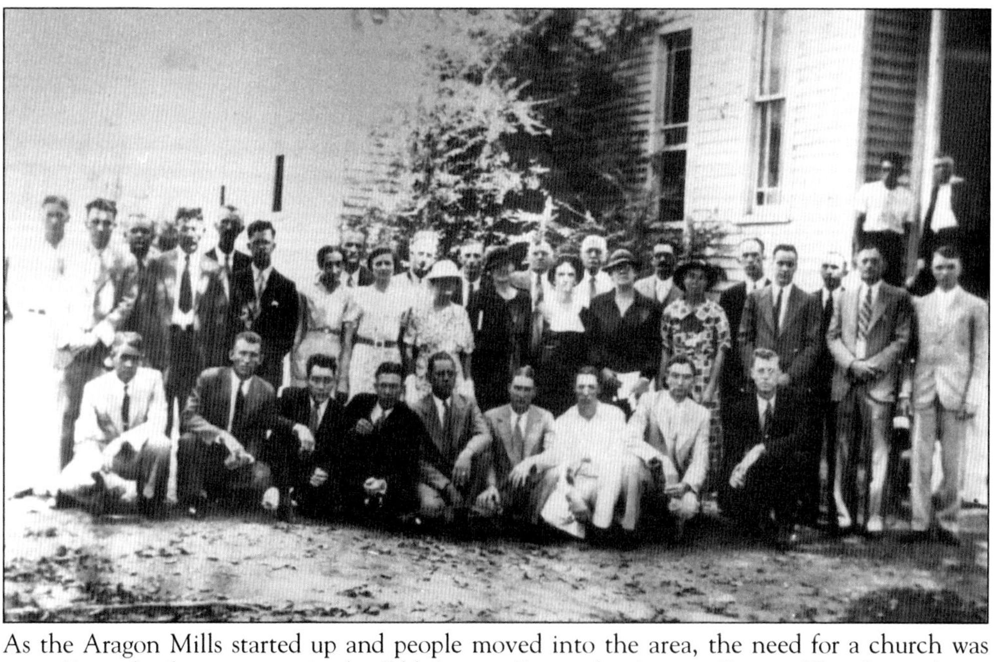

As the Aragon Mills started up and people moved into the area, the need for a church was seen. From the first meeting in the Old Aragon Store, the Aragon Baptist Church was born. Incorporation took place in 1901, and the founders' vision was realized when the church building was completed the next year.

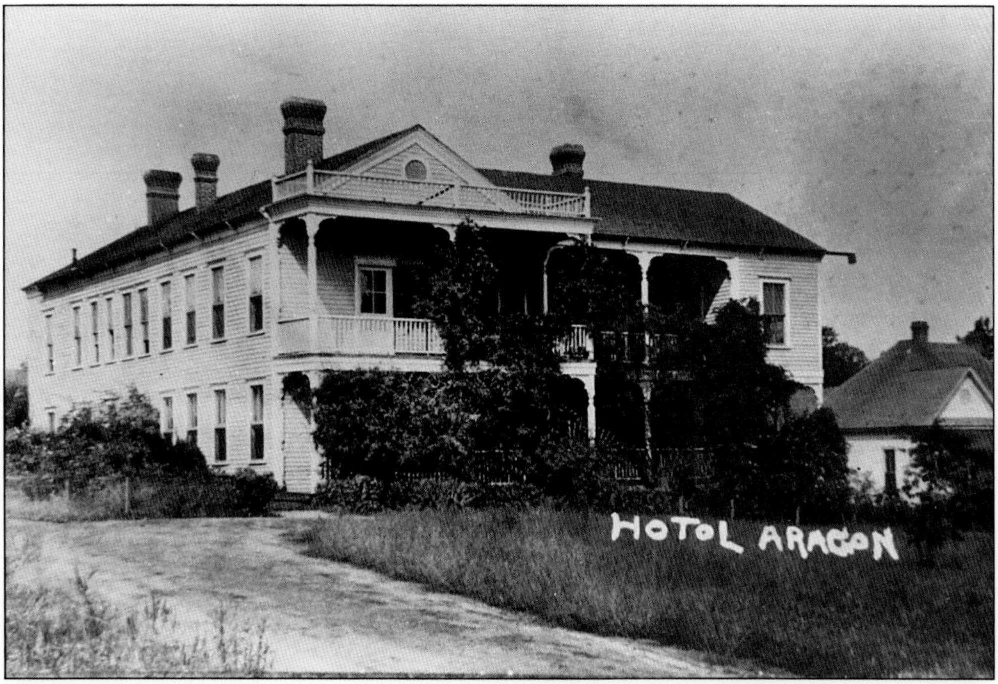

Lying on the Southern Railway and the Cartersville branch of the Seaboard Railway, Aragon got its start in 1898 when a two-story brick textile mill was built and chartered to manufacture several weights of high-grade duck. The Aragon Hotel, pictured here in 1907, doubtless accommodated business visitors to Aragon Mills, but it is no longer standing.

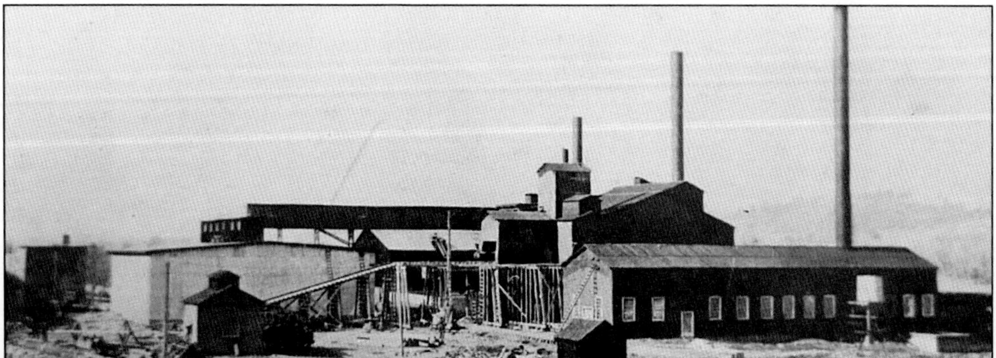

Along the east bank of Euharlee Creek, the Davitte Lime Company operated kilns which had existed for many years. In 1908, Davitte sold his company's lime kilns and limestone quarries. The new owner, the Piedmont Portland Cement Company, built their cement plant near Aragon along the Seaboard Air Line Railroad 1.5 miles northeast of Aragon Mills. Unfortunately, it did not prosper.

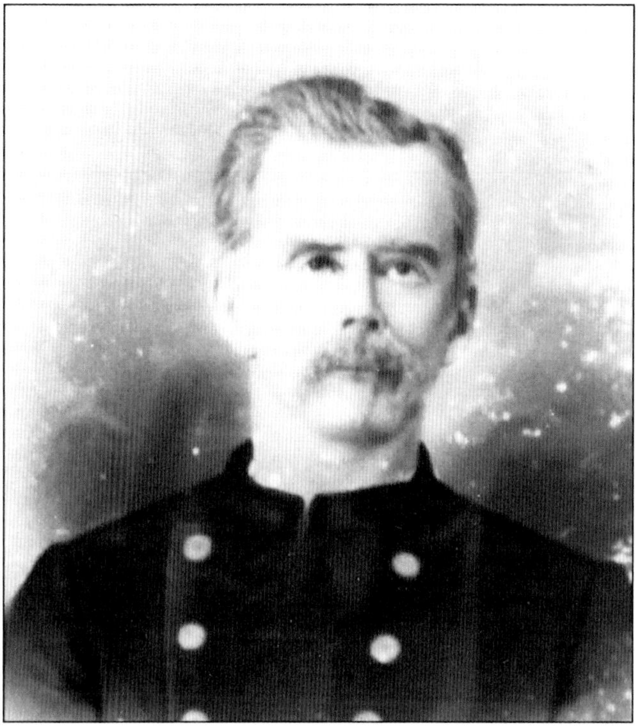

Jacob Scott Davitte was the son of John C. Davitte, who settled in the Cherokee Territory in 1831 near what is Aragon today. Davitte farmed and took an active part in church and community affairs. He helped to establish the Piedmont Institute and supported it with contributions. The flag stop, once called Davittes, became Portland when the cement plant was established, and a tiny community developed.

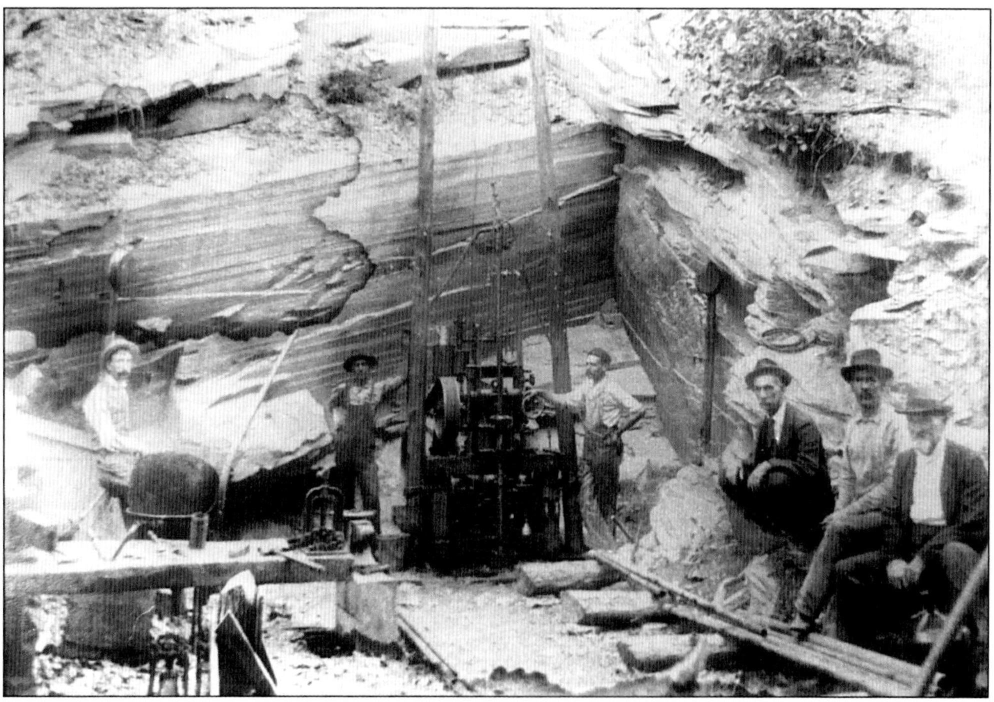

Workers were photographed in a limestone quarry located in the Aragon area, with what appears to be a drilling rig. Limestone in the area was roasted in kilns to make lime, in a process which predates the Civil War. The individuals are not identified, but the third individual from the right is believed to be Jake Davitte.

Six

Hamlets

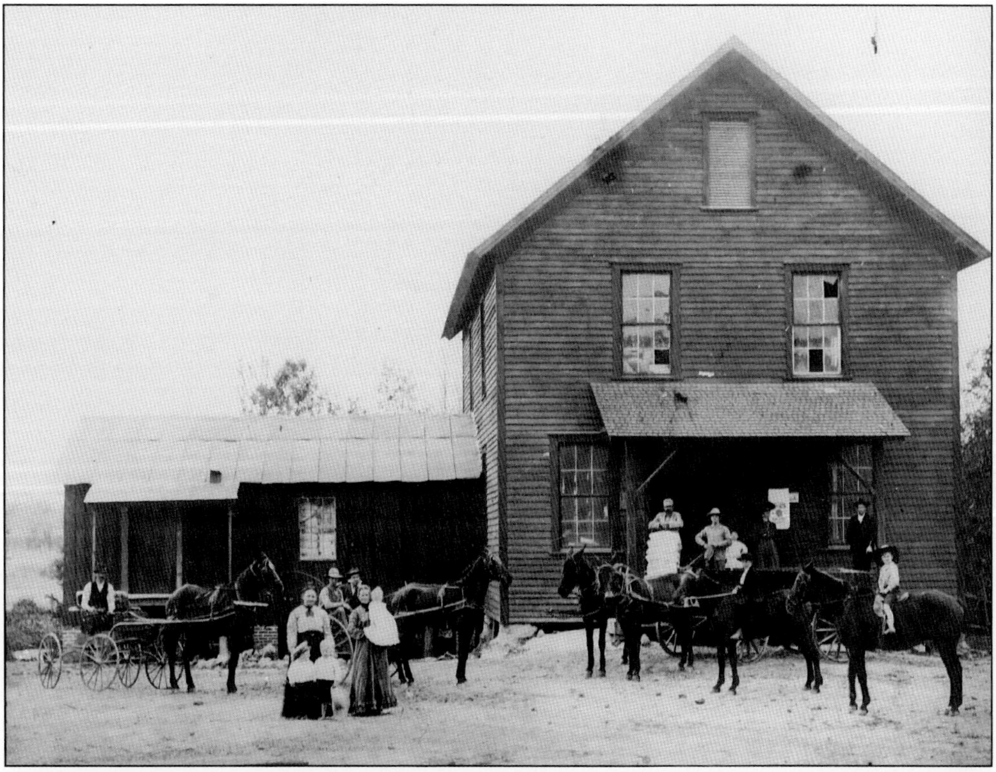

People and horses pose for the photographer in 1907 at Lovvorn's general store in the Friendship community. The Rev. W.J. Lovvorn, standing on the porch at the extreme right, owned this general store and also operated a cotton gin and gristmill on the same site. Ballenger Gravelly, the first settler in Cedar Valley according to local tradition, built his home nearby in the early 1830s and was one the few whites to teach his children the Cherokee language. (Courtesy Georgia Department of Archives and History.)

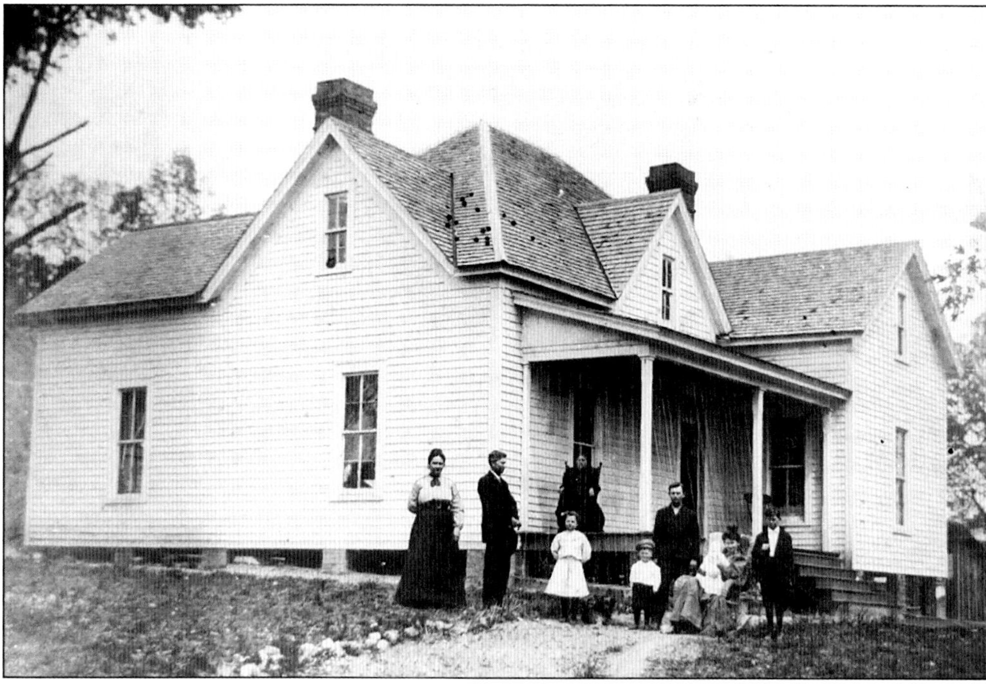

The Lovvorn family gathers at the home of the Rev. William Jeptha Lovvorn Sr. in 1907. The Reverend Lovvorn was pastor at the Friendship Baptist Church. From left to right, the Lovvorn family is as follows: Mrs. Lovvorn; Reverend Lovvorn; Mary; W.J. Jr.; Homer; Minnie (then Mrs. W.O. Hamrick with baby, Ruth); and Hoyt. Mrs. Lovvorn's mother, Mrs. Matilda Upchurch, is seated on the porch.

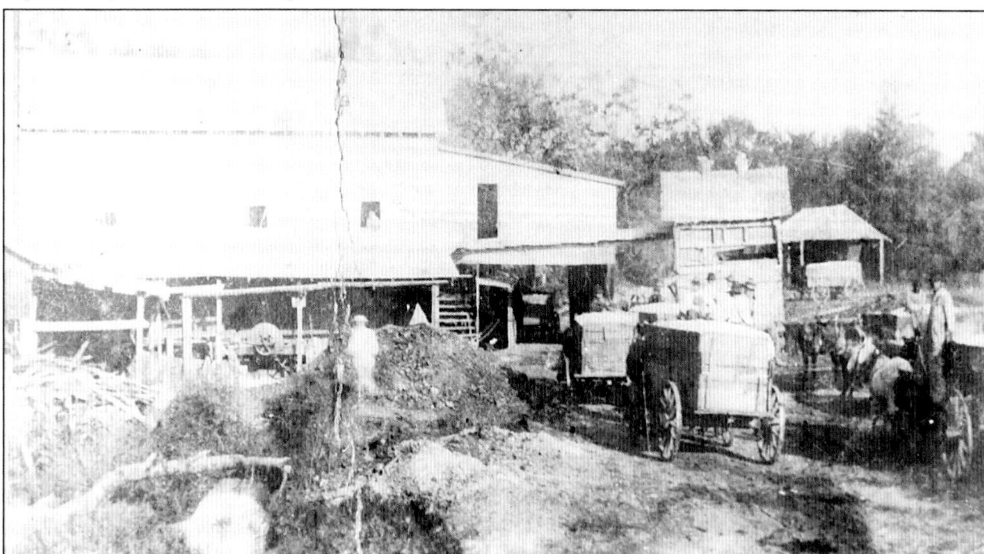

Earlier known as Lovvorn's Mill, by 1910 when this photograph was taken, the gristmill and cotton gin on Cedar Creek was known as Sutton's Mill, the name today of the tumbledown remains. Cotton was picked by hand and hauled to the gin from the fields by wagons drawn by horses or mules, as shown in this image. (Courtesy Georgia Department of Archives and History.)

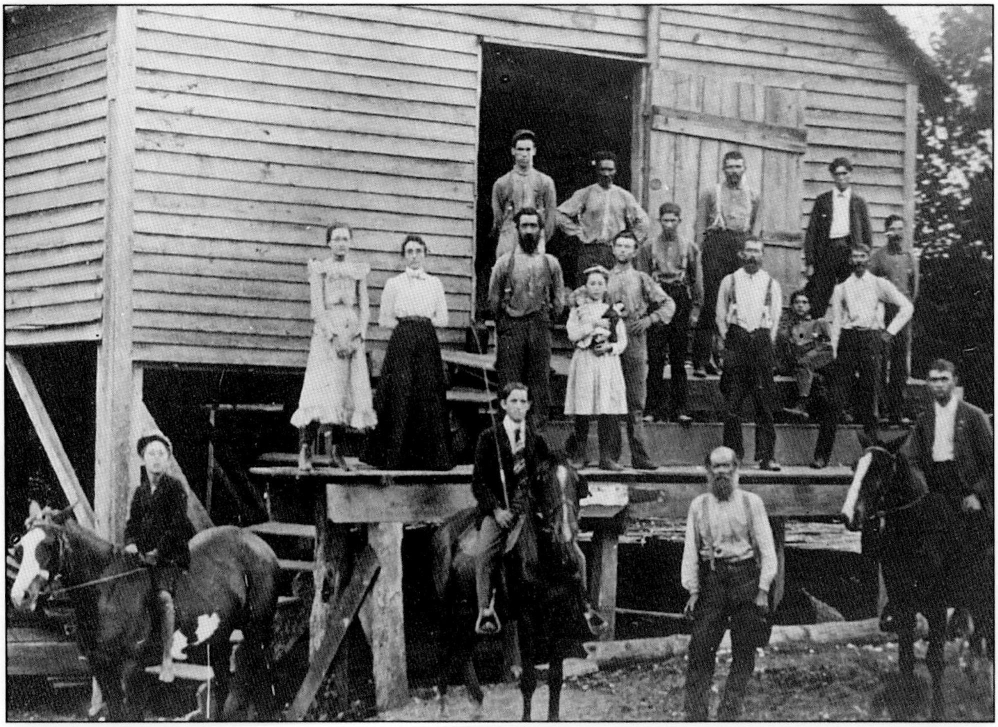

Ray's Mill was also located on Cedar Creek, upstream from Sutton's Mill and closer to Cedartown. It is believed that Ray's became known as Brock's Mill. The mill which ground corn and wheat for the Friendship community has disappeared.

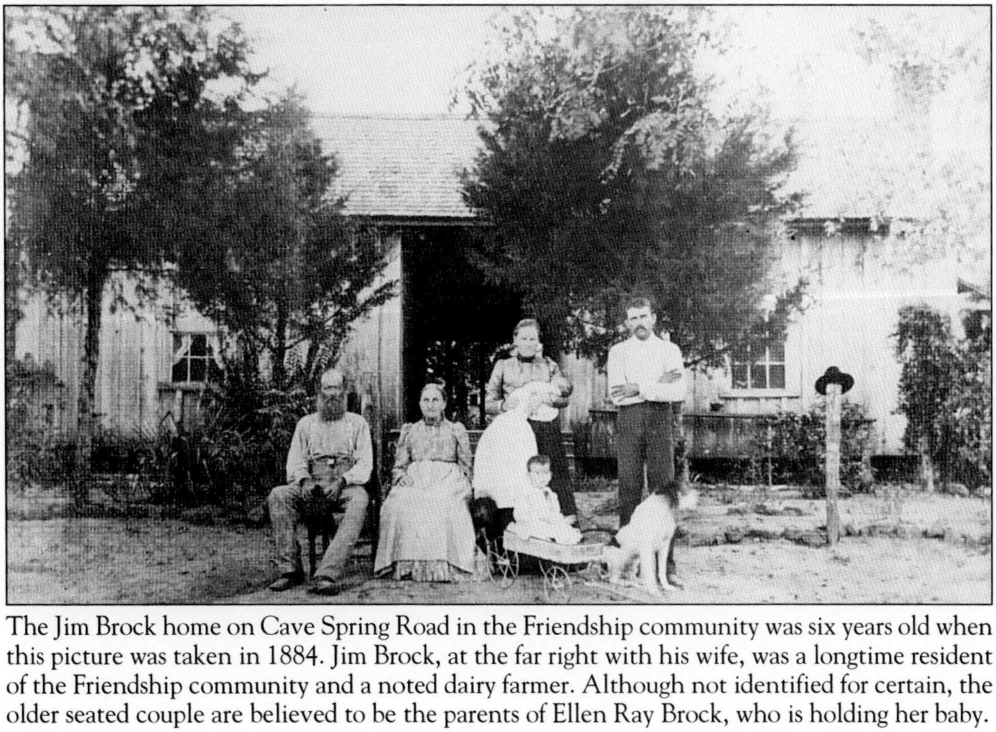

The Jim Brock home on Cave Spring Road in the Friendship community was six years old when this picture was taken in 1884. Jim Brock, at the far right with his wife, was a longtime resident of the Friendship community and a noted dairy farmer. Although not identified for certain, the older seated couple are believed to be the parents of Ellen Ray Brock, who is holding her baby.

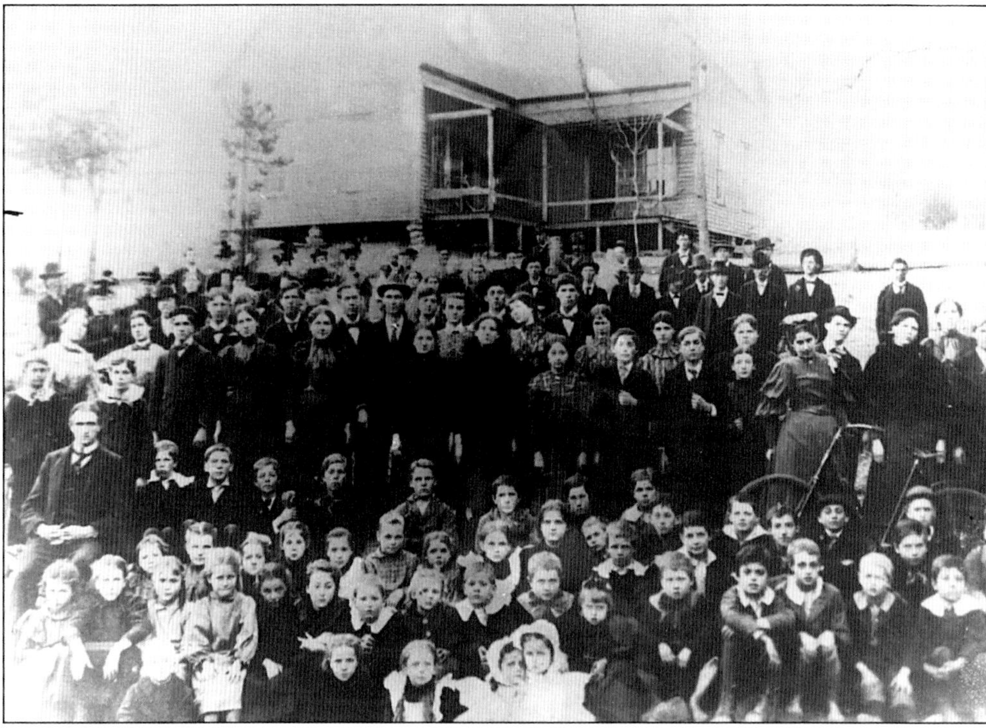

The two-room school, shown here in 1895, served the Friendship community. Pictured at an unknown event, the schoolchildren are seated with visitors standing in back. The principal, John W. Sutton, is seated on the left. He later became the superintendent of schools for Polk County.

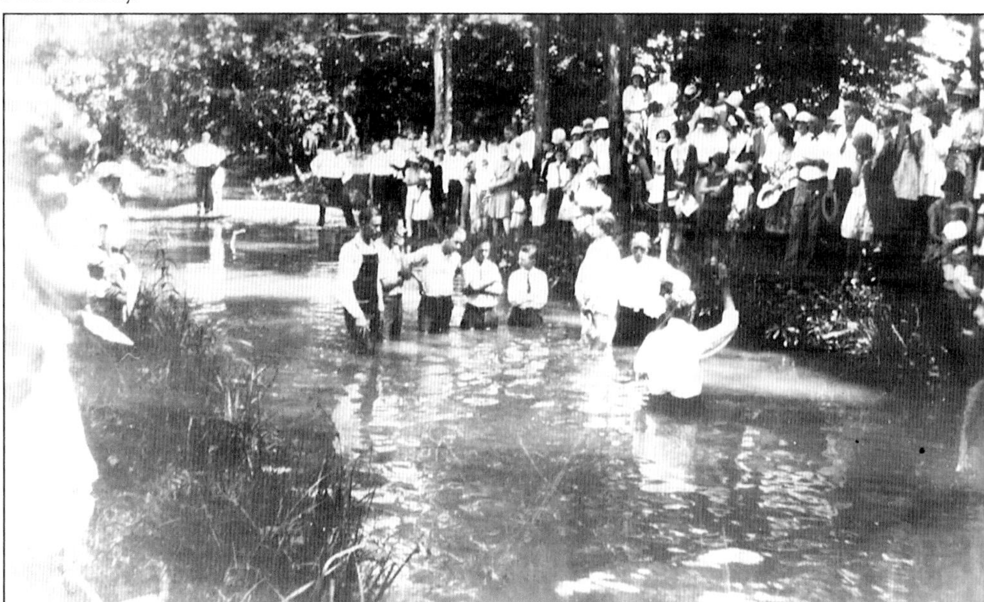

The Reverend Randolph W. Hamrick, the pastor of the Friendship Baptist Church, performs an old-style baptism ceremony in Cedar Creek, *c.* 1929. (Courtesy Georgia Department of Archives and History.)

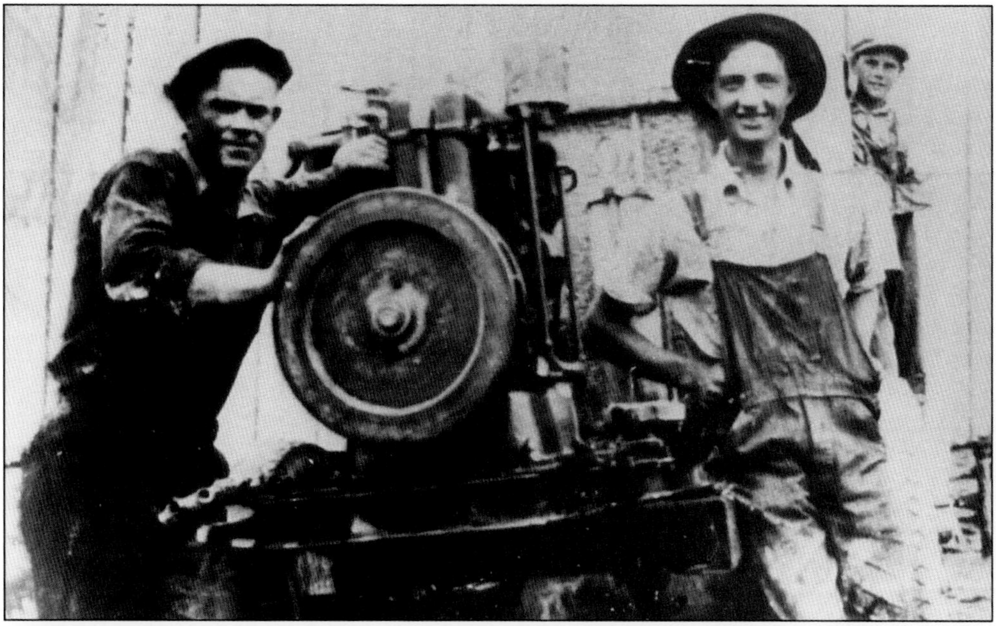

This insecticide-spraying machine was used in the orchards at Treat Mountain. Between roughly 1920 and 1940, the Treat Packing Company operated some 700 acres of apple and peach orchards, employing at times as many as 500 workers. Apples in boxes made in the sawmill were transported by horse and wagon, later by truck, to the Seaboard Railroad crossing in Esom Hill.

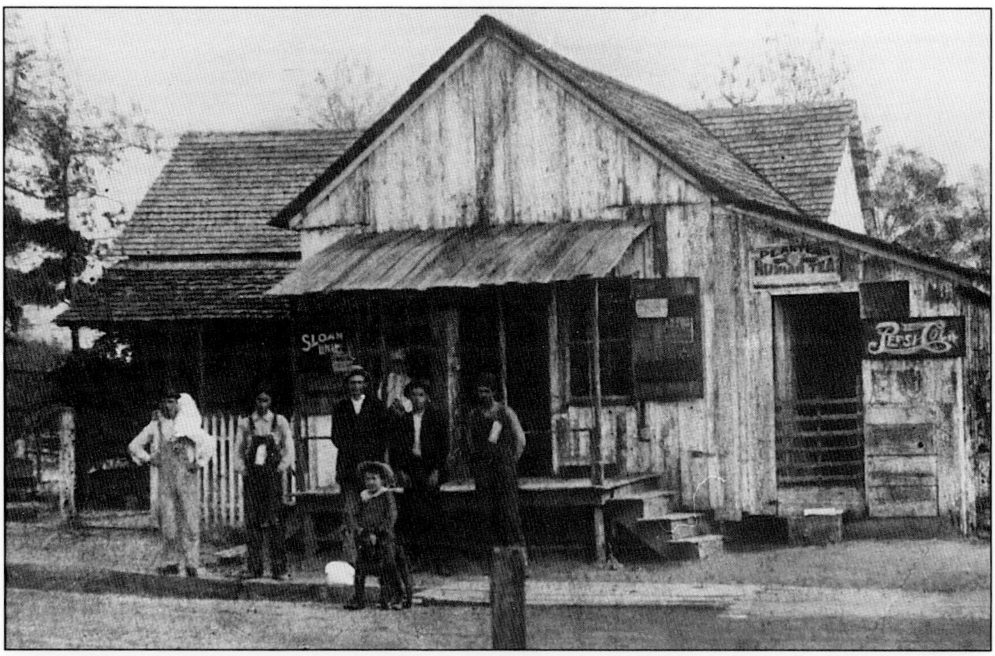

About 1885, Columbus M. Isbell settled at Ake's Station 3 miles east from Esom Hill and raised his family there. He built the house shown here and operated a general store in the front room of his home for a number of years. Later his son, William, took over the operation of the store. The structure stood until a few years ago, when it was demolished.

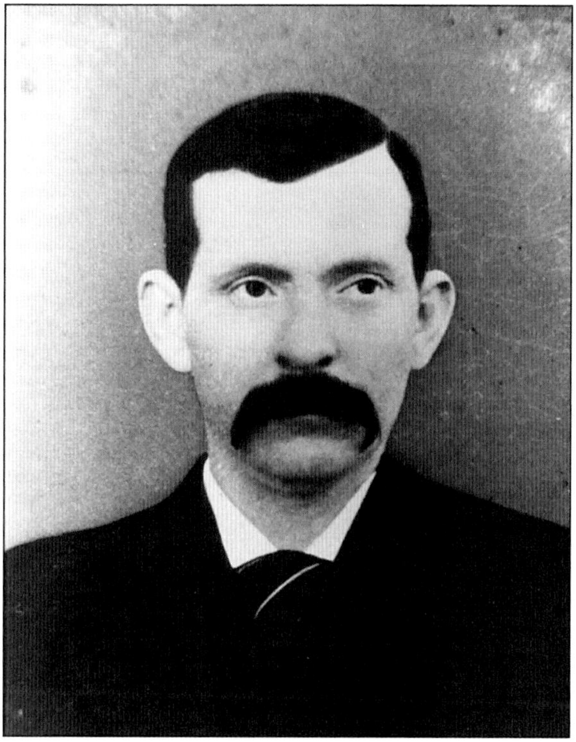

Among the early settlers in Esom Hill was the Reverend Van Allen Brewster, a Baptist pastor, who left Haralson County in 1860 and moved to Esom Hill with his family. His son, Joseph P.S. Brewster, shown here, operated a general store with the Esom Hill post office, as well as a cotton gin. In the 1920s, the Brewster family moved into Cedartown, where they established another general store.

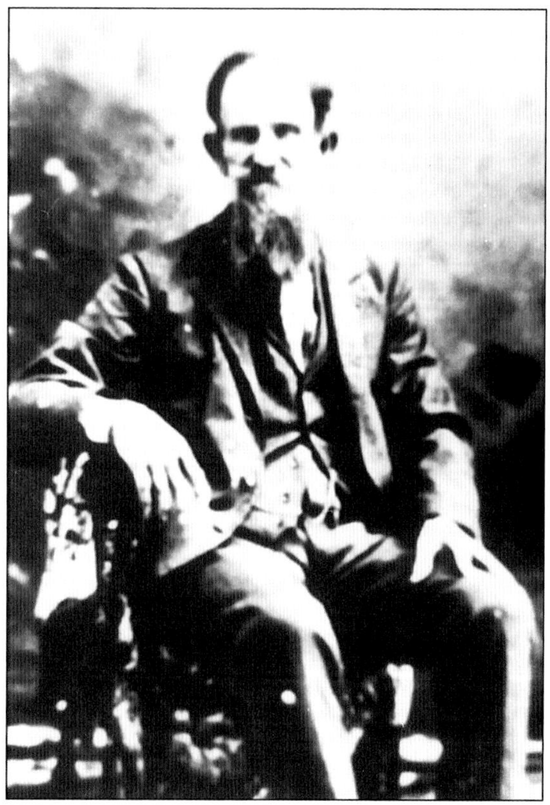

Jeremiah M. Isbell served in the U.S. Civil War with his eldest son. His father, Pendleton Isbell, made an even greater contribution, serving with eight of his sons and three of his grandsons. All returned home safely except one son and one grandson, who were killed. When Jeremiah Isbell returned to Floyd County from the war in 1865, he found that his family had "refugeed" to Esom Hill.

The Brewster and Isbell families lived next to each other in Esom Hill, and were formally linked when Laura Jane Isbell, shown here, and Joseph P.S. Brewster married in 1879. Twelve children were born to the couple, contributing considerably to the family of the proud grandfather. Jerre Isbell boasted in his 81st year that, out of his 198 living descendants, there was "not an idiot nor invalid nor a deformed one."

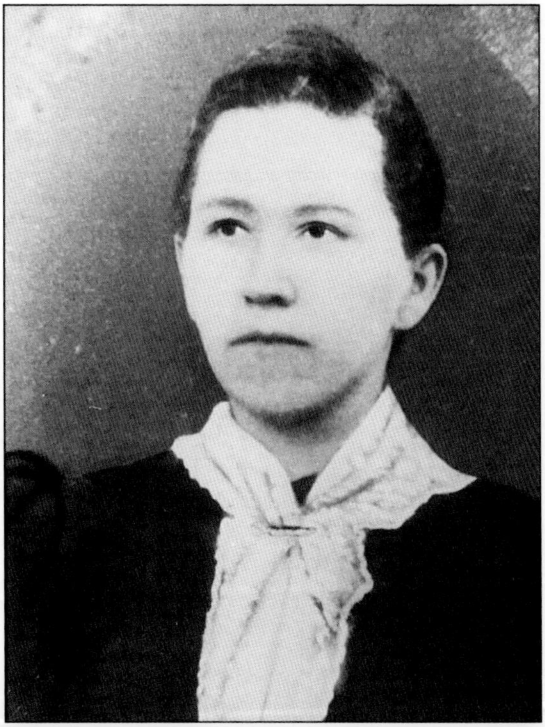

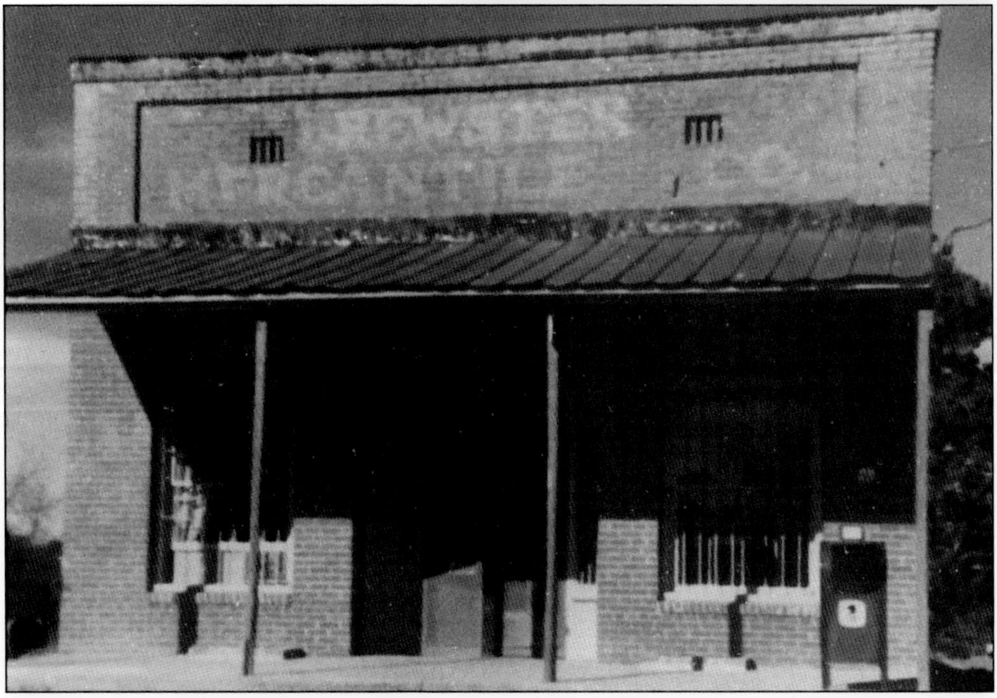

In 1881, Esom Hill had five general stores to serve a population of 169. One was owned by J.P.S. Brewster. Shown here is the Brewster Mercantile Company, built in 1901 after Brewster's first store burned. Besides operating a post office in the store, Brewster carried every kind of merchandise needed by farming families, from toothpicks to two-horse wagons.

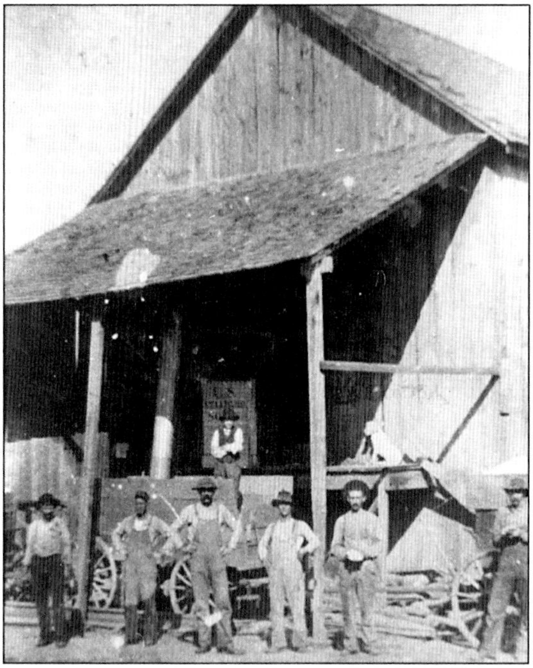

J.P.S. Brewster built his gin about 1900 near the tracks of the East and West Railroad of Alabama (later the Seaboard Air Line). Farmers coming to Esom Hill could sell their cotton at the gin and pick up supplies at the nearby Brewster Mercantile. The farmers usually operated on credit and paid their bills when they could harvest their crops. Barter was often used, with the farmers trading chickens, eggs, or vegetables for merchandise.

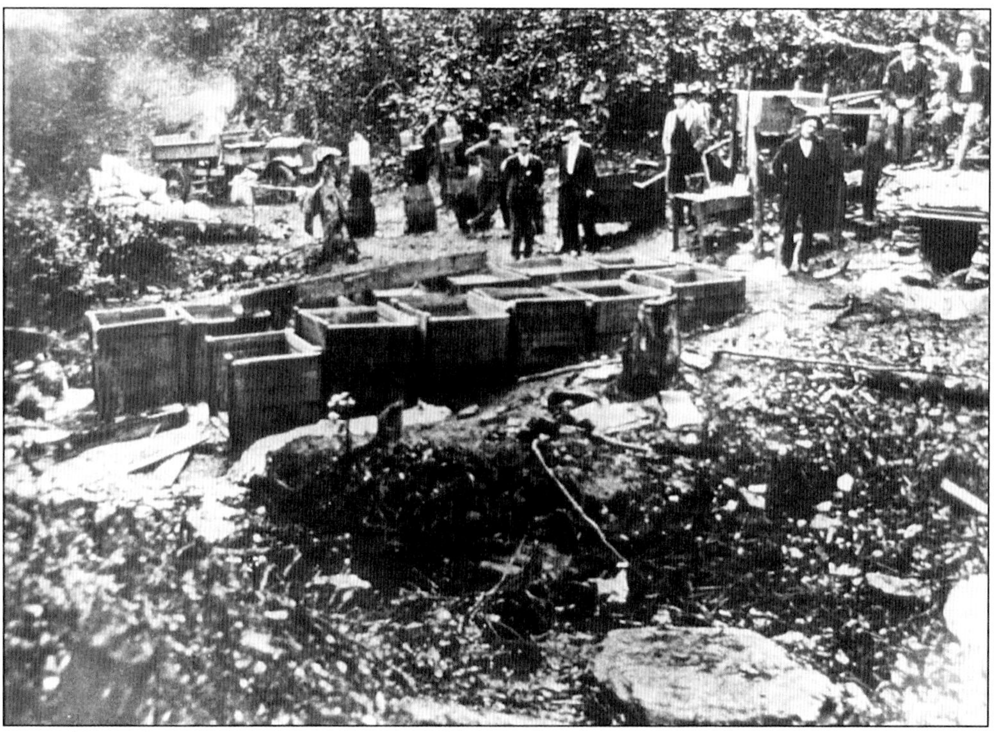

Law officers destroyed this moonshine still near Esom Hill, *c.* 1928. That town had a long-standing reputation for producing corn liquor. One legendary moonshiner was Will Smith, known as Bell Tree Smith. His customer would leave an empty jug and payment by the Bell Tree, ring a bell, and leave. When the bell rang again, he returned for his filled jug. Will Smith was shot and killed in a fight in 1909.

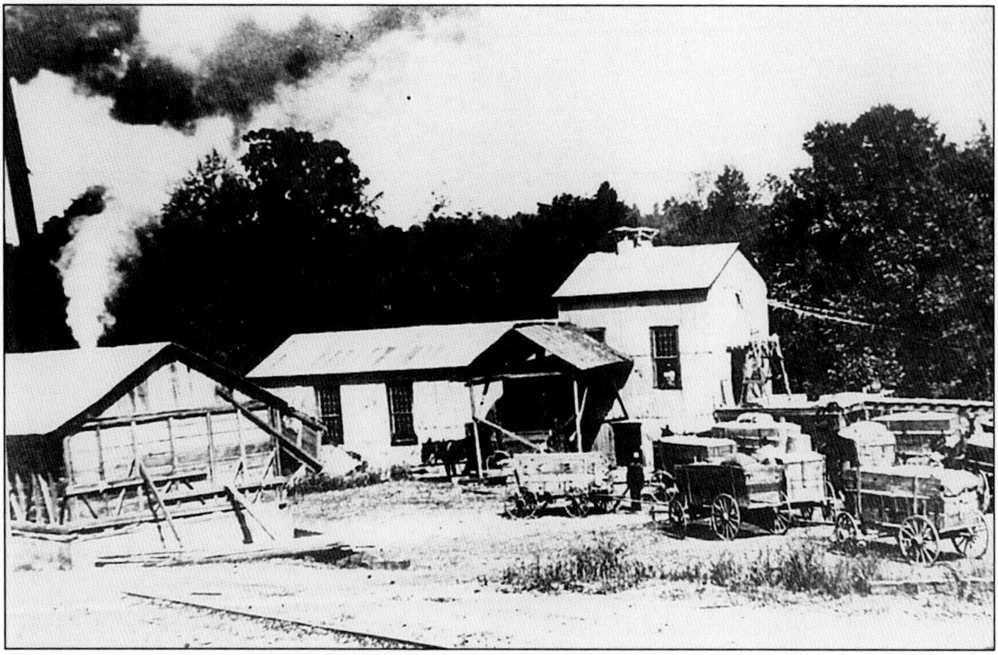

Wagons of cotton stand waiting to be ginned at Young's Grove in 1925. Cotton was the dominant crop and corn was second, with other crops being wheat, hay and forage, and oats.

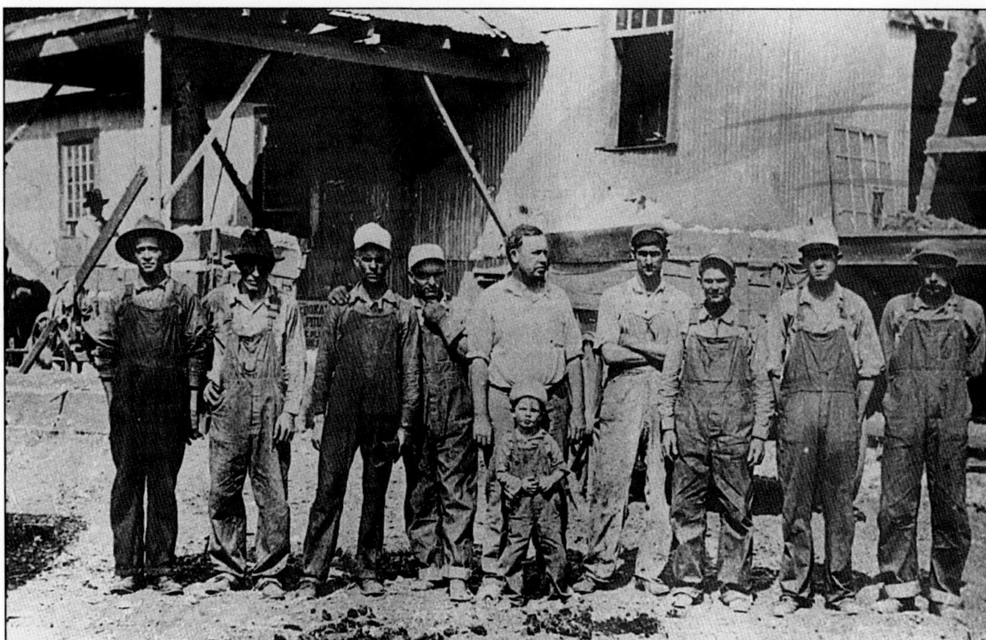

Workers at the Young's Station cotton gin pose in this 1925 picture. From left to right, they are as follows: Duley Pilgrim, Son Rudesal, Arthur Rudesal, Oliver Brown, Gus Henderson with Gus Henderson Jr. standing in front, Lloyd Stevens, Jim Bowens, Sid Johnson, and Horace Powell.

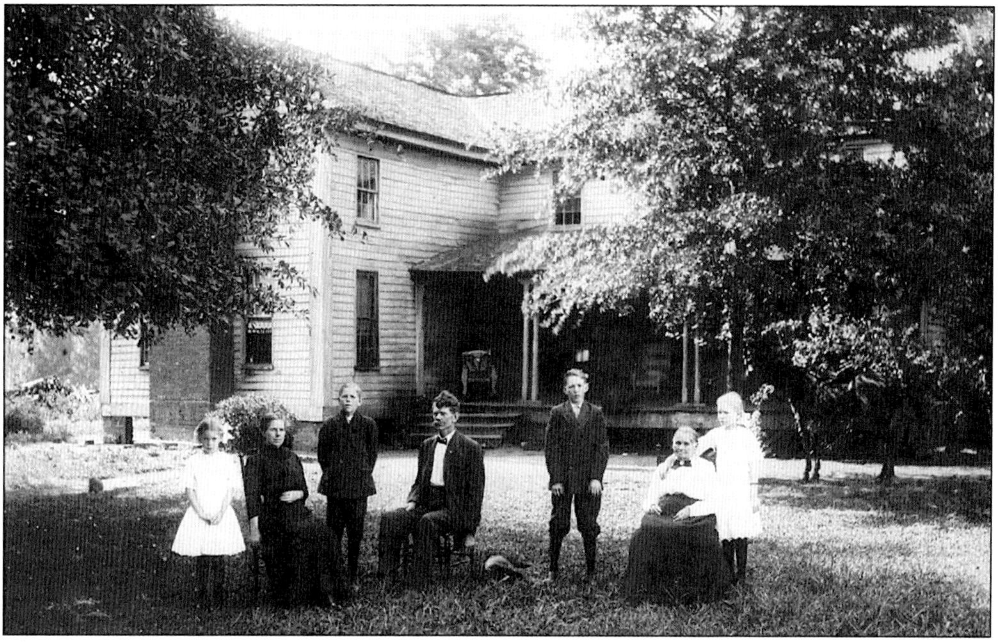

The Raper family gathered in their Sunday best for a family portrait in 1913 in front of their home at Prior's Station. The house was built by one of the Prior family, possibly Haden Prior. His first home was burned in 1864 by Union troops, and the structure shown is likely the house rebuilt sometime later by the Priors.

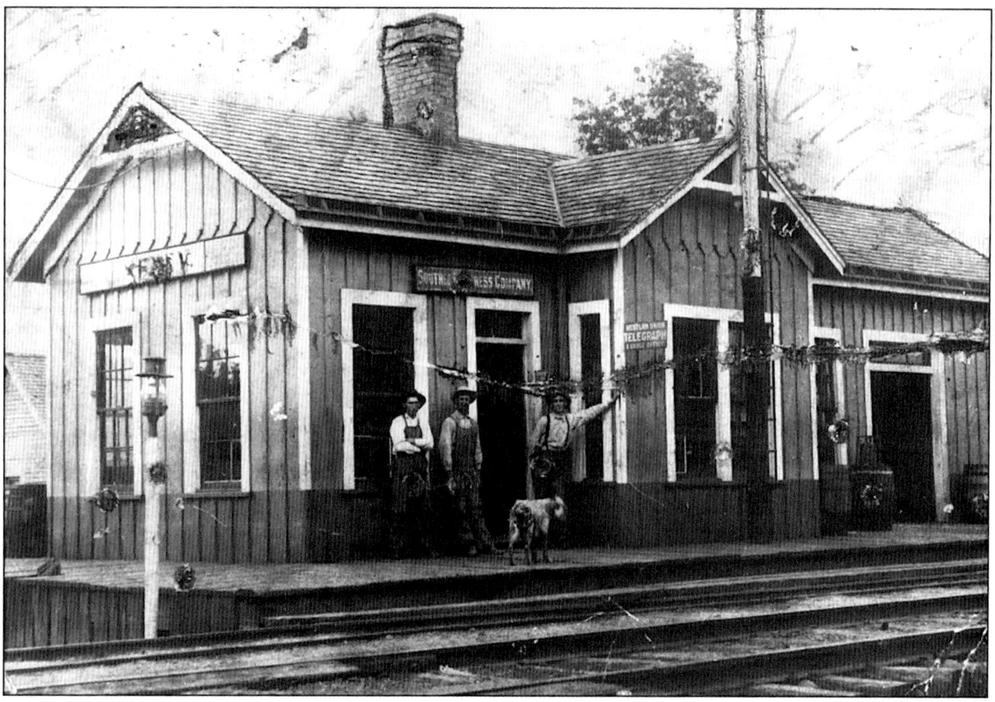

In 1881, the East Tennessee, Virginia & Georgia Railroad was extended from Rome to Atlanta, and from this, Seney—the "little half and half" town—came into existence. In 1900, the town had a population of 121, half in Polk County and half in Floyd County.

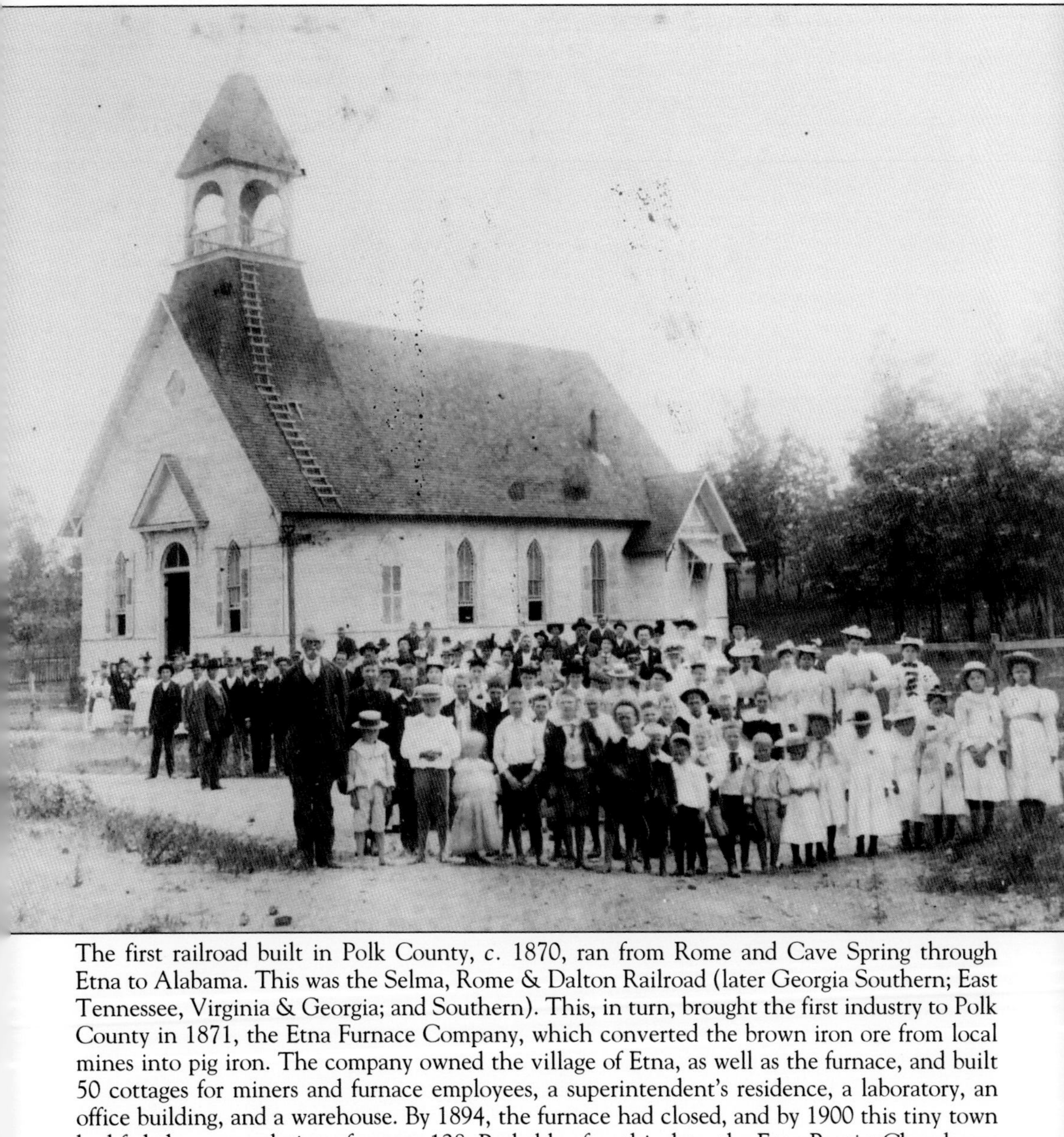

The first railroad built in Polk County, *c.* 1870, ran from Rome and Cave Spring through Etna to Alabama. This was the Selma, Rome & Dalton Railroad (later Georgia Southern; East Tennessee, Virginia & Georgia; and Southern). This, in turn, brought the first industry to Polk County in 1871, the Etna Furnace Company, which converted the brown iron ore from local mines into pig iron. The company owned the village of Etna, as well as the furnace, and built 50 cottages for miners and furnace employees, a superintendent's residence, a laboratory, an office building, and a warehouse. By 1894, the furnace had closed, and by 1900 this tiny town had faded to a population of a mere 128. Probably after this date, the Etna Baptist Church was photographed with its congregation.

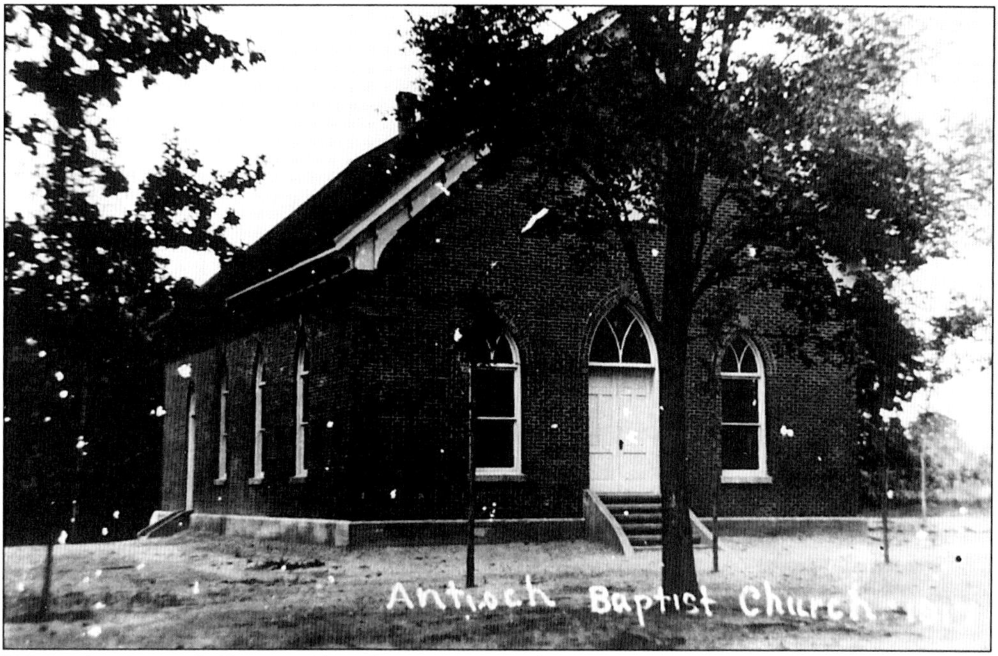

When the Antioch Baptist Church was organized in 1843, it was located in the village of Shades, which later became Antioch. The church was shared equally between the Baptists and the Methodists, with services for each being held on alternate Sundays.

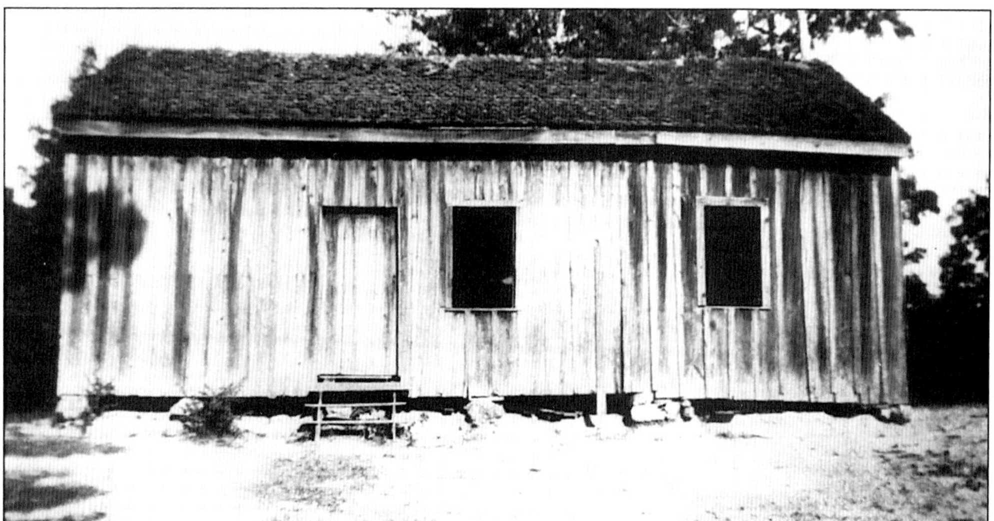

The tiny New Harmony Baptist Church was built in 1888, halfway between Esom Hill and Etna. Until a school was built in 1926, the building was used as a school as well as for church services. In 1934, a new church was built, and the dilapidated structure was taken down piece by piece to be reassembled and used for a home.

Seven

School Days

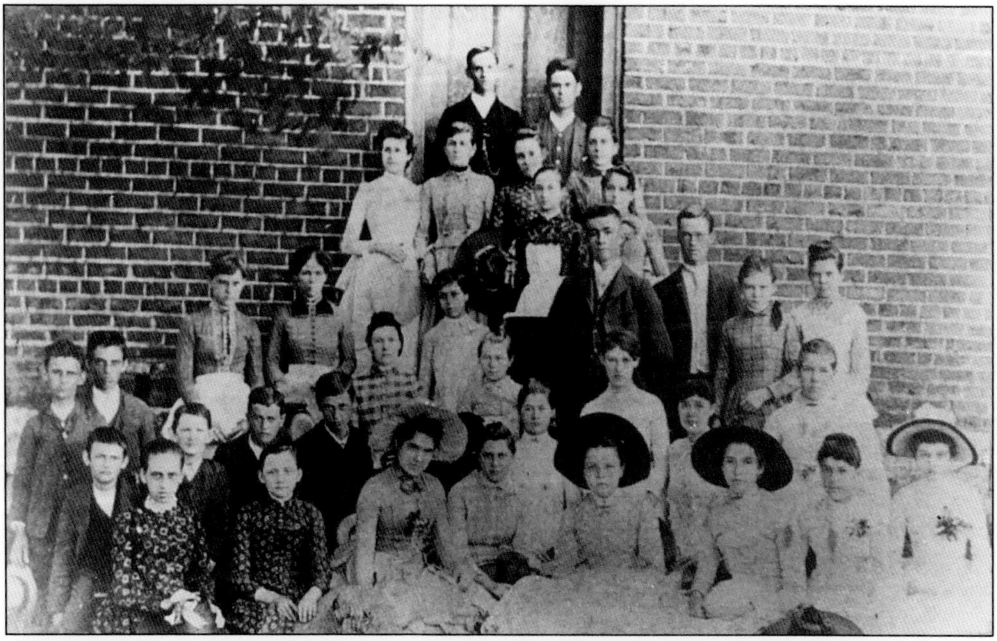

This group of students appears to be posed at the College Street School, possibly in 1889, when the building was completed. Children attended private schools, usually sponsored by churches, until 1887, when Georgia legislated public schools for Polk County. Before completion of the first public school, classes were held in the courthouse and an adjacent store building. At the same time, a school for black children was established, and classes were held in a Methodist church. In 1891, the first high school class graduated, consisting of just three students. Entertainment of any kind was rare in those days, and the widely varied program of commencement exercises was an enjoyable break in everyday routine, although the audience had to endure three hours.

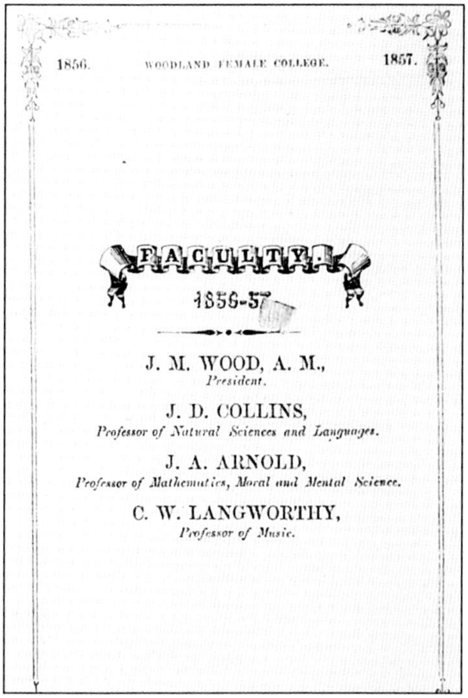

1856. WOODLAND FEMALE COLLEGE. 1857.

FACULTY.

1856-57

J. M. WOOD, A. M.,
President.

J. D. COLLINS,
Professor of Natural Sciences and Languages.

J. A. ARNOLD,
Professor of Mathematics, Moral and Mental Science.

C. W. LANGWORTHY,
Professor of Music.

The Woodland Female Academy catalogue for the school year 1856–1857 lists Jesse Wood as president, with 51 female students from across Georgia and Alabama. A school for boys, the Mosely Academy, had been established earlier.

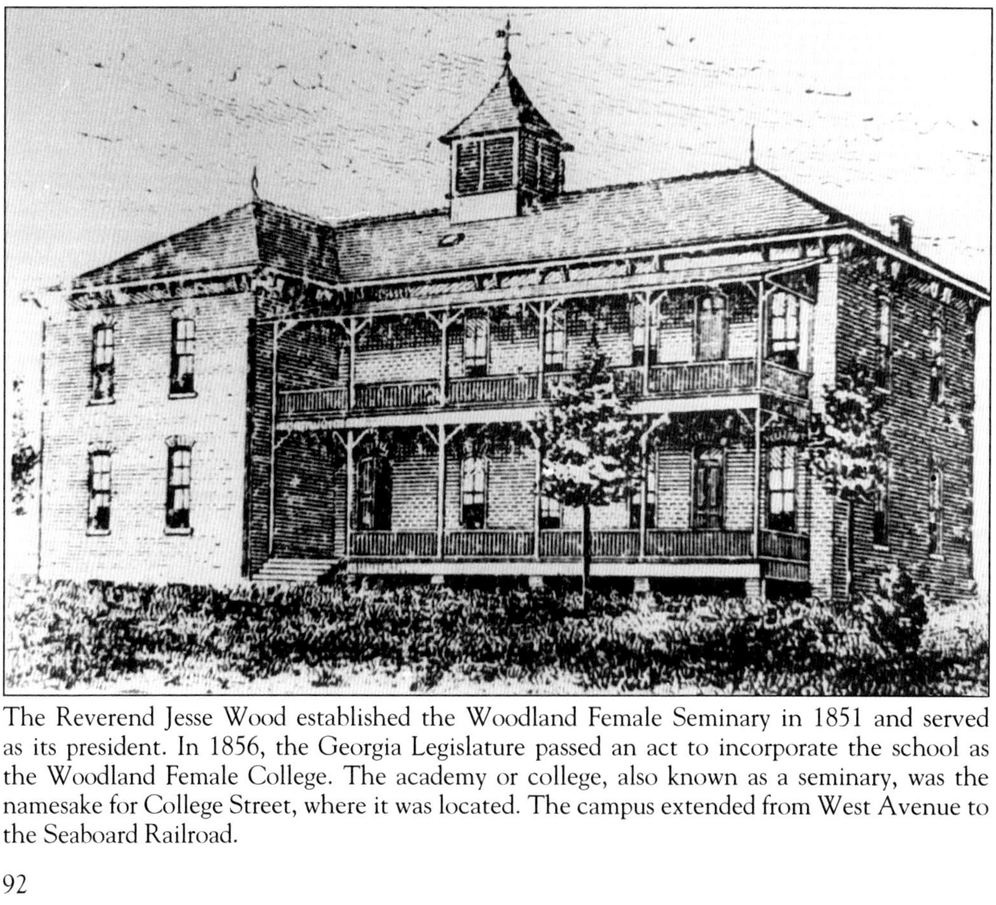

The Reverend Jesse Wood established the Woodland Female Seminary in 1851 and served as its president. In 1856, the Georgia Legislature passed an act to incorporate the school as the Woodland Female College. The academy or college, also known as a seminary, was the namesake for College Street, where it was located. The campus extended from West Avenue to the Seaboard Railroad.

An impressive array of subjects and fees was published in this 1877 *Cedartown Express* advertisement. The school "year" lasted a brief three months. It would be ten years before the Georgia Legislature passed a bill to create public schools in Polk County. The town academy was probably the building on Main Street which the Presbyterian congregation used on Sundays.

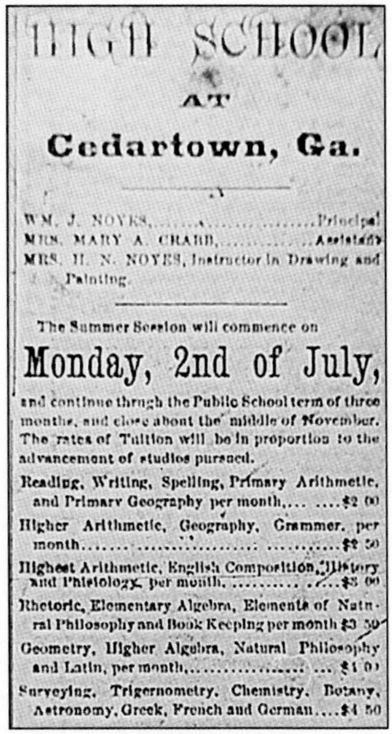

HIGH SCHOOL

AT

Cedartown, Ga.

WM. J. NOYES,........................Principal
MRS. MARY A. CRABB,...............Assistant
MRS. H. N. NOYES, Instructor in Drawing and Painting.

The Summer Session will commence on

Monday, 2nd of July,

and continue through the Public School term of three months, and close about the middle of November. The rates of Tuition will be in proportion to the advancement of studies pursued.

Reading, Writing, Spelling, Primary Arithmetic, and Primary Geography per month,... ....$2 00
Higher Arithmetic, Geography, Grammer, per month....... ....$2 50
Highest Arithmetic, English Composition, History and Phisiology, per month, ...$3 00
Rhetoric, Elementary Algebra, Elements of Natural Philosophy and Book Keeping per month $3 50
Geometry, Higher Algebra, Natural Philosophy and Latin, per month,...................... ... $4 00
Surveying, Trigernometry, Chemistry, Botany, Astronomy, Greek, French and German....$4 50

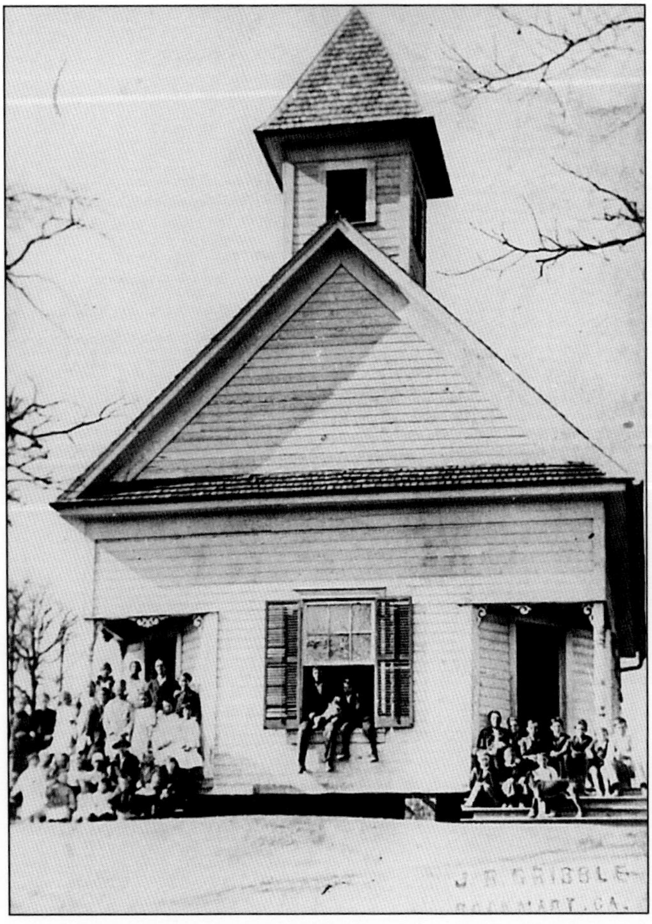

Kids cover the stairs and hang out of the windows at the Morgan Valley School in this *c*. 1918 picture. In the early 1900s, J.R. Gribble made many photographs of scenes around Rockmart such as this. Gribble was affectionately known as "Nickel Jim" by the children who bought candy in his candy/photography store. (Courtesy Georgia Department of Archives and History.)

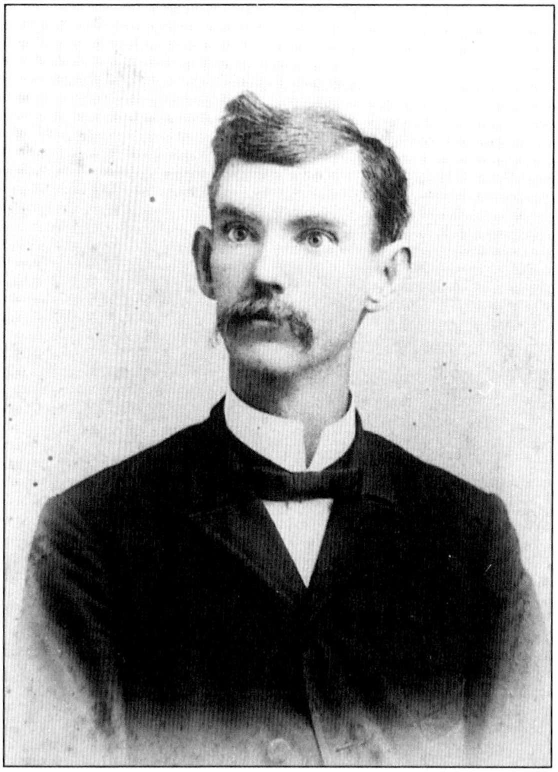

The Reverend Elbert W. Ballenger was a highly respected educator and Methodist minister who campaigned vigorously for a school in Rockmart. The founder and president of the Piedmont Institute arrived in Rockmart in 1888 and served as the minister of the Methodist Episcopal Church for a short time. He served at the institute until 1898, when he retired in poor health and was replaced by the Reverend O.L. Kelley.

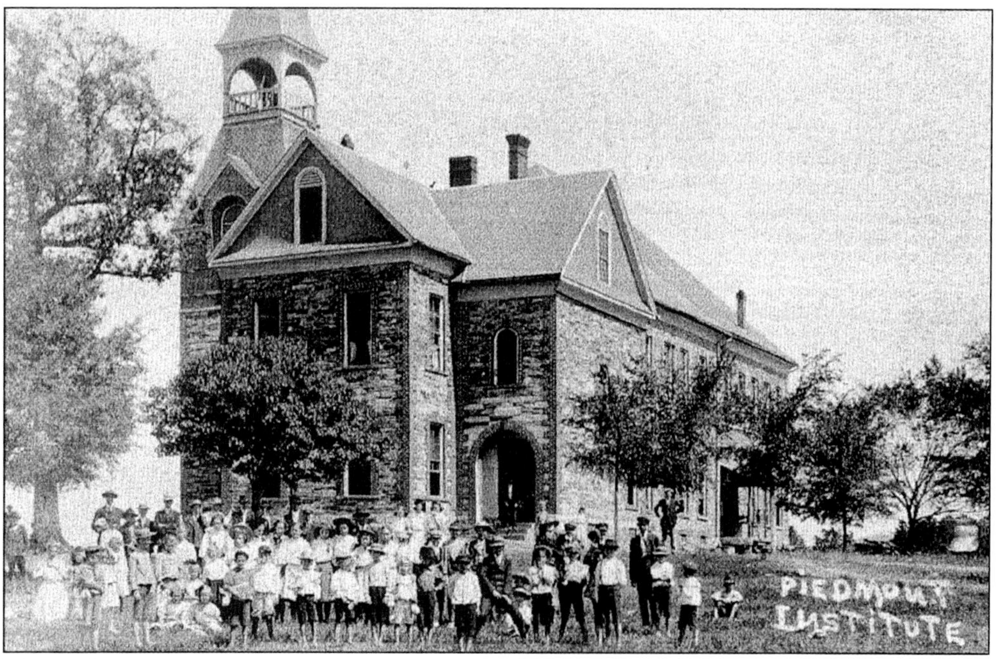

The Piedmont Institute, shown here *c.* 1902, was built in 1889 by the Methodist Conference under the leadership of the Reverend E.W. Ballenger. Although the school operated for only 22 years and produced approximately 110 graduates in that time, the education was comparable to two years of college, and graduates were held in high esteem. (Courtesy Bob Basford.)

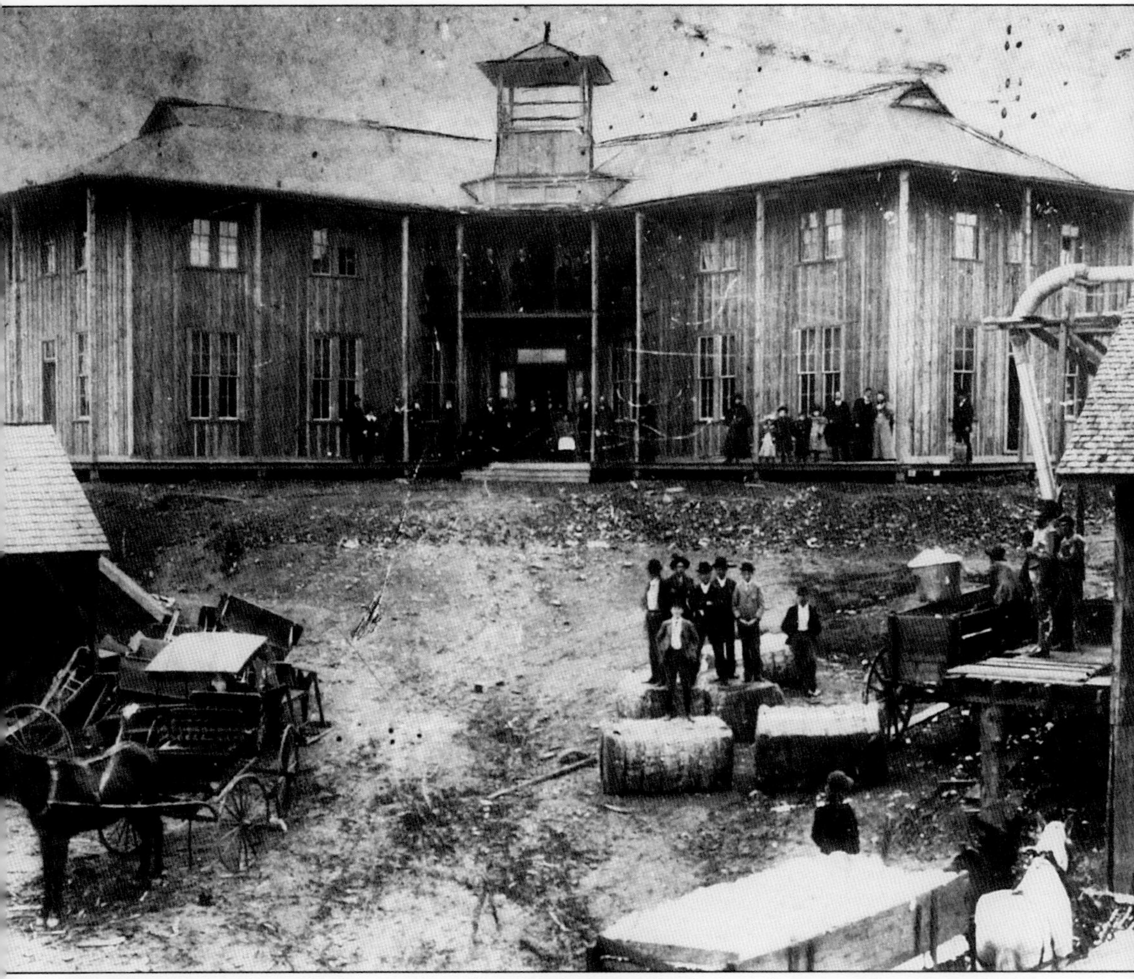

Benedict School overlooks wagons of cotton being unloaded to the gin. The two-story frame building, which contained both a dormitory and school rooms, was built in 1895 by the Reverend George Benedict and his brother, who named it the Samuel Benedict Memorial School, in honor of their minister-father. In the early days, a Benedict diploma was accepted as the equivalent of two years of college. Some children boarded at the school, and day students were transported from Cedartown by a horse-drawn bus with spring seats along the sides.

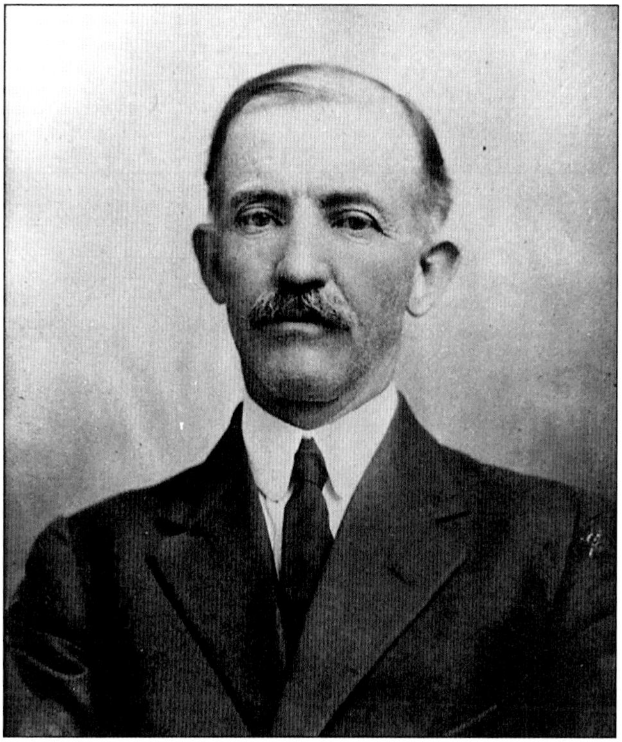

In February 1892, the Reverend George Elliot Benedict came from Virginia to serve as rector of the St. James Episcopal Church in Cedartown. While in this position, he established the Benedict School, with the Reverend John S. Lightburn serving as principal until 1904, when Reverend Benedict could be freed of his parish duties to serve the school for the next five years.

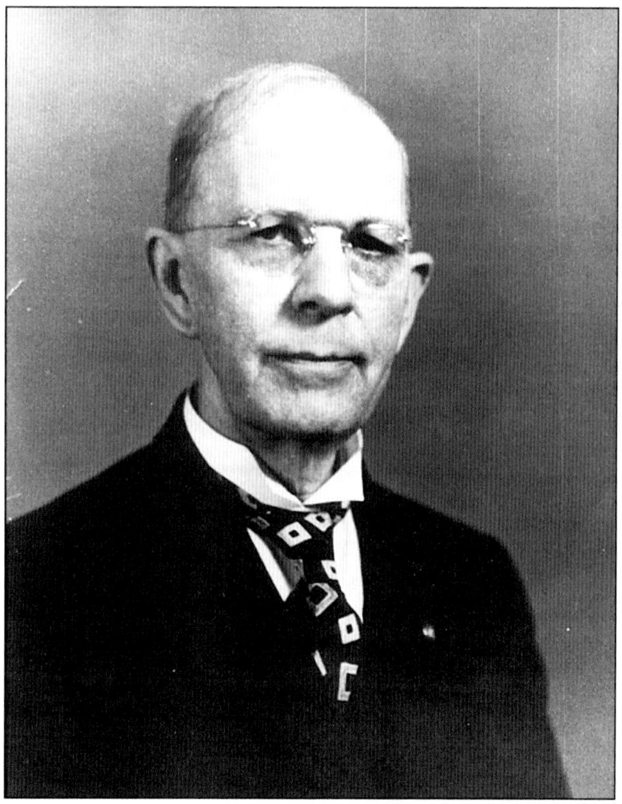

John Edwin Purks, shown with his customary stand-up collar, came to Cedartown in 1907 from West Point, Georgia, to become the superintendent of Cedartown schools, a position he would hold for 42 years. At that time there was one white school with 10 teachers and 375 students and one black school with 2 black teachers and 136 students. Mr. Purks is credited with founding the present Cedartown Public School system.

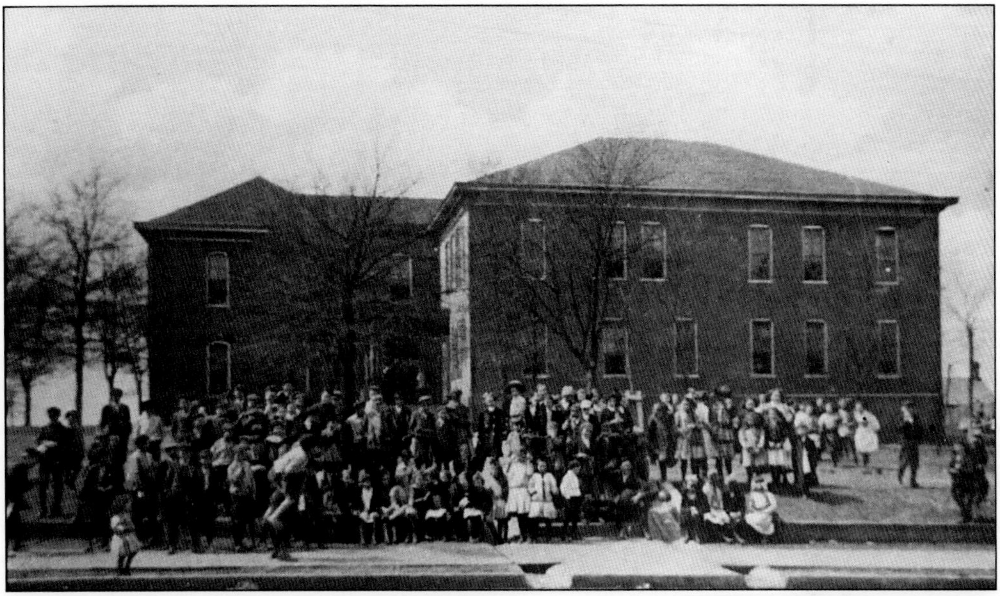

The College Street School was built in 1889, the first school after state legislation to provide public schools in Polk County. In 1907, the Gibson Street School was built, the first of five schools built under the leadership of J.E. Purks. Over a 42-year period, enrollment increased five-fold.

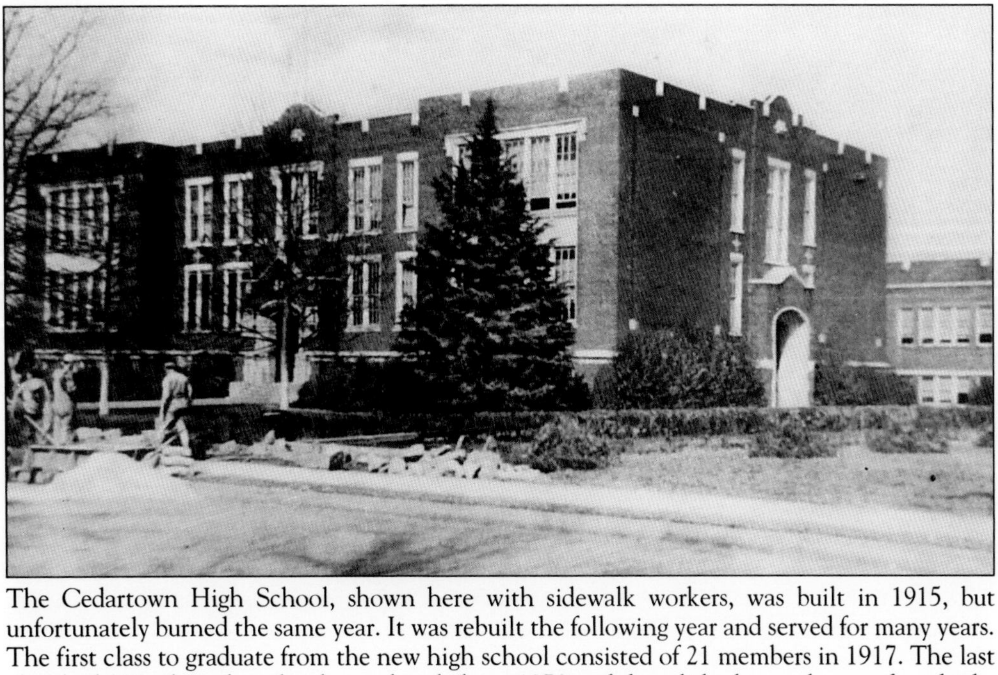

The Cedartown High School, shown here with sidewalk workers, was built in 1915, but unfortunately burned the same year. It was rebuilt the following year and served for many years. The first class to graduate from the new high school consisted of 21 members in 1917. The last class had 219 when the school was closed about 1970 and demolished to make way for a high-rise apartment building.

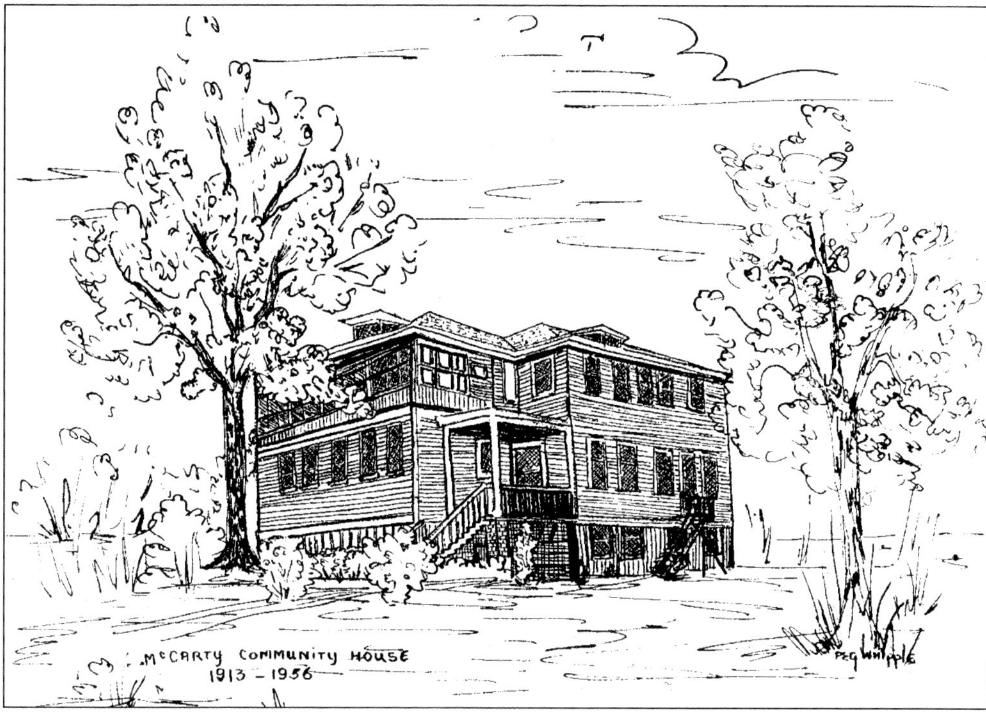

The Women's Home Missionary Society held educational programs in an unused textile mill, the Wahneta (Juanita) Knitting Mill, after it had closed in 1905. However, with the passing years, the numbers participating in the programs overwhelmed the old mill building, eventually requiring more space. In 1915, the society erected the McCarty Settlement House to accommodate the school-mission.

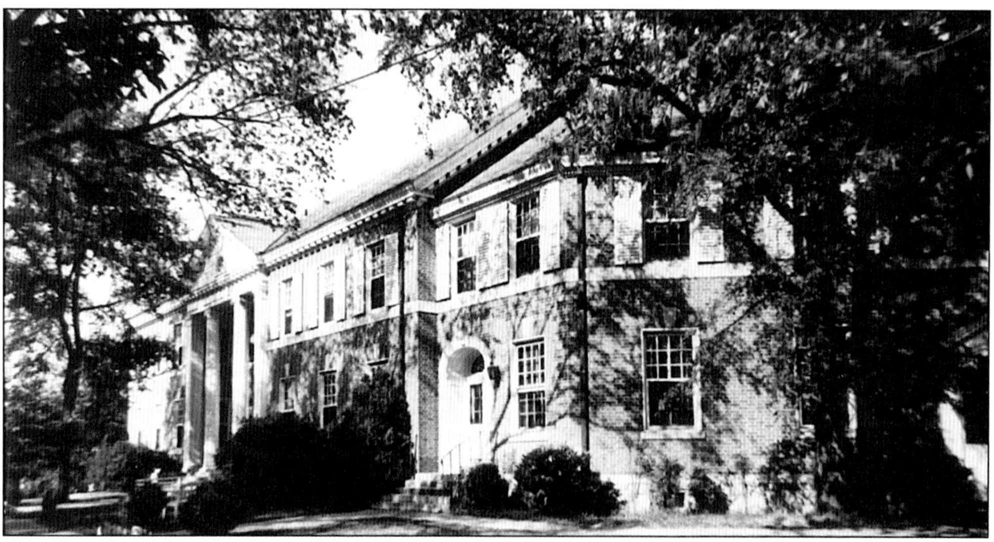

Miss Ethel Harpst came to the McCarty Settlement House in 1915 and started to take in orphaned children. In 1924, she received the gift of a seven-room house, and the Ethel Harpst Home was founded. A home for black orphans was started in 1931 by Sarah Murphy, and the two were eventually combined, becoming the Murphy-Harpst Home. Pictured is Merner Hall, erected in 1933 on the beautiful hilltop campus.

Eight

Some Notable Nabobs

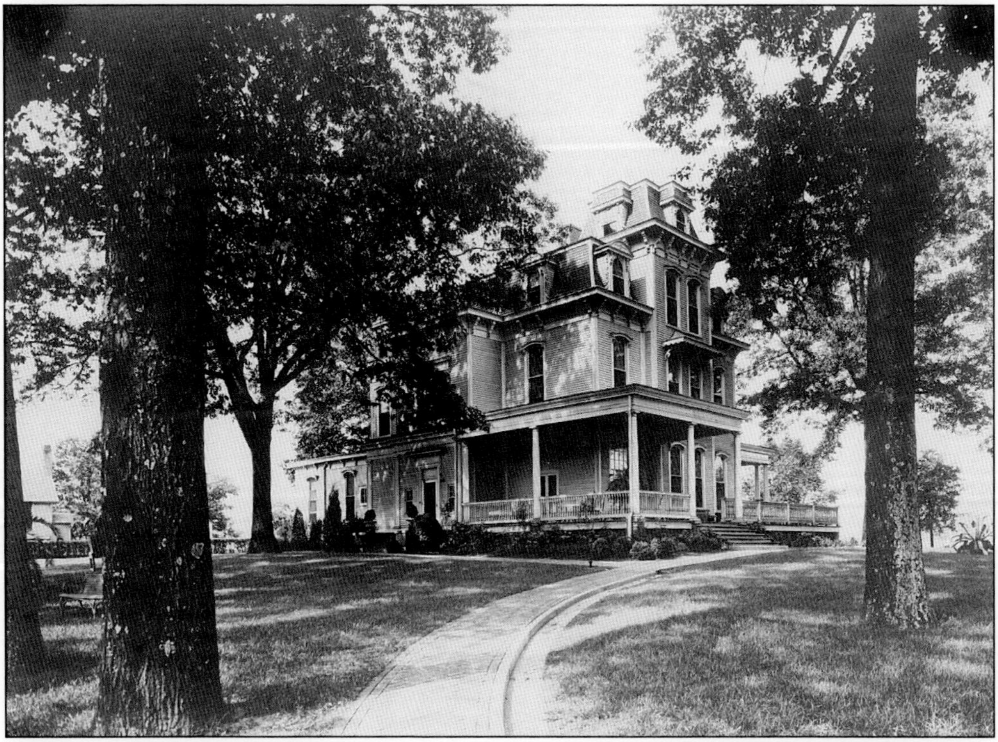

Built in 1873 by Amos G. West on the corner of West Avenue and College Street, this elegant home was acquired by Thomas Adamson. After his death in 1911, his son, Charles, brought his family down from Philadelphia and settled into the house, pictured here in 1927. Amos West might not recognize his fine home after 50 years: Charles Adamson had exercised his passion for architecture with extensive additions to his mansion, such as pleasant bays and extra wings, both open and covered piazzas, sleeping porches and sun-rooms. The property later changed hands, and after several years of standing vacant, the fine old home was demolished in the 1950s to make way for Casey's Market.

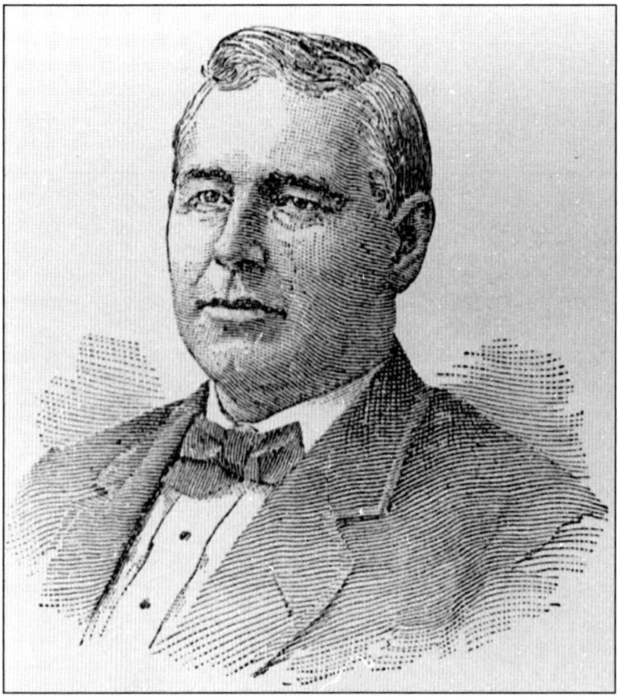

Amos G. West, known as the "Iron King of the South," founded the Cherokee Iron Company in 1873, bringing the first industry to Cedartown. He acquired the East & West Railroad, renamed it the Cherokee Railroad, and extended it from Rockmart to Esom Hill. West leased convicts from the state to operate both the iron mines at Grady and the iron furnace in Cedartown. In 1880, Cedartown's population of 843 included 152 convicts, held in the prison stockade.

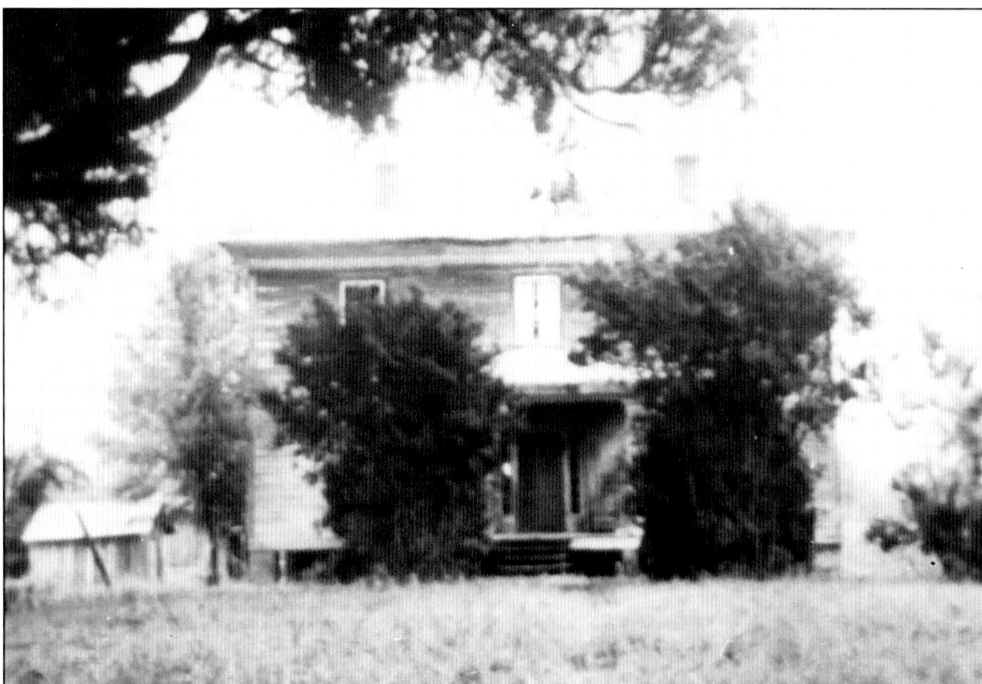

On a stormy night in 1883, when mysticism was popular, an electrical storm mysteriously transformed a 14-year-old girl. The young girl, Lulu Hurst, became strangely endowed with amazing powers which no one could explain. At the time, the Hurst family lived in the old Whatley home, shown here in 1970. Lulu went on stage and, in a short two years, paid off the family's mortgage with her earnings.

Lulu soon developed her mystical powers into three acts and began to appear as a professional entertainer. The popularity of her acts grew, first in Georgia and then across the country. In her "Chair Act," shown in this July 26, 1884 illustration from *Frank Leslie's Illustrated Newspaper*, Lulu would lift a man seated in a chair while other men drawn from the audience tried to resist Lulu.

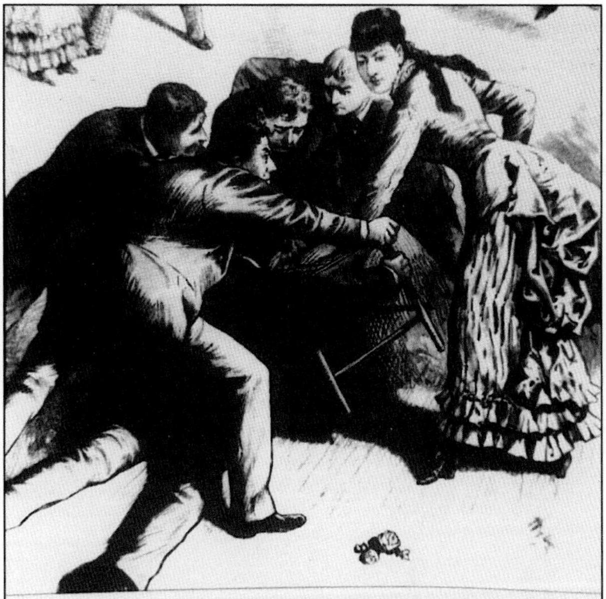

An artist at one of Lulu Hurst's performances illustrated two variations of "The Chair Act" for a news article in Frank Leslie's *Illustrated Newspaper* on July 26, 1884.

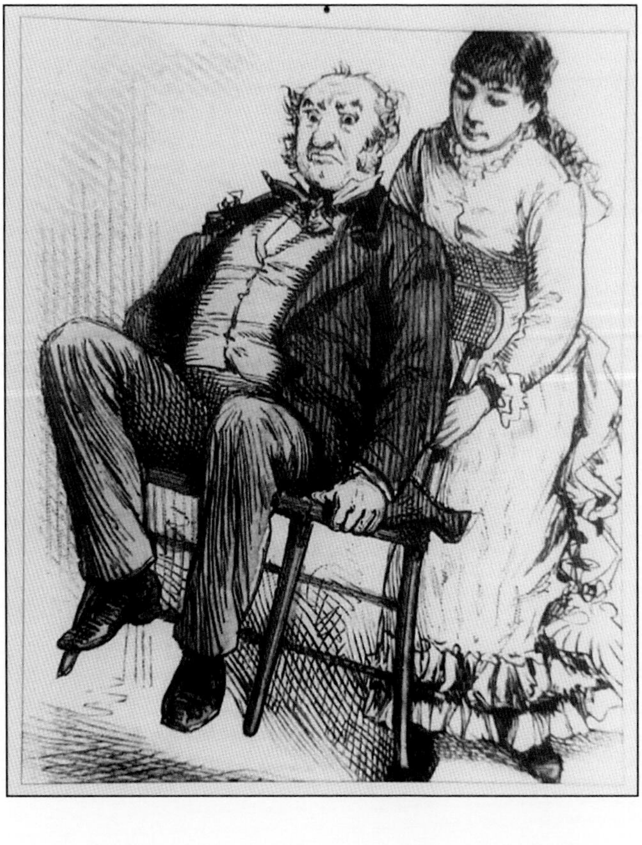

Lulu's audiences believed her powers could be attributed not to muscular strength, but to some magnetic, electric, or spiritualistic source. While some sought to explain the puzzling powers, others tried to discredit the "Georgia Wonder" as a fraud. However, even Lulu herself was never able to successfully explain the phenomenon.

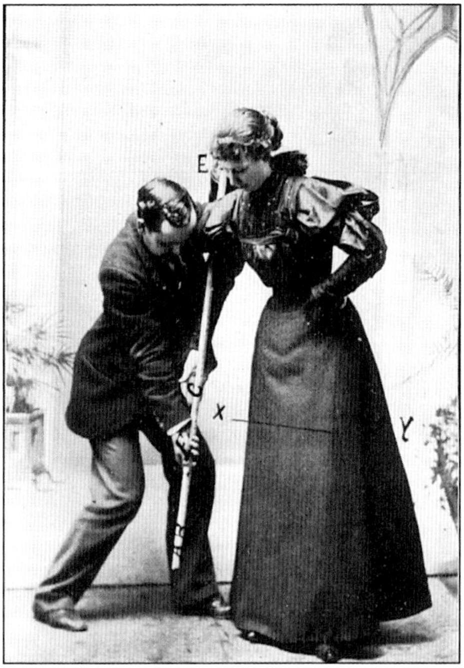

In her "Walking Cane Act," a strong man could not move the walking cane while the young Cedartown girl merely rested her fingers on the cane. (Courtesy the Hargrett Rare Book and Manuscript Library, University of Georgia.)

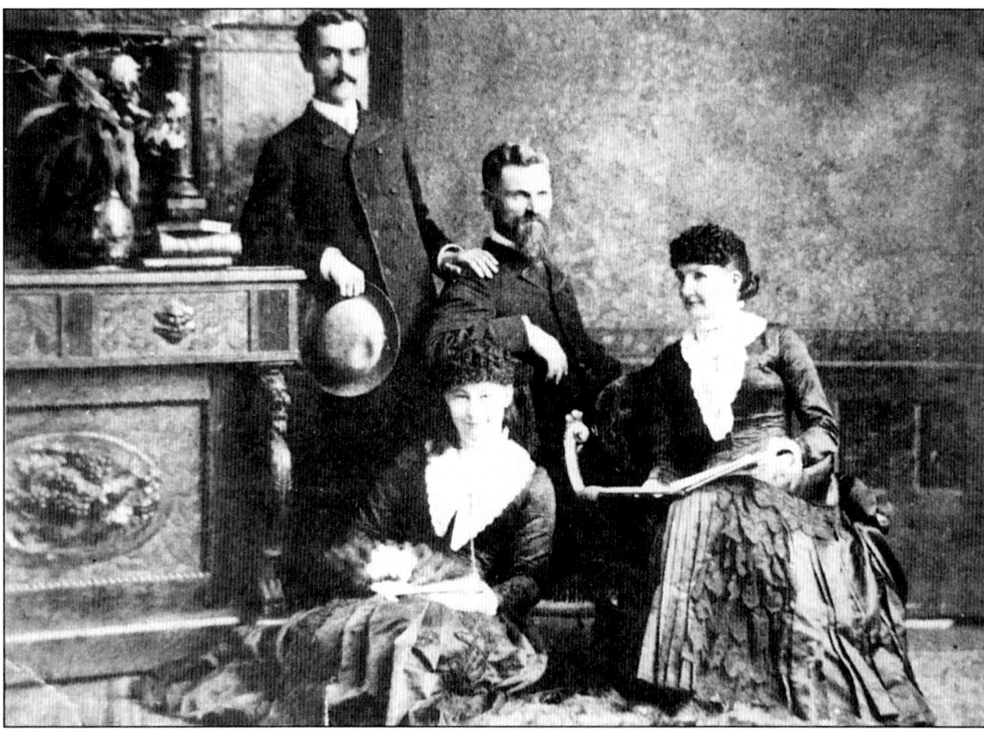

After experiencing two years of growing stage fame, Lulu retired from the stage and enrolled at Shorter College in Rome, Georgia. She had grown tired of being a curiosity. Her manager during her brief career, Paul Atkinson, eventually married Lulu. The young married couple are shown in this picture, with Lulu's parents, Will Hurst and Sally Wood Hurst.

Dr. T.F. Burbank was Cedartown's first registered druggist. He was a native of Meriweather County and served in the 63rd Georgia; his brother served in the Union army. He studied medicine and pharmacy in New York City, and while there, met three owners of a Cedartown general store. Dr. Burbank accepted their invitation to open a pharmacy in their store and arrived in Cedartown in 1873.

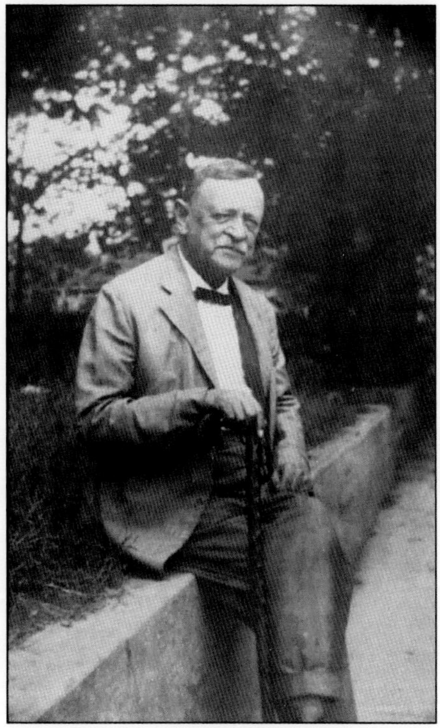

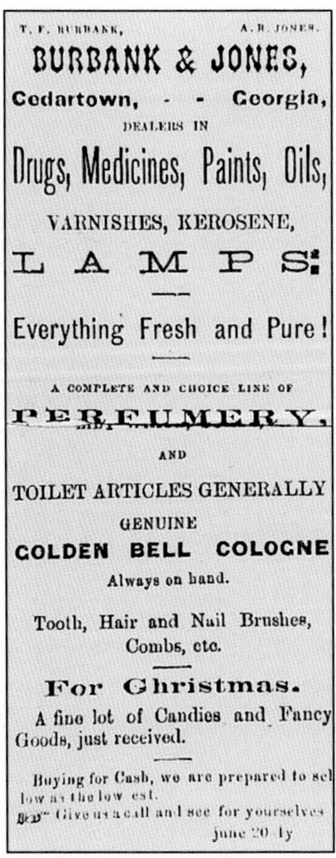

All kinds of drugs and chemicals could once be sold over the counter without restriction, including morphine and opium. In addition to the drugs, paints, and kerosene declared in this 1875 ad, Dr. Burbank also concocted special remedies, such as worm candy, cough medicine, and his "celebrated pills."

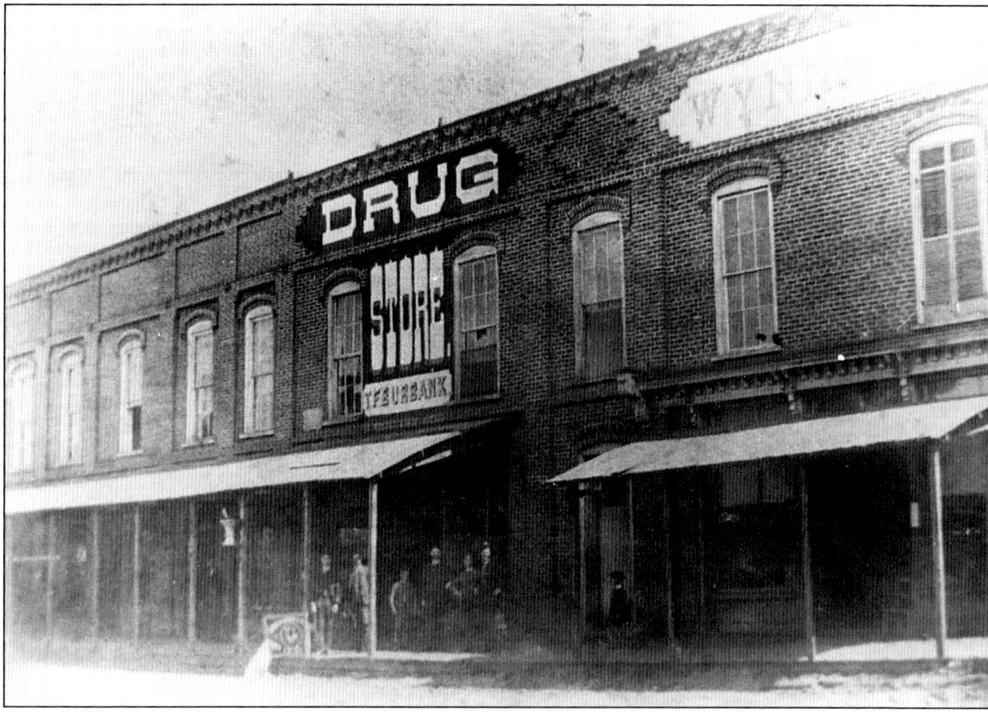

Dr. Burbank built the block with his drugstore at 305 Main Street. His first drugstore was located in a general store on the town square, near the location of the present Polk County courthouse.

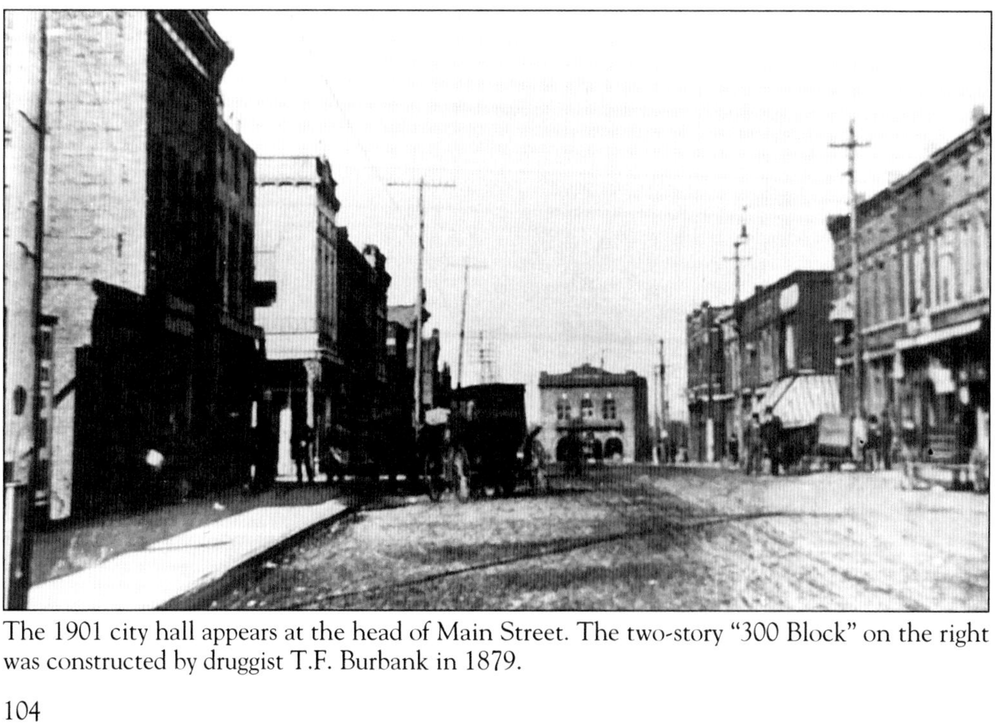

The 1901 city hall appears at the head of Main Street. The two-story "300 Block" on the right was constructed by druggist T.F. Burbank in 1879.

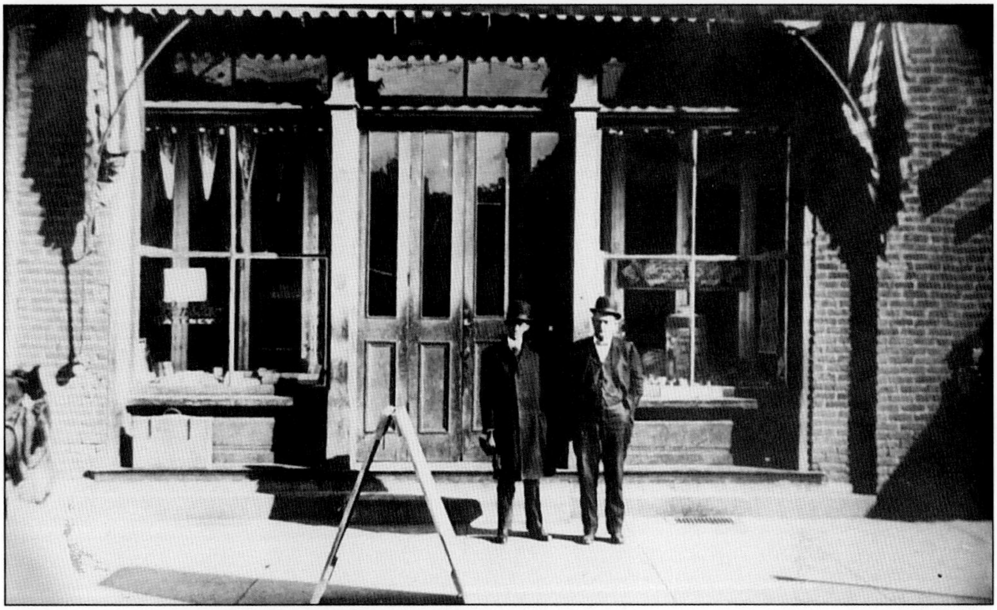

In this picture on Main Street, Dr. Burbank stands in front of his drugstore, with Dr. Seals Whitely at left. The cement sidewalk appears to have been a recent installation which many businesses provided to complement the granite curbing that was installed by the City in 1904. The street would remain unpaved for several more years.

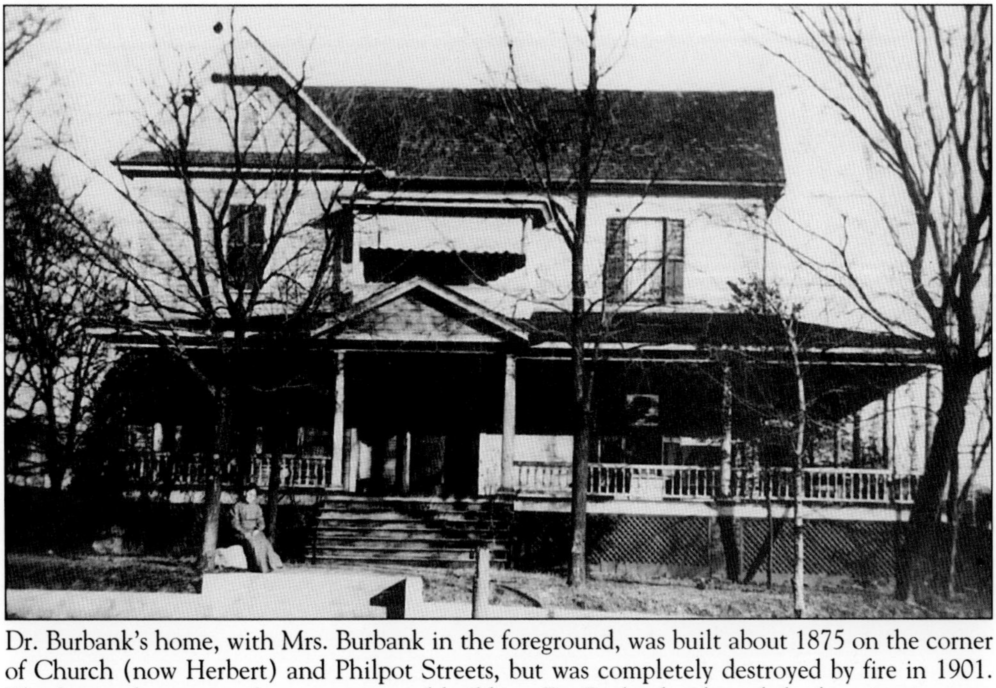

Dr. Burbank's home, with Mrs. Burbank in the foreground, was built about 1875 on the corner of Church (now Herbert) and Philpot Streets, but was completely destroyed by fire in 1901. The house shown was the reconstructed building. Dr. Burbank selected the location in town within walking distance of his drugstore to avoid having to hitch up horse and buggy for the daily trip to his store.

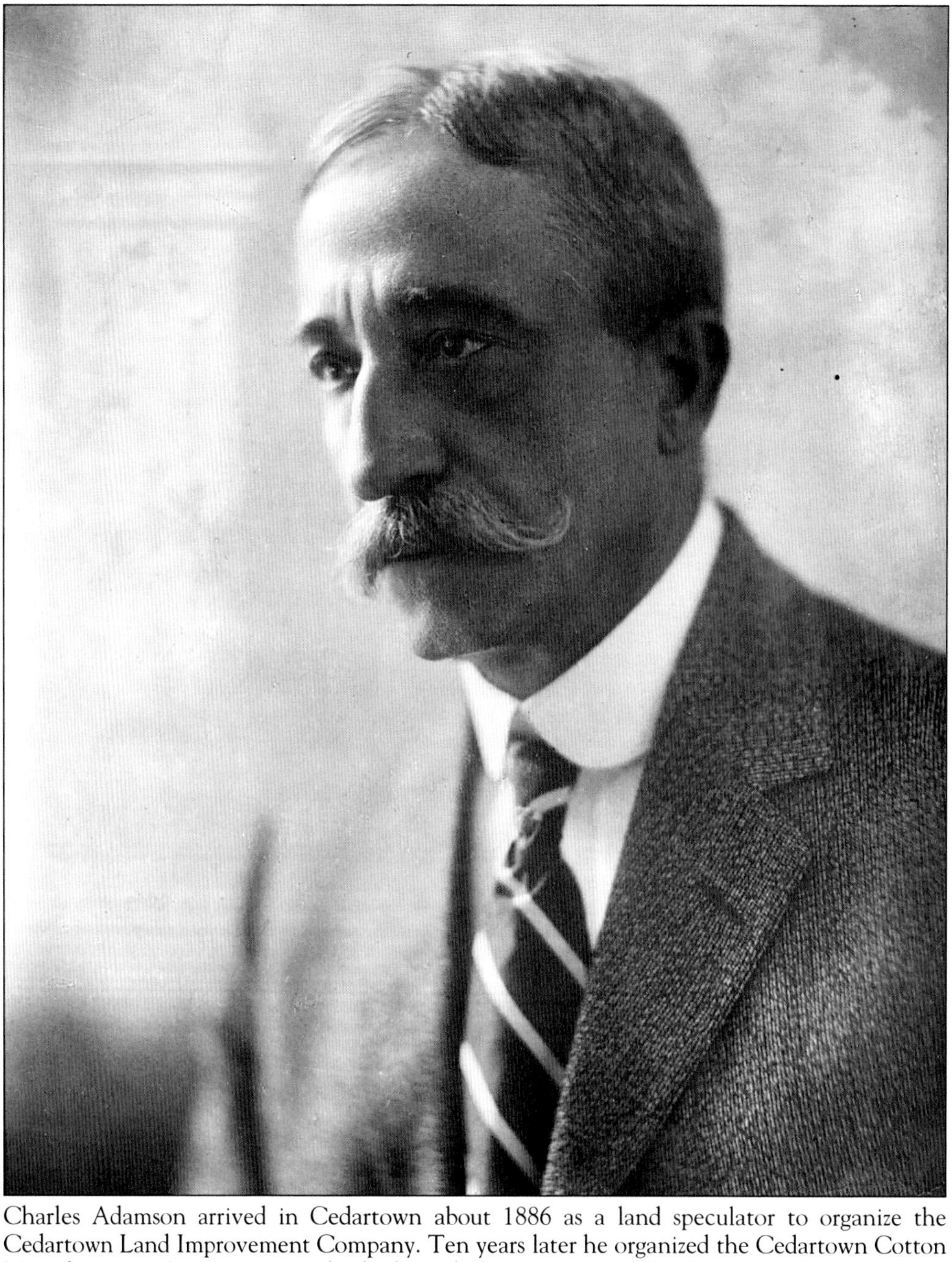

Charles Adamson arrived in Cedartown about 1886 as a land speculator to organize the Cedartown Land Improvement Company. Ten years later he organized the Cedartown Cotton Manufacturing Company to make high-grade hosiery yarn. After he acquired the adjacent Paragon Mills, he operated the combined textile mills as the Cedartown Cotton Company until 1925, when he sold the mills to the Goodyear Tire & Rubber Company. During his 45 years in Cedartown, Adamson had acquired considerable wealth, but at the time of his death in 1931, the Great Depression and the advent of rayon had wiped him out.

Adamson married the former Katherine Brand Cook in 1897, but the couple maintained their home in Philadelphia until sometime after 1911. In her youth, she had helped to support her family as a seamstress, and in later years, she made all of her husband's shirts. Her years in Cedartown were some of the happiest of her life—she loved being the grand lady in her grand house.

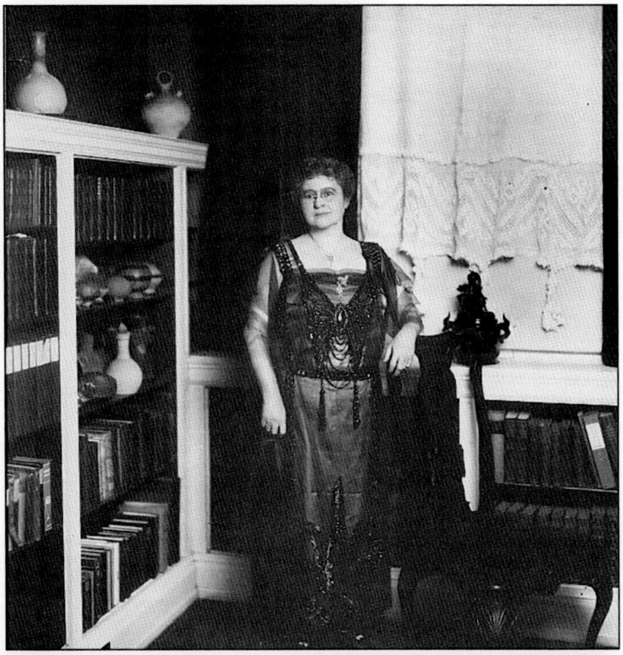

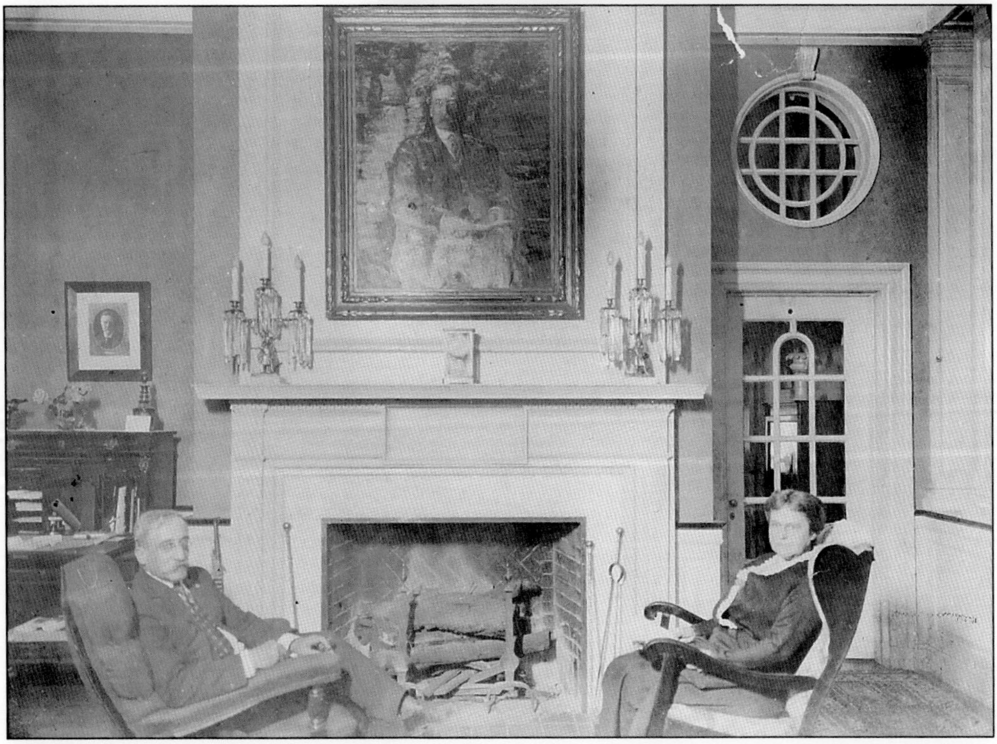

Charles Adamson and wife, Katherine, relax in their luxurious home, which was built by Cedartown's "Iron King of the South," Amos G. West, in 1873. The three-story residence had high ceilings and numerous long windows and French doors. Mr. Adamson's portrait, hanging above the mantel, was presented to the Polk County Historical Society by his granddaughter, Mrs. Margaret Coco, and now hangs in that organization's museum.

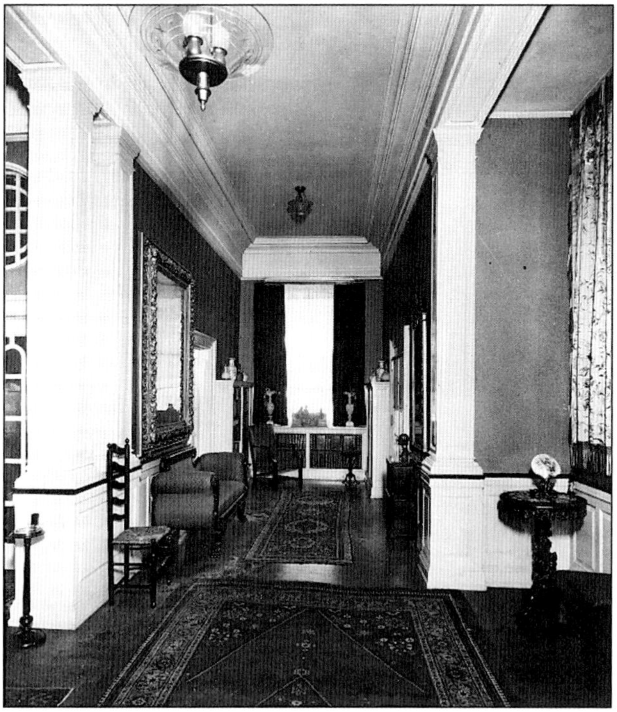

A visitor to the elegant Adamson home in 1927 would be greeted by this view of the entrance hall. The hand-carved moldings demonstrate the careful workmanship used throughout the structure, arguably the finest home ever built in Polk County.

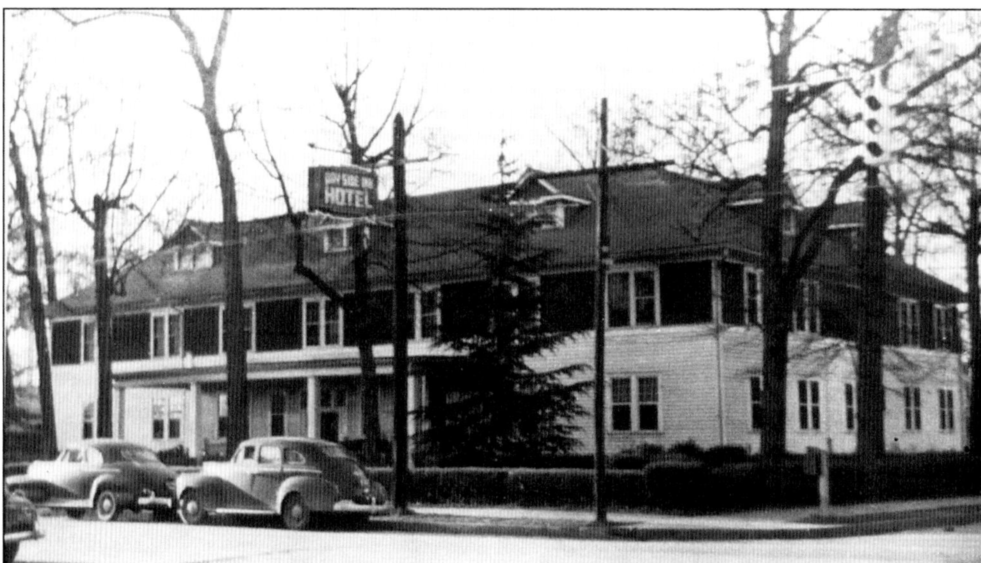

In 1920, Charles Adamson ordered this 32-room "mill hotel" as a package from the Aladdin Company of Bay City, Michigan. Each piece was individually cut and numbered. All of the pieces needed for the hotel were shipped by rail, ready for assembly at the site. Although Aladdin named their mill hotel after the 1716 historic inn of Longfellow fame, *Tales of a Wayside Inn*, in Sudbury, Massachusetts, Adamson's inn bears no resemblance to the original. (The archivists in Sudbury have never heard of Cedartown's inn.) The Wayside Inn offered rooms for travelers and a fine restaurant, popular for years, which attracted patrons from miles around.

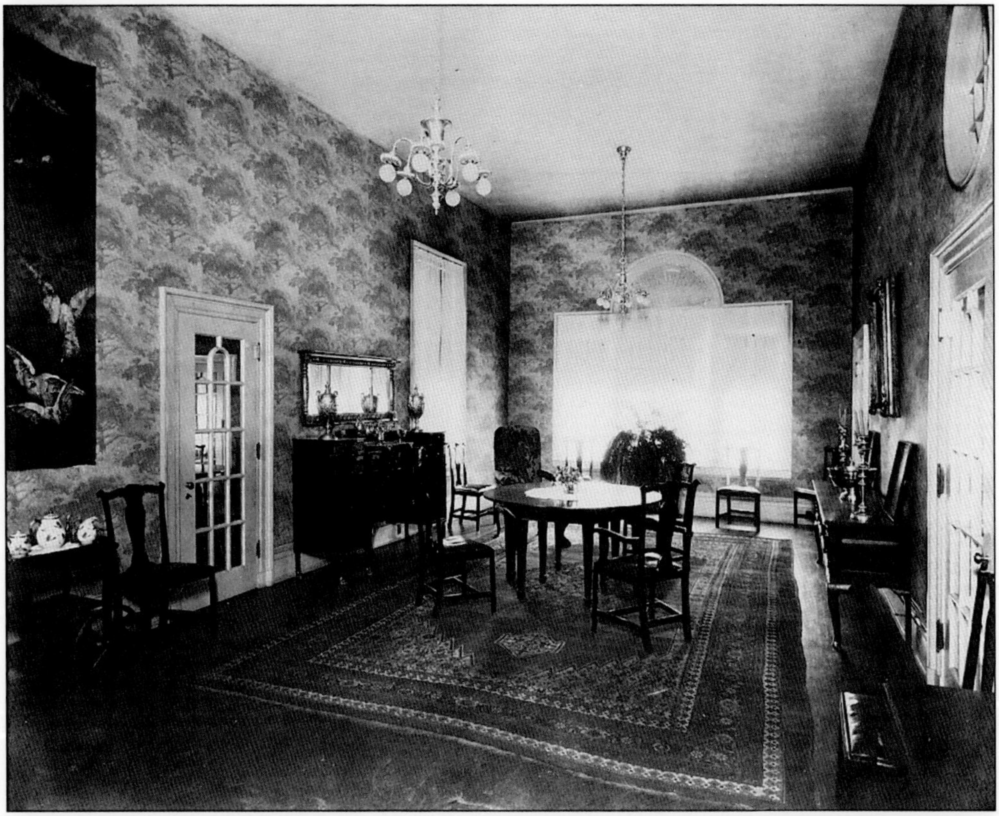

Mrs. Adamson furnished her home not with antiques, but with custom-made copies of classical styles of furniture that she commissioned in Philadelphia and had shipped to Cedartown. Rare, old Chinese rugs, possibly obtained by the elder Adamson during his years of consular service in many corners of the world, partially cover polished floors in this view of the dining room, as they did in other rooms.

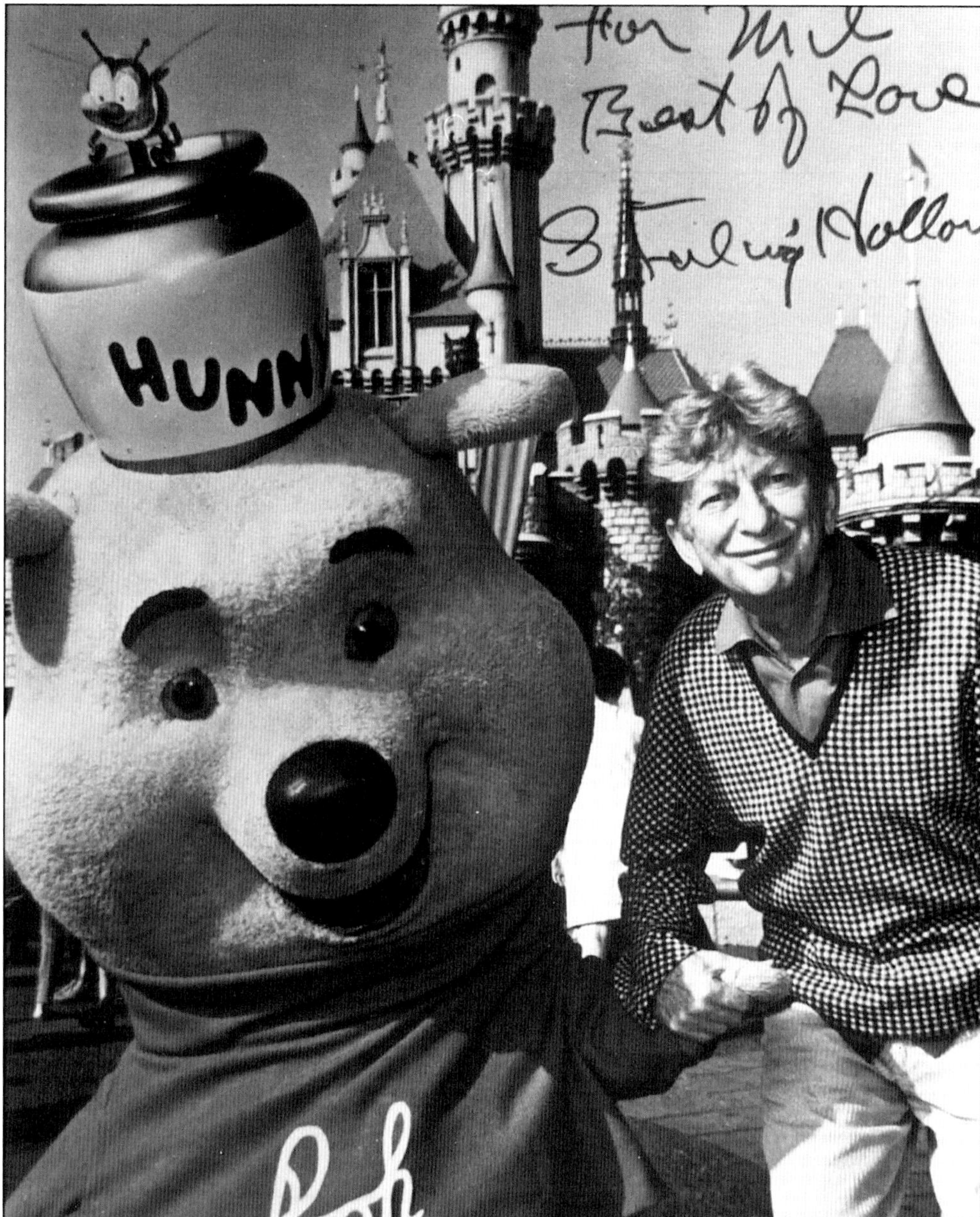

Of all his cartoon characters, Sterling Holloway may best be known for his Oscar-winning voiceover in Walt Disney's Winnie-the-Pooh series. When "Pooh" suffered a heart attack in the late 1970s, one small fan by the name of Amy asked her daddy to call and wish a fellow Georgian well. That daddy was President Jimmy Carter.

The younger Holloway sits in the lap of an unknown girl, while the elder Sterling Price Holloway, "S.P.," sits proudly at the wheel of his new automobile, dressed in a "duster" coat, leather gauntlet gloves, and jaunty cap. Halloway obtained his new Lozier, shown here, c. 1910. According to one old-timer, the first automobile in Cedartown was purchased by John Booz in 1902.

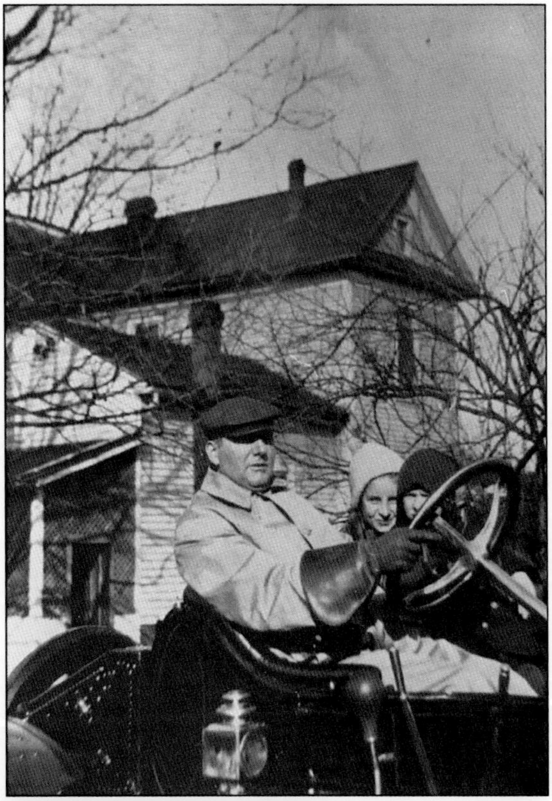

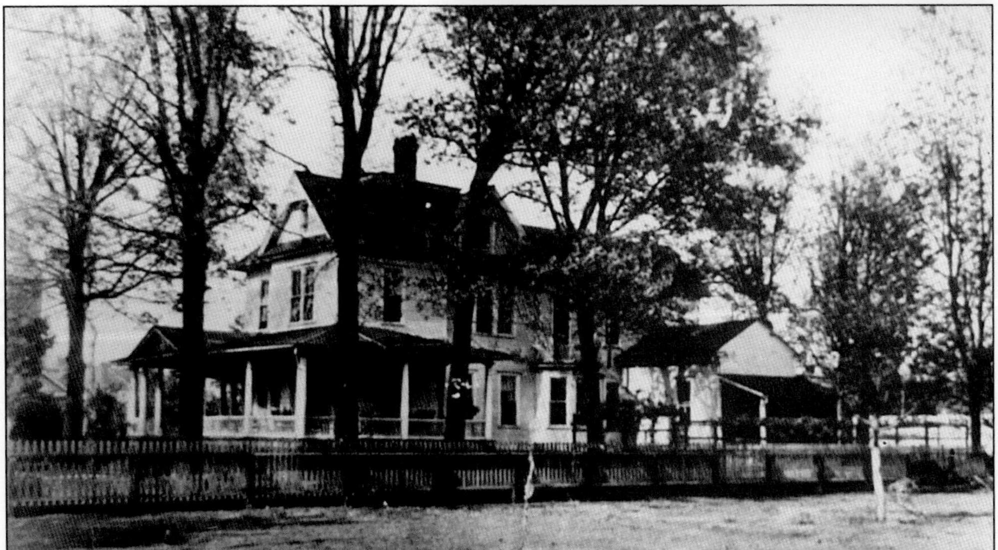

Holloway's birthplace was located on College Street in Cedartown. As a youth, Holloway staged plays in his garage loft with the help of neighborhood friends that he drafted into his company. He set his sights on an acting career at an early age, and his determination never faltered. Although Holloway reached prominence as an actor, he never forgot his roots, and over the years visited old friends in Cedartown.

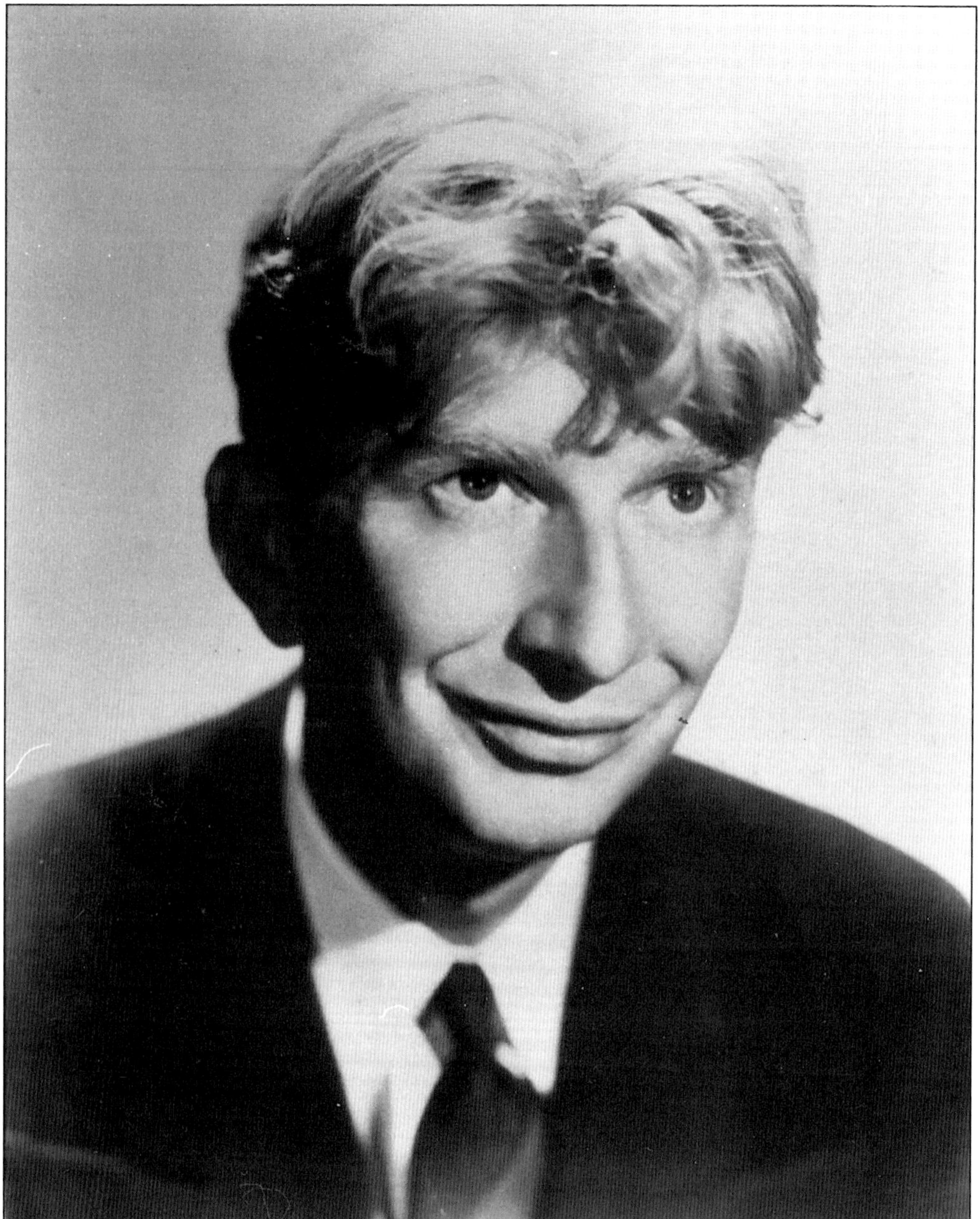

Sterling Price Holloway Jr. had a career spanning 70 years of work in every entertainment medium of the century: stage, screen, radio, records, and television. He made over 100 movies, several as the sidekick of Gene Autry, and later, capitalized on his "furry" voice in Disney cartoons. In television, he was probably best known for his appearances as a regular with William Bendix in *The Life of Riley*.

The young Holloway attended school in Cedartown but "was a rotten scholar," according to his father, who packed him off to the Georgia Military Academy. For almost three years he led a miserable life as a military cadet, but managed to produce and perform in stage productions, which further reinforced his resolve to become an actor.

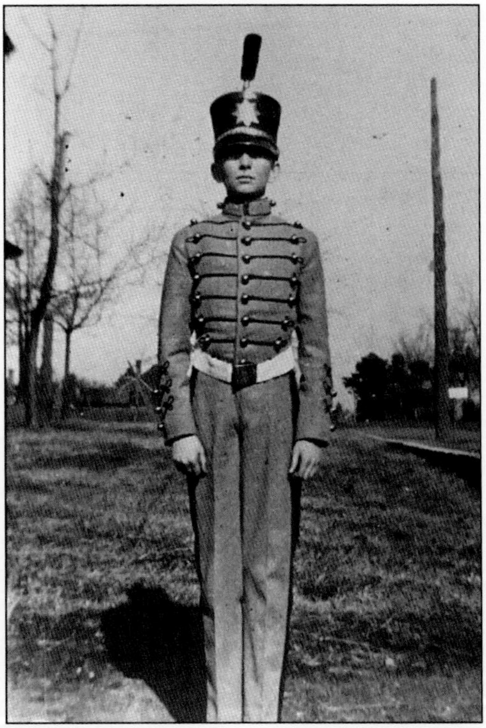

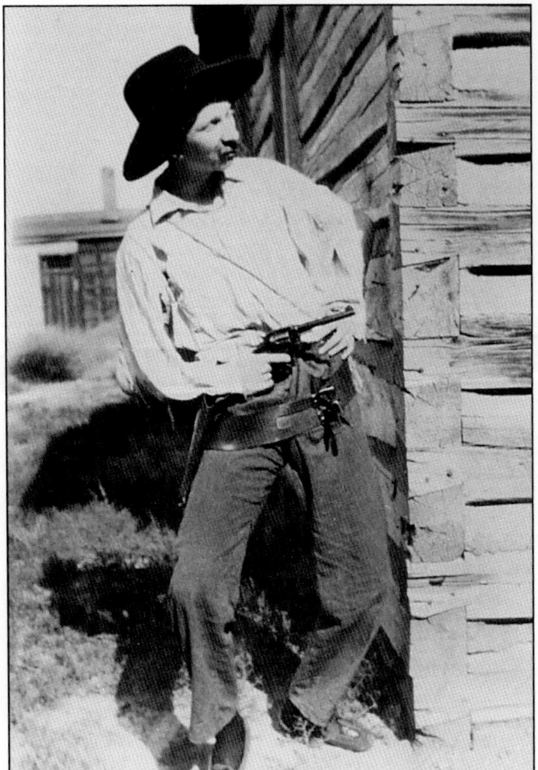

A youthful Holloway plays the gunfighter in this undated image. He is fully outfitted with six-gun, holster, cowboy hat—even a mustache.

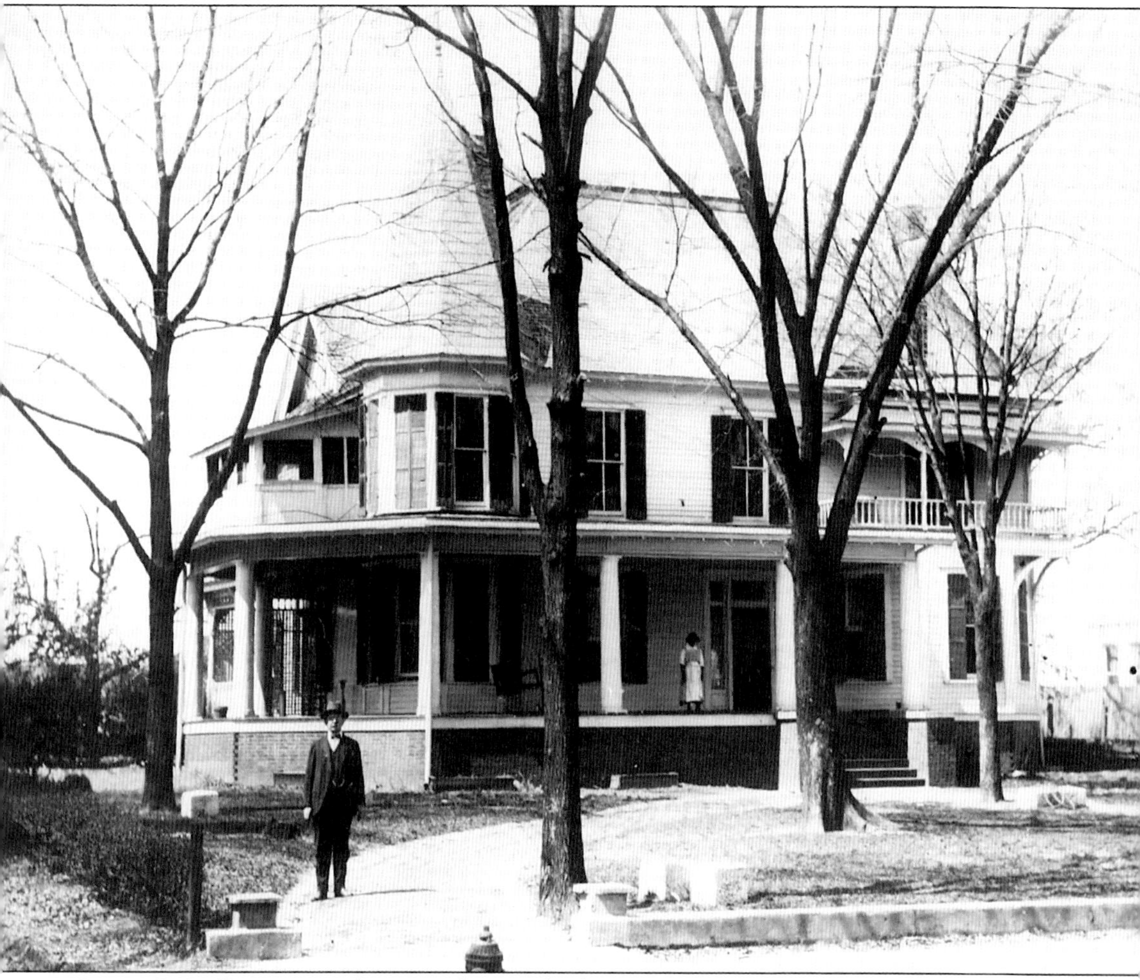

Lewis S. Ledbetter was the son of a Methodist preacher who died leaving 14 children. Ledbetter had to help support the family and consequently, was mostly self-educated. After serving in Company E, 2nd Georgia, he managed to take a dentistry course in Baltimore and graduated in 1870, after which he came to Cedartown and established his dental practice. Dr. Ledbetter served Cedartown as a dentist but left that practice in 1887 because of ill health. He represented many of the major insurance companies in writing fire insurance policies. He owned several rich iron ore deposits in the county and was a director in the Land Company, as well as serving as town treasurer, notary public, and justice of the peace. Ledbetter is shown in this picture in front of his home on College Street, built in 1898 by G.A. Artope. The structure was razed about 1950 to make way for Casey's Market. (Courtesy Georgia Department of Archives and History.)

Senator William J. Harris was elected and served from 1918 to 1932 as the U.S. senator from Georgia. Earlier he had served in the Georgia Senate from 1911 to 1912. He also held positions in the federal government as the director of the U.S. Census Bureau 1915–1916 and as the secretary of commerce. His wife was Julia Wheeler Harris, the daughter of the famous Confederate general "Fighting Joe" Wheeler.

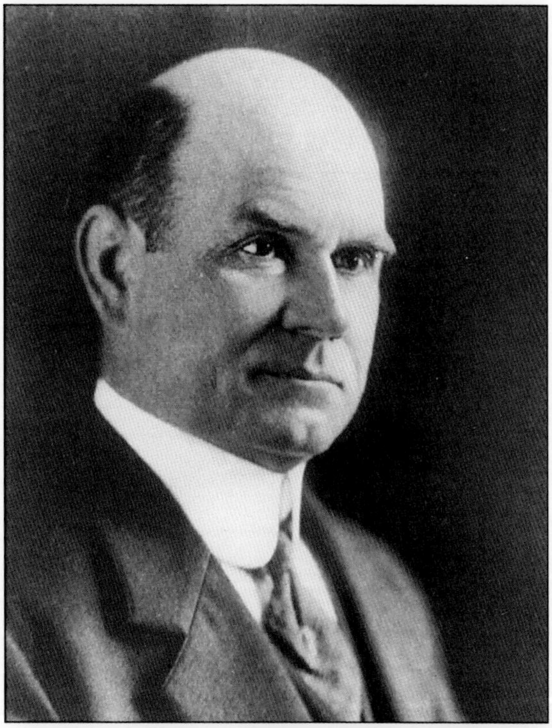

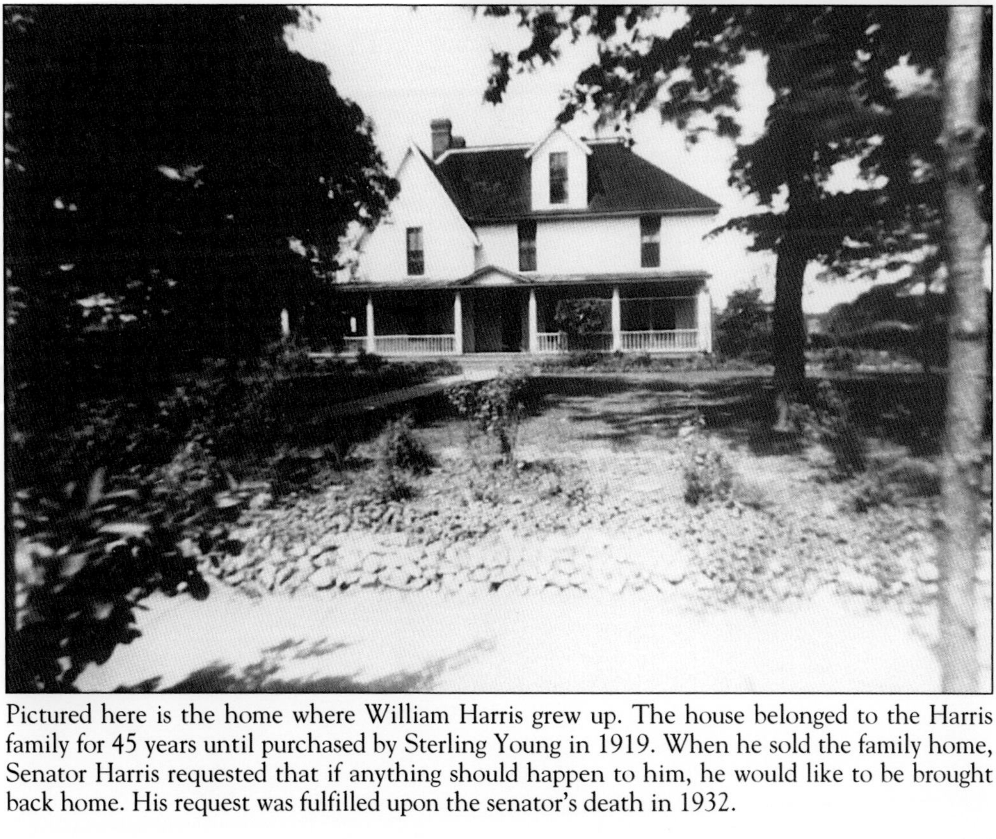

Pictured here is the home where William Harris grew up. The house belonged to the Harris family for 45 years until purchased by Sterling Young in 1919. When he sold the family home, Senator Harris requested that if anything should happen to him, he would like to be brought back home. His request was fulfilled upon the senator's death in 1932.

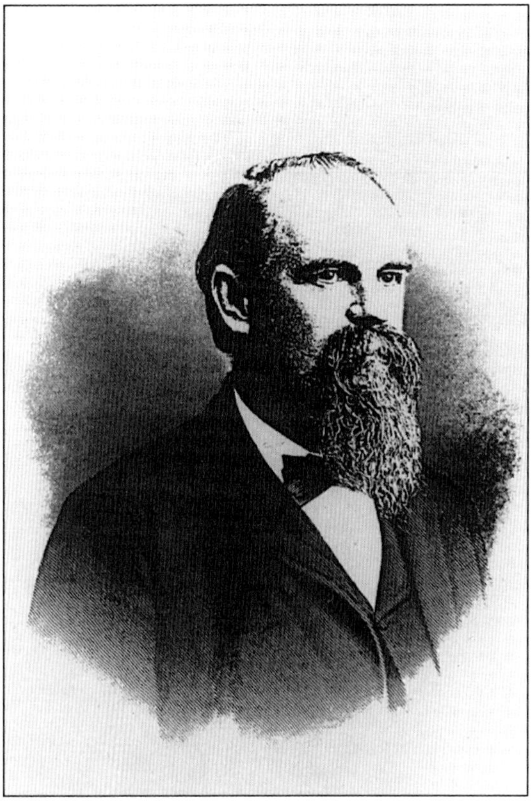

Robert William Everett graduated from Mercer College and taught school for a number of years. A successful farmer, Everett took pride in the fact that he never bought any supplies that could be produced on his farm. He served several terms in the State Legislature, and in 1891 was elected to Congress, the only Polk County man ever to serve the Seventh District in the U.S. Congress.

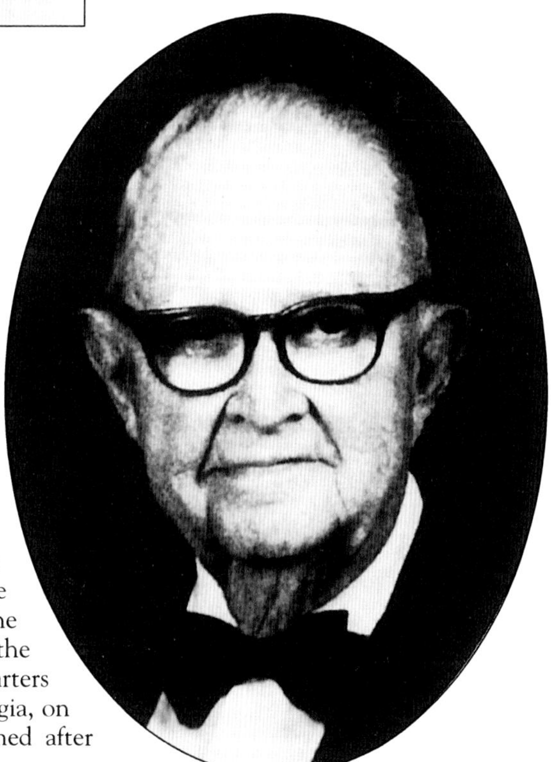

W.D. Trippe served in the Georgia General Assembly as both a representative and senator. For 22 years he served on the Georgia Ports Authority (GPA), holding the position of chairman twice. The headquarters of the GPA is located in Savannah, Georgia, on W.D. Trippe Boulevard, which was named after him to recognize his service to that body.

Nine

Lighter Moments

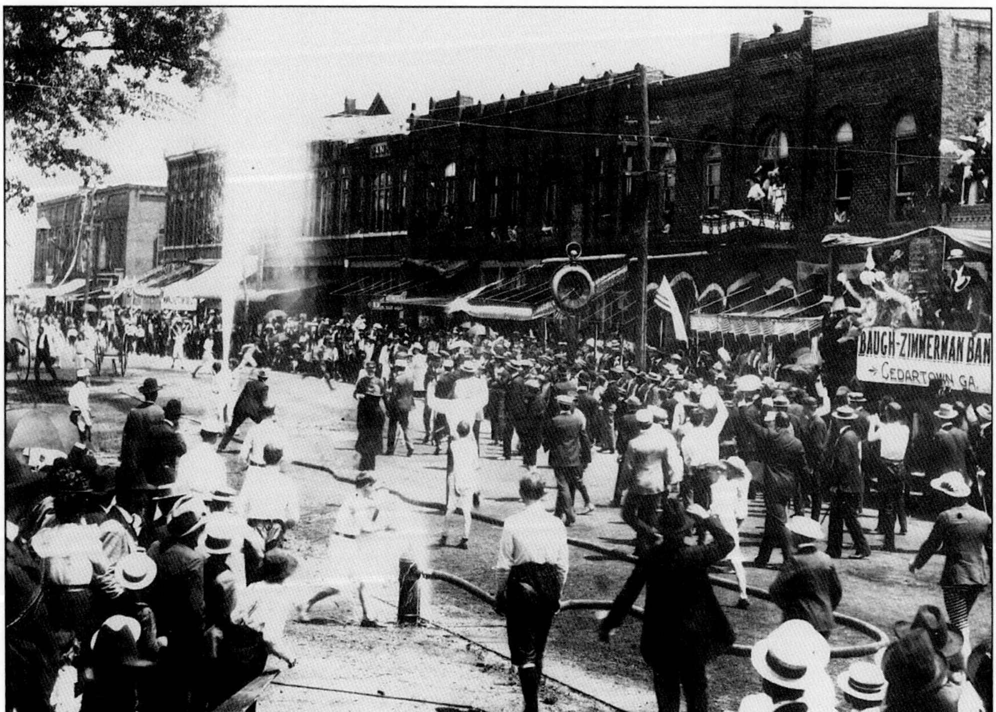

In this 1895 view looking south on Main Street from Stubbs Street, a giant pocket watch in the center of the picture, the clock of W.W. Turner's Jewelry, rises above the crowd gathered for the spring festival and fire tournament. Cedartown organized a volunteer fire department in mid-1892 when the City started operation of the Water and Light Plant with 6 miles of water mains and 50 fire hydrants. In the first pressure test of the system, a stream of water was directed from a hose over the spire of the courthouse—to the satisfaction of everyone. In the 1970s, Robert Wilkerson gathered information and photographs from a number of people and published them in a pamphlet about the fire department. Many of these images have been included in this history of Polk County.

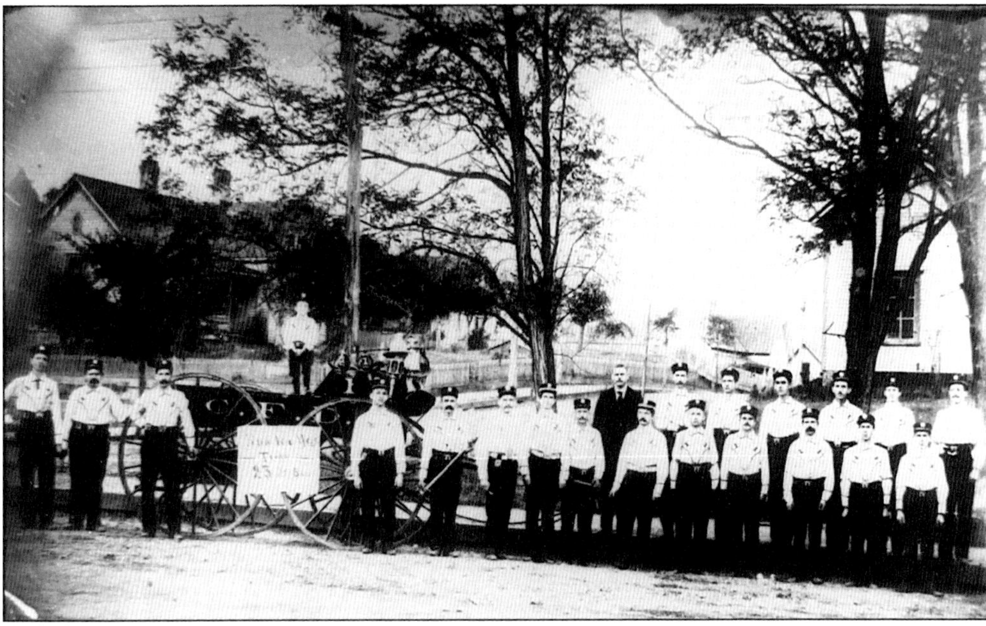

Firetruck drivers were the only paid members of the volunteers; the department also had two surgeons. Number 1 Company, shown here, was located on Main Street and was outfitted in black and white uniforms. The Number 2 Company, located on Gibson Street, dressed in red and black. In this 1894 picture, the company celebrates their 100-yard run which came within a fraction of a second of the record.

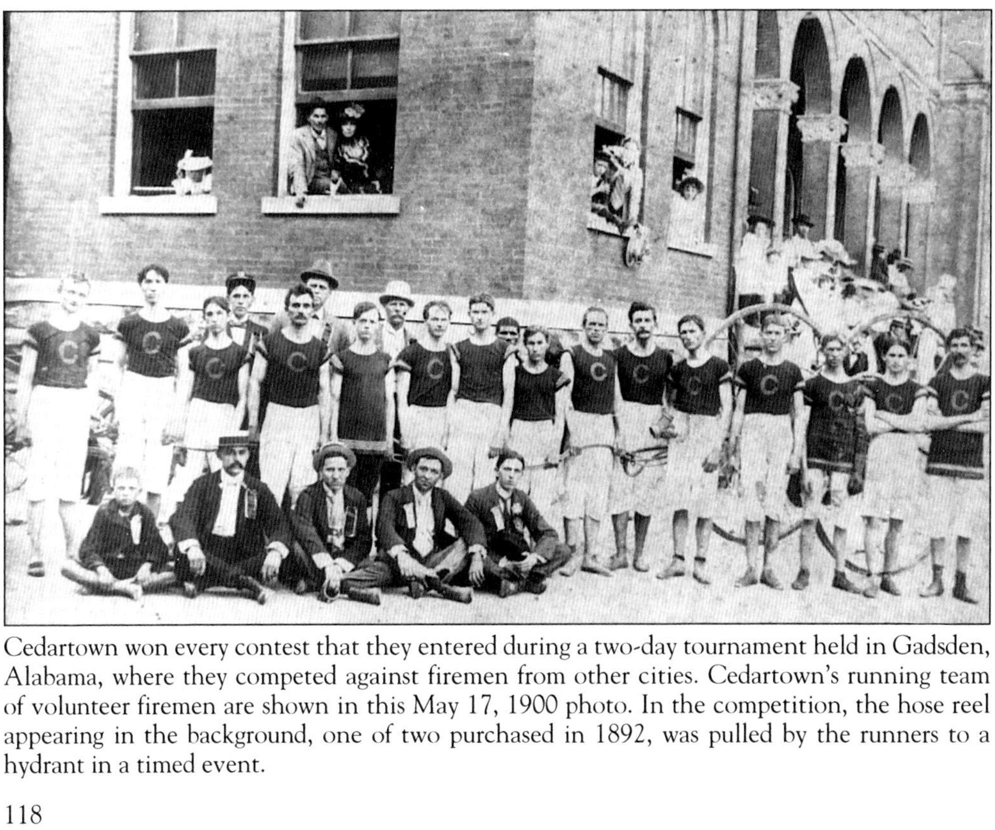

Cedartown won every contest that they entered during a two-day tournament held in Gadsden, Alabama, where they competed against firemen from other cities. Cedartown's running team of volunteer firemen are shown in this May 17, 1900 photo. In the competition, the hose reel appearing in the background, one of two purchased in 1892, was pulled by the runners to a hydrant in a timed event.

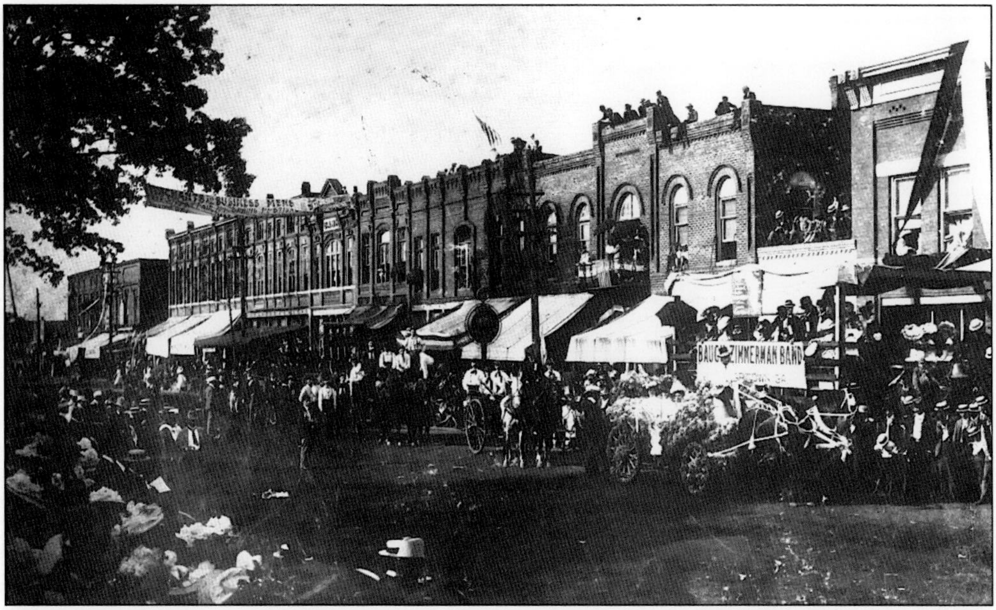

The gathering of fire companies from northwest Georgia and neighboring Alabama cities for the annual competition was the occasion for celebration with a festive parade of decorated carriages and wagons filled with ladies and gentlemen decked out in their finest togs.

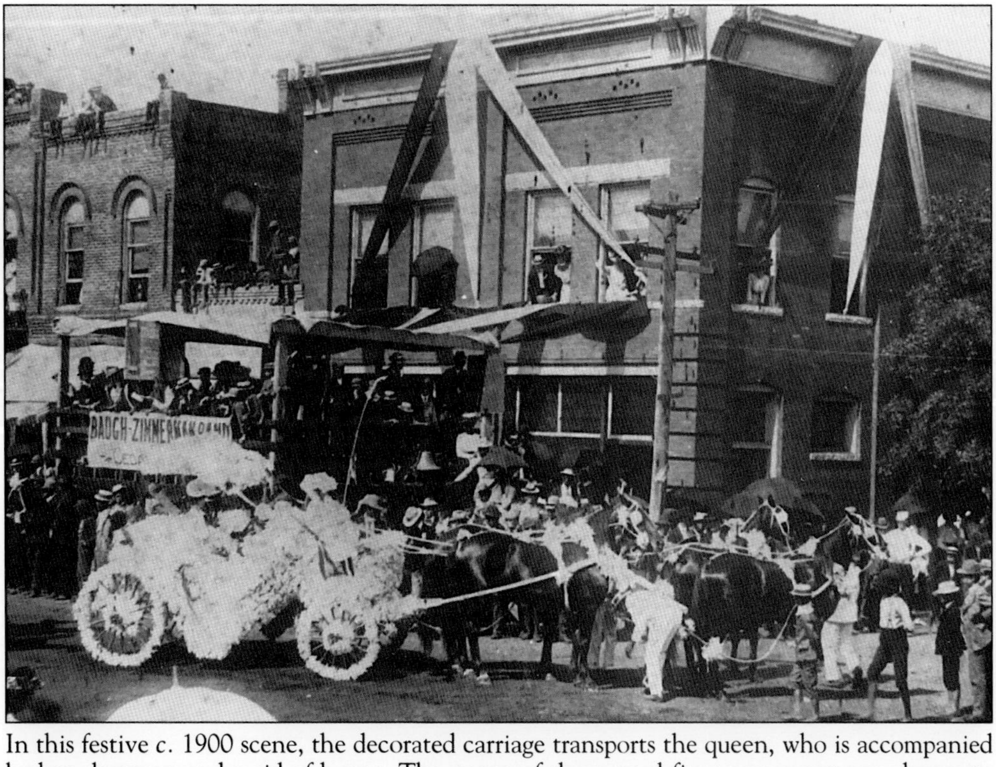

In this festive *c.* 1900 scene, the decorated carriage transports the queen, who is accompanied by her chaperon and maid of honor. The queen of the annual fire tournament was chosen to reign over the festival. In the bandstand next to the carriage, the Baugh-Zimmerman band plays for the gala parade.

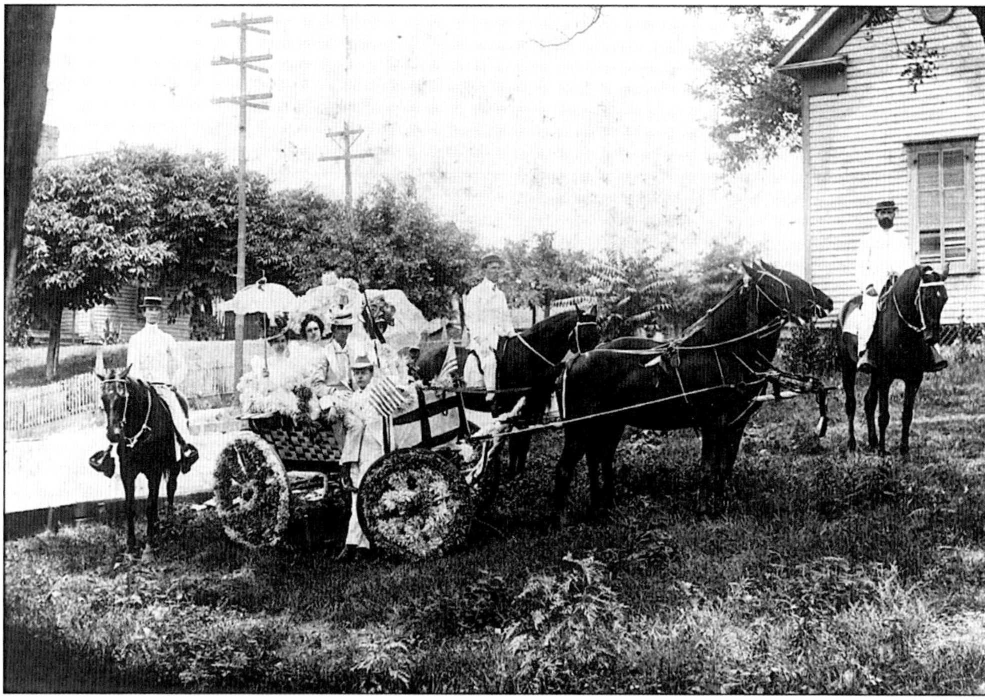

This handsomely decorated wagon with elegantly attired ladies and gentlemen representing Fire Company Number 1 posed for the photographer while ready to join the Fourth of July parade in 1900. They are as follows: Albert H. Lane, driver; Miss Mary Barton, sponsor; Miss Rena May Ledbetter, maid; Mrs. W.C. Bunn, chaperon; and escorts J.V. Stubbs, Dr. William Chapman, Albert M. Lane, Henry T. Bunn, and Charles K. Henderson Jr.

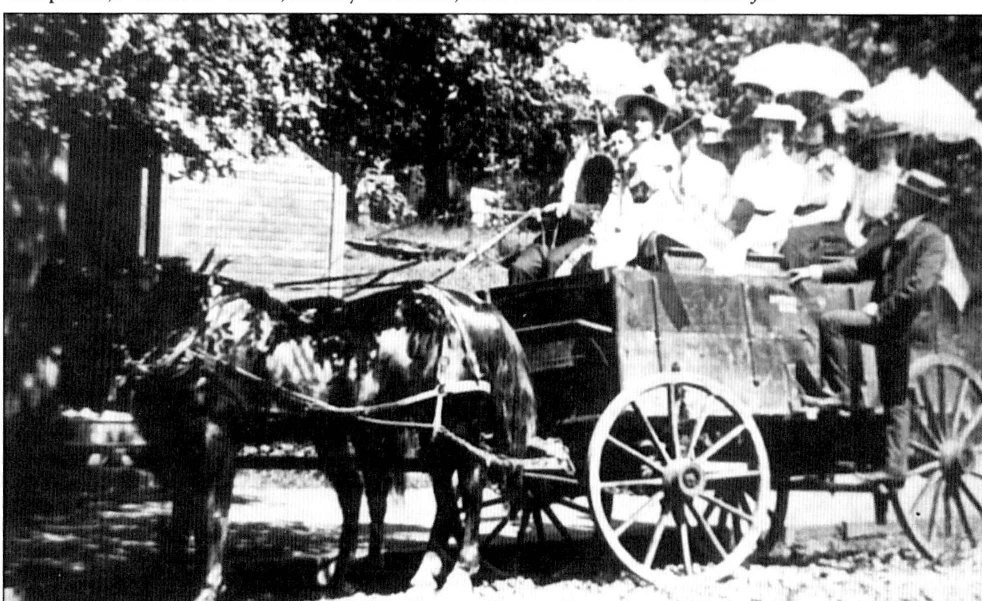

This photograph, dated July 4, 1900, suggests the wagon-load of ladies may have been about to join in the Main Street parade. A swain might rent a horse and buggy to take his girl out riding, but in this case it seems a wagon was necessary to carry all of her girlfriends, too.

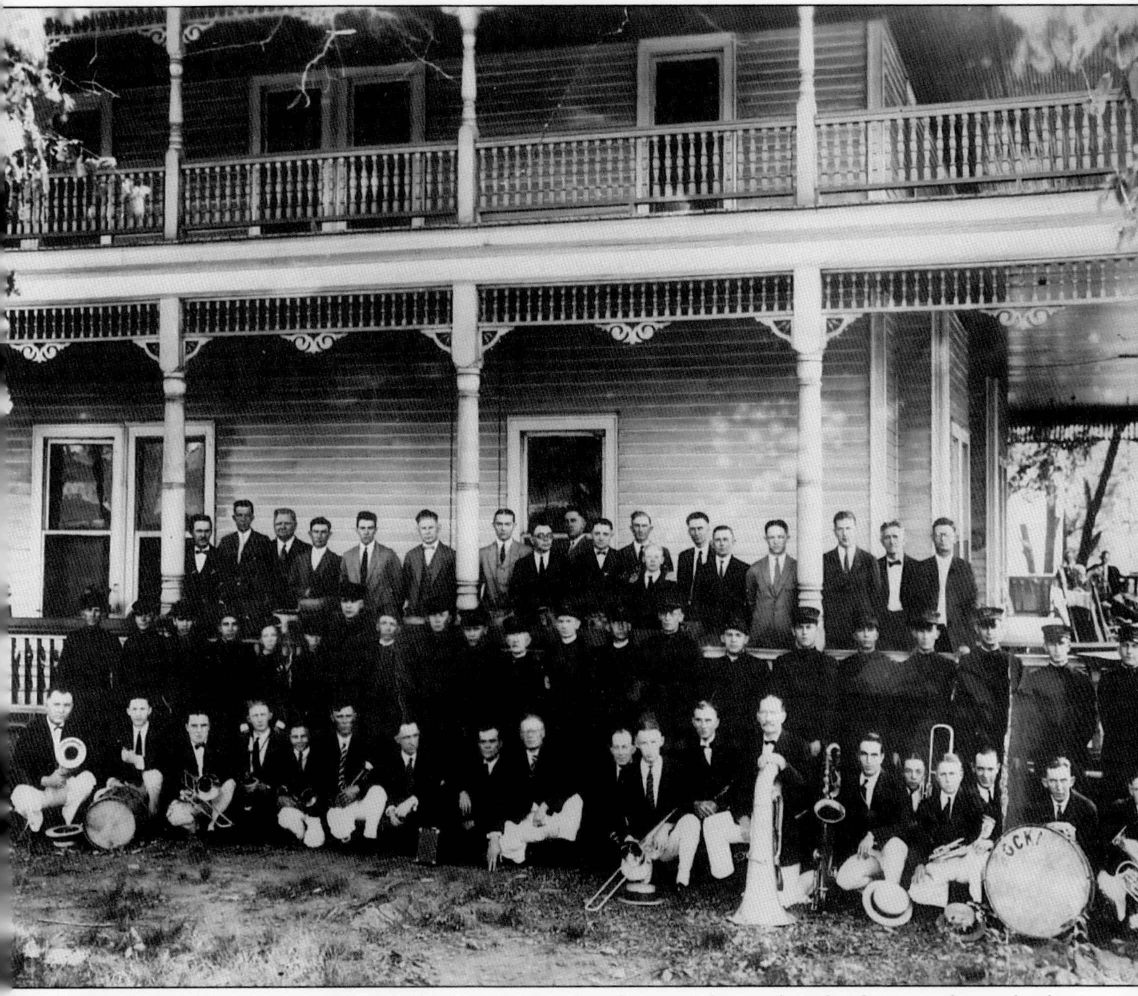

Three bands pose at the Marble Hill Hotel, where a dance band often performed; the Rockmart band occupies the front row, Aragon's the second, and Cedartown's the third. In the early 1900s, popular bands such as these pictured were in great demand in the county and beyond, appearing in various auditoriums and halls, playing for dances, and giving concerts. Band performances at the auditorium of the Piedmont Institute celebrated a variety of occasions, such as graduations, political rallies, and Fourth of July festivities. (Courtesy Georgia Department of Archives and History.)

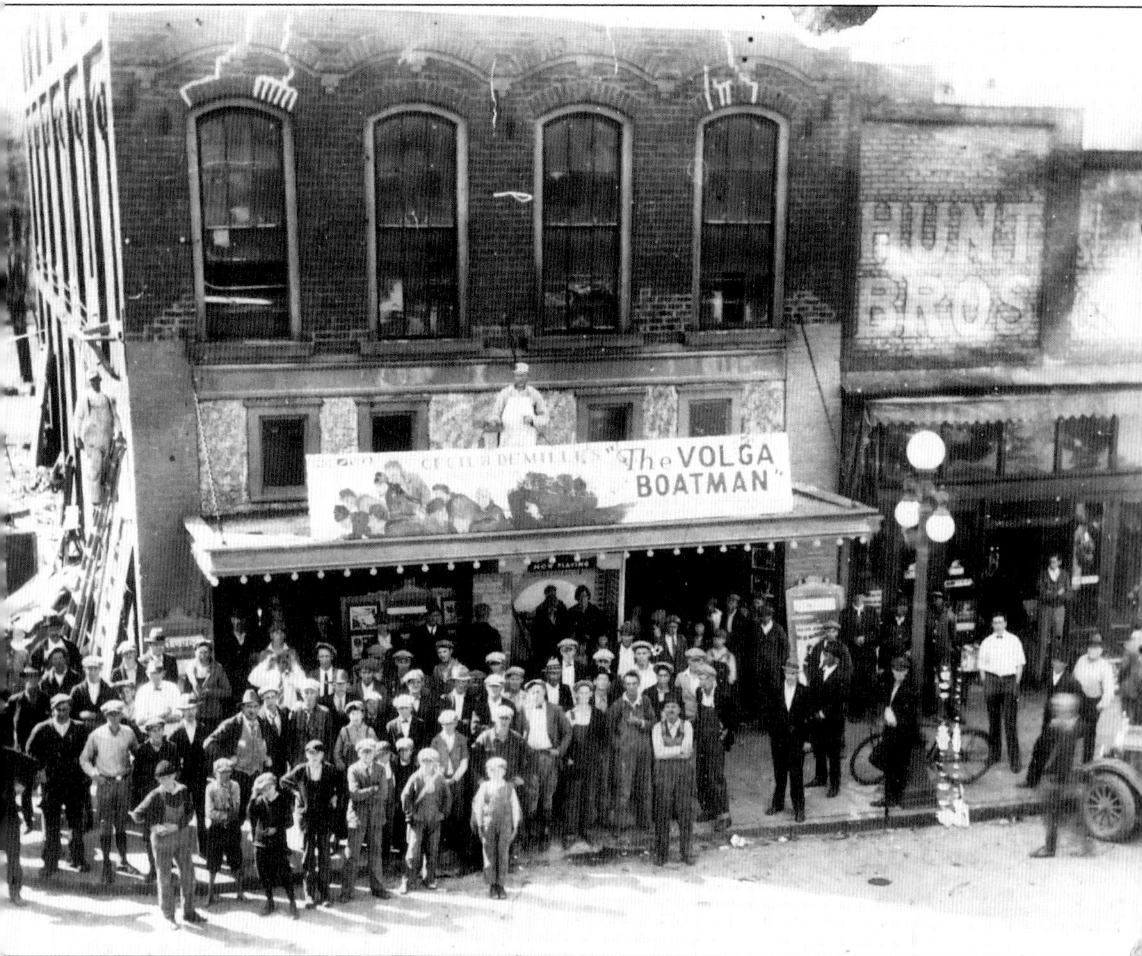

The Grand Theater at the corner of Woodland and Main Streets drew a crowd of men and boys in this *c.* 1927 image, maybe for a matinee. The first "picture shows" were held in 1909 at the old city hall and were sponsored by T.F. Thompson. Later, Thompson established the Elite Theater, which burned several years later. After the Elite, the Grand Theater, shown in this picture, was opened, but again the building was destroyed by fire. Thompson next operated the Princess Theater, and several years later, when "talking pictures" made their appearance, he opened the Palace Theater, which later became the Cedar Theater. (Courtesy Georgia Department of Archives and History.)

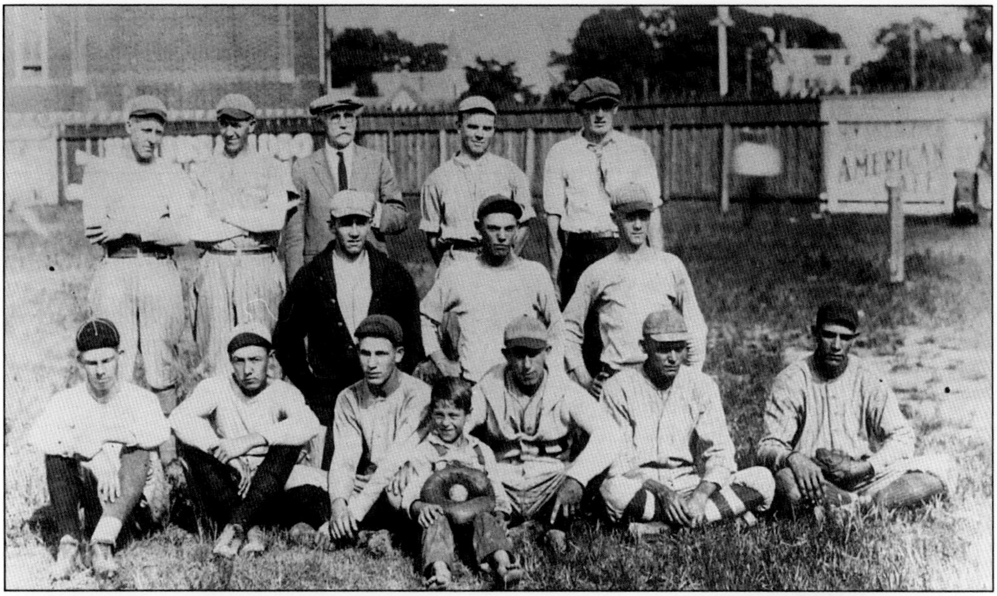

Although the record of the 1920 Cedartown High School baseball team is unknown today, this determined-looking crew with their distinguished patron, Charles Adamson, must have made a good showing.

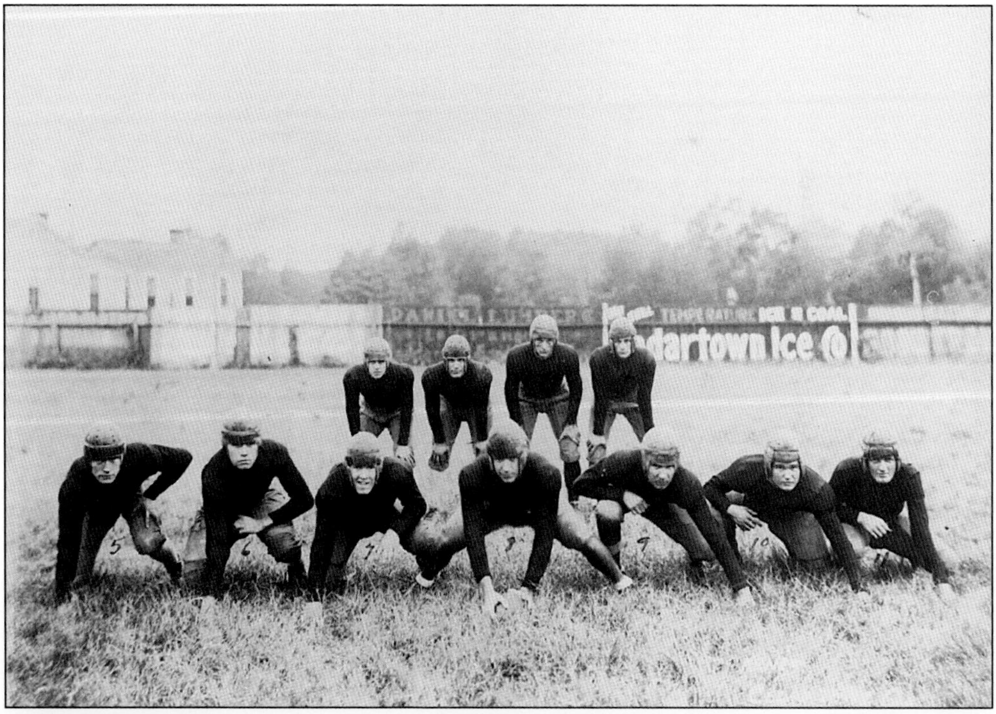

Football is the oldest sport at Cedartown High School. The school had its first undefeated team in 1922. The record-setting team of 1928, shown here, not only won all nine of their games, but scored 327 points while allowing only one touchdown by all of their opponents. That year Frank Lott was captain, and a huge total of 225 points was made by one player, Bunn Wood.

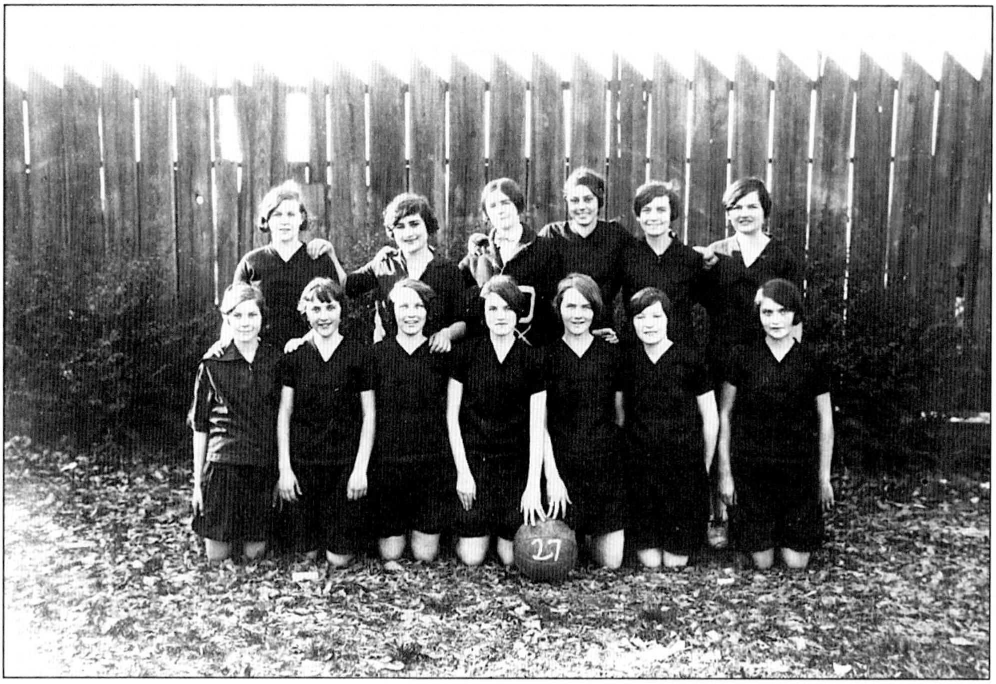

The 1927 girls' basketball team, posed here by the high school, played several teams from other schools in the area. They might be called a "fair-weather" team because the high school did not have an inside gym, and all the basketball games were played on an outdoor court.

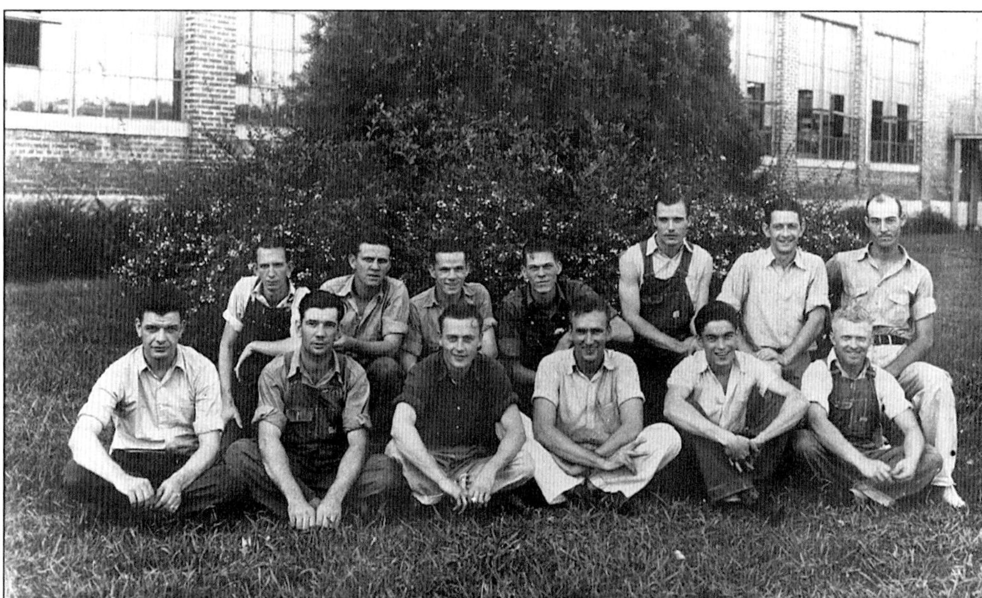

The various mills commonly sponsored ball clubs and scheduled regular games. In 1936, this rugged-looking team from Goodyear's Spinning Department won the championship in softball.

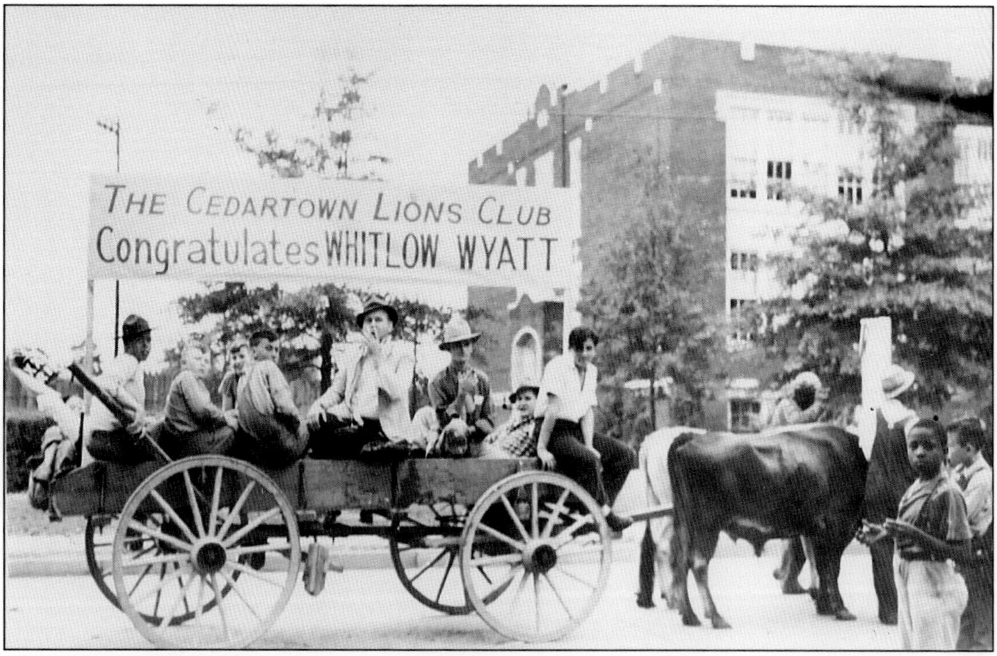

This Whitlow Wyatt Day celebrates a baseball great who grew up in Cedartown and in the early 1930s played high school sports. Wyatt played six-plus years with the Brooklyn Dodgers and Philadelphia Phillies. After his career as a player, he managed the Atlanta Crackers baseball team and later became the pitching coach for the Milwaukee-Atlanta Braves. (Courtesy Georgia Department of Archives and History.)

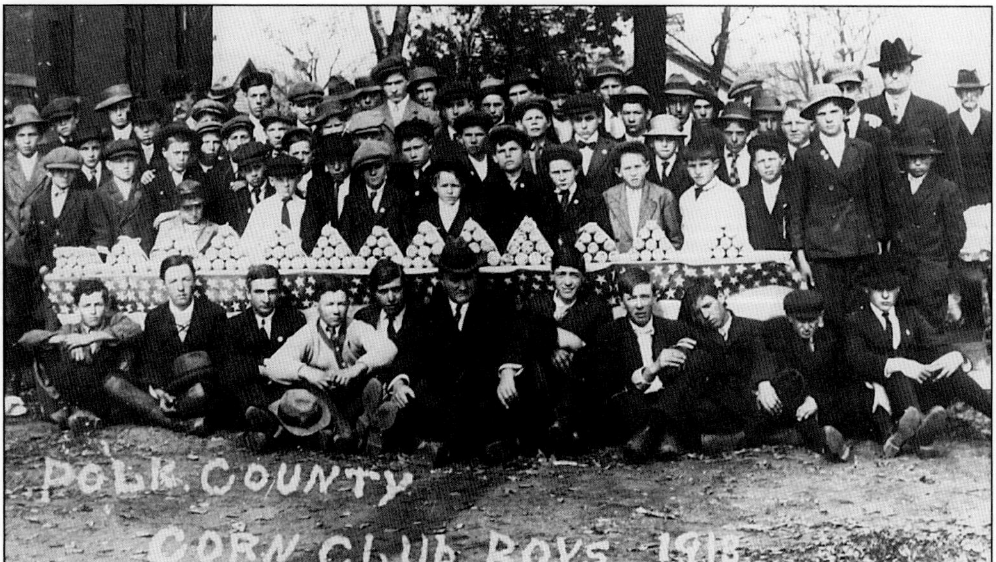

In this 1913 photo, the Corn Club Boys, as they called themselves, pose by the courthouse with their ears of corn. Each boy raised his own corn in competition with others in the club, which eventually became a 4-H Club. It is interesting to note one difference from today's young farmers: there are no girls in the club.

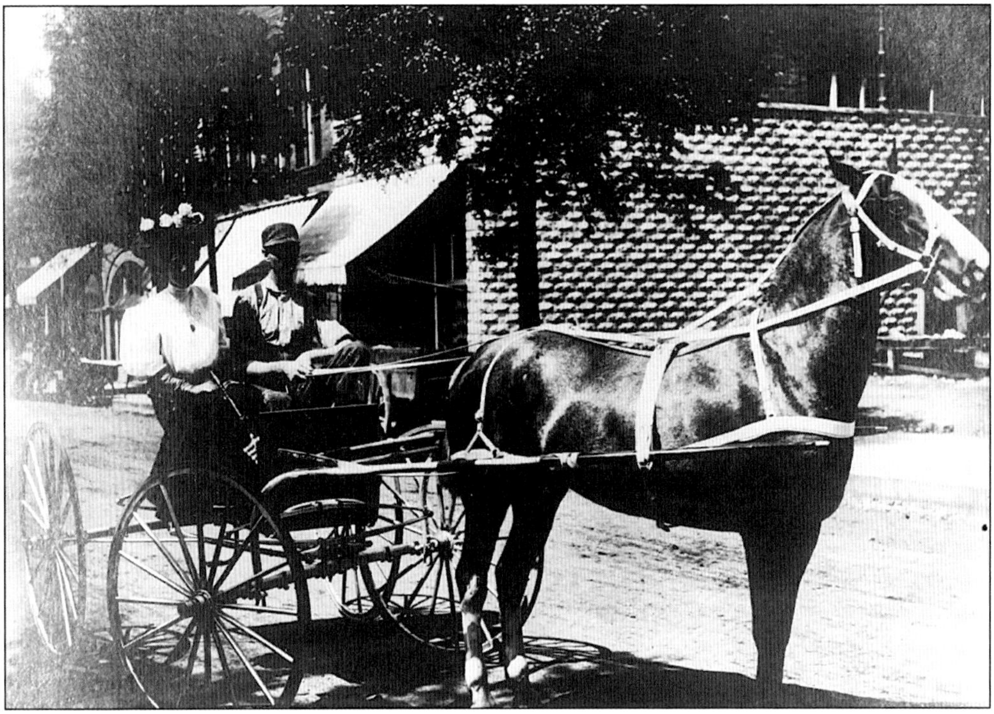

On Sunday afternoons, people would get out their buggy, hitch up a horse, and go for a drive around town or out in the countryside. This couple poses on Main Street *c.* 1910 with their handsome horse and what appears to be a new buggy.

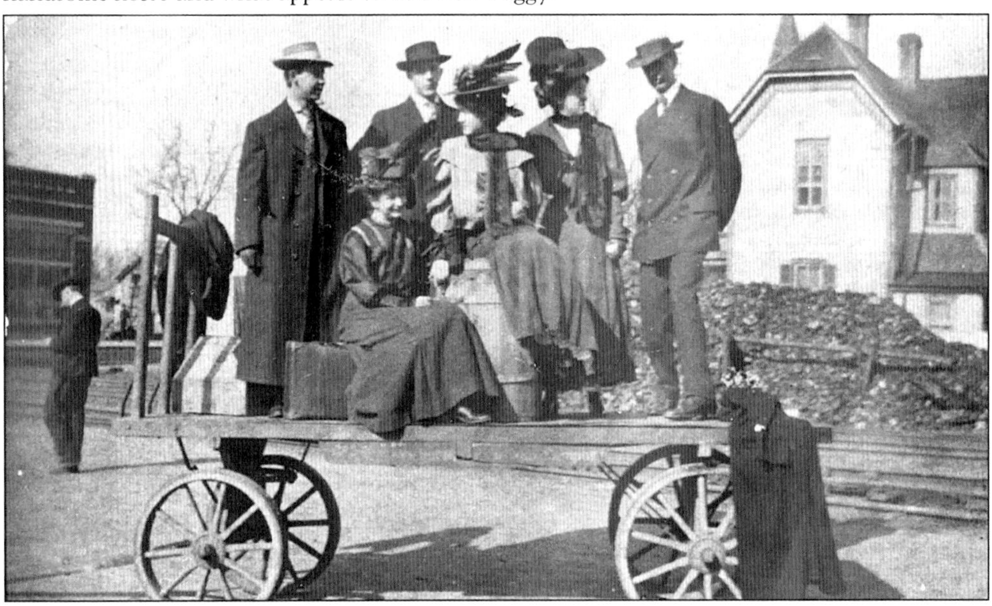

By the turn of the century, train travel had become the great convenience—faster and more enjoyable than travel by horseback or horse and buggy. Here, three handsomely decked-out couples stand on a railway wagon waiting expectantly for their train. The people and date of the picture are not identified, but the location is just east of Main Street, Cedartown, at the site of the Seaboard depot, which was completed in August 1904.

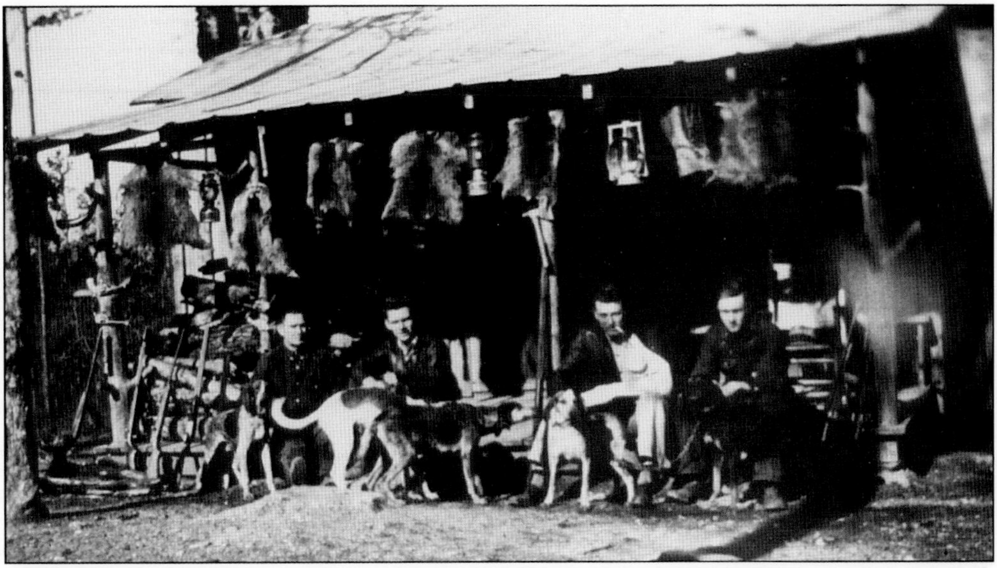

Hunting was a necessity in pioneer days. Today hunters enjoy bagging quail and dove, a sport which is one of Polk County's most popular pastimes. These four unidentified hunters and their "coon" dogs have had some success hunting for raccoons, as evidenced by the pelts hanging from this rustic lean-to in the Esom Hill vicinity.

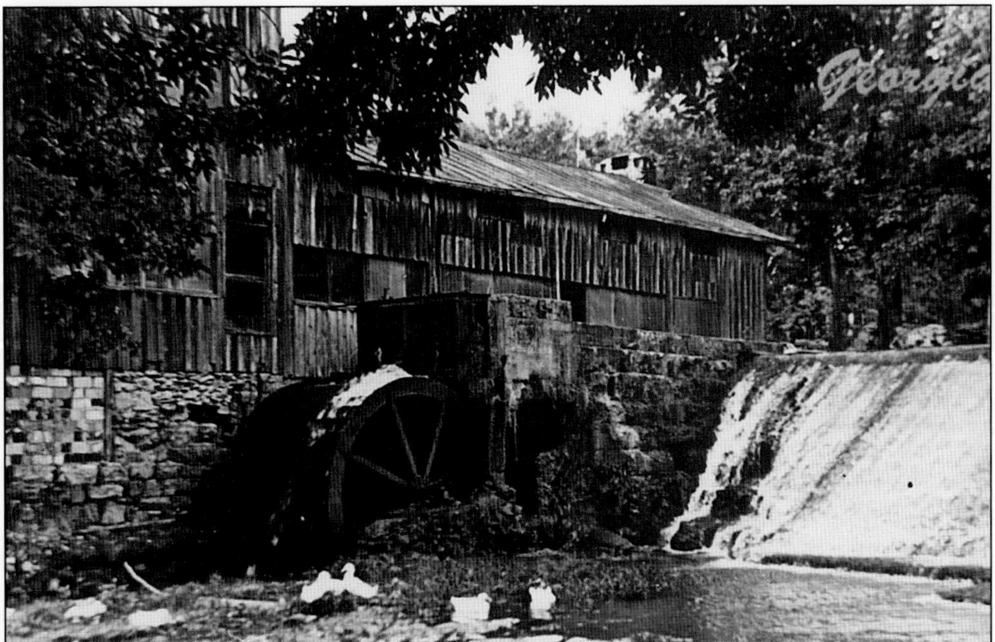

The Old Mill has survived for more than 150 years and is a beloved landmark in Polk County. Robert L. Stevens partially restored the structure in 1960 when he opened the Old Mill Restaurant, a favorite dining spot for 31 years.

ACKNOWLEDGMENTS

Over the years, residents have shared family materials by donations to the Polk County Historical Society, including many rare old photographs, which constitute the core of this pictorial history. Unfortunately, the names of many contributors have gone unrecorded. The most outstanding collection is that of Watson Dyer, who, in his position as editor of a genealogy periodical, traveled northwest Georgia for 16 years to copy priceless old pictures. For a number of years, Hoyt Worthington has added to that collection.

Many images were obtained from the Vanishing Georgia collection at the Georgia State Archives. Dozens of old postcards were graciously made available by Jim Lankford. Donnie Jarrell also shared his collection of postcards and Sterling Holloway memorabilia. The Rockmart Library graciously permitted their collection of photographs to be copied. We are grateful to the *North Georgia Journal* for permission to reproduce parts of Polk County articles.

In gathering and copying the photographs and researching much of this "new" history, Dr. David Wiggins has been most helpful and reliable. Jim Hurt applied his photographic skills in copying hundreds of images.

We gratefully acknowledge the many photographers who captured history on film, and the individuals who have made their materials and images available: Ralph and Jane Ayers, Evelyn Bailey, Ralph Baker, Mr. and Mrs. Ray Barber, Bobbie Barnette, Bob Basford, Virginia Berry, Phillip H. Brewster, G. Allen Carter, Margaret Coco, Edna Coleman, Elizabeth Herring Colquhoun, Dr. Robert E. Davis, Watson Dyer, Bob Fluornoy, James R. Gribble, Debbie Carter Grogan, Mrs. Charles K. Henderson, Dennis Holland, Mrs. Boothby Holloway, Cora Belle Honea, Mrs. Harold Hurt, Donnie Jarrell, Jim Lankford, Charlotte T. Marshall, Mr. and Mrs. Hugh M. McRae Jr., Leonora F. Mintz, Catherine Moody, Faye Prickett, Genevieve W. Seymour, Sue Isbell Stone, Annie Laura Waite, Ann White, Dr. David Wiggins, Robert Wilkerson, Hoyt Worthington, Georgia Wyatt, and Annie Jane Zuker.